Jackie

Reclaiming the Curriculum

Specialist and Creative Teaching in Primary Schools

Crown House Publishing Limited
www.crownhouse.co.uk

First published by
Crown House Publishing Ltd
Crown Buildings, Bancyfelin, Carmarthen, Wales, SA33 5ND, UK
www.crownhouse.co.uk

and

Crown House Publishing Company LLC
PO Box 2223, Williston, VT 05495, USA
www.crownhousepublishing.com

First published 2018.

Cover image and page 280 © Jackie Holderness.

Photographs: Page iv © Ed Read. Page 26 © Jonathan Bishop. Page 27 © Samantha Kerr. Page 41 © Jackie Holderness.
Page 55 © Jack Cornell. Page 67 © Jonathan Bishop. Page 83 © Marion Mills. Page 99 © Susan Perry. Page 115 © Zoe Steel.
Page 125 © Dawn Basnett. Page 141 © Jackie Holderness. Page 155 © Jackie Holderness. Page 169 © Jenifer Smith.
Page 183 © Lynn Knapp. Page 195 © Jackie Holderness. Page 209 © Ed Read. Page 223 © James Veness. Page 237 © Stephanie Daley.
Page 253 © Nicholas Mynheer. Page 263 © Jess Tweedie. Pages 283 and 284 © Nicholas Mynheer.

Quotes from Ofsted and Department for Education documents used in this publication have been approved under an Open
Government Licence. Please see: http://www.nationalarchives.gov.uk/doc/open-government-licence/version/3/.

British Library of Cataloguing-in-Publication Data

A catalogue entry for this book is available from the British Library.

Print ISBN: 978-178583306-9
Mobi ISBN: 978-178583346-5
ePub ISBN: 978-178583347-2
ePDF ISBN: 978-178583348-9

LCCN 2018941948

Printed and bound in the UK by
TJ International, Padstow, Cornwall

For Alex Laar

Contents

Acknowledgements

We would like to thank all the schools and teachers who have contributed so generously to the book. We would also like to thank the editorial team at Crown House Publishing, and other professional colleagues, for their advice and encouragement.

Preface

This book sets out to document educational practice of notable quality in a range of primary schools across the country, exemplifying effective, imaginative and innovative treatment of major aspects of the curriculum. The work described succeeds in cultivating pupils' cognitive and creative development in many ways and enhancing their learning and understanding in the broadest sense.

This comes at a time when the approach of many schools to pupils' curriculum entitlement is shaped, and significantly constrained, by their perception of a governmental emphasis on the core curriculum at the expense of the rest. This bias is reflected in the major importance attached to national testing, assessment and league tables as indicators of school effectiveness. Schools have come to believe that their success, as measured by Ofsted, largely relates to ongoing attainment in English and mathematics, with little more than limited reference to other subjects and aspects of the curriculum.

Many head teachers and teachers increasingly fear that their effectiveness, their standing, their reputation with parents and the community, and, indeed, the professional evaluation and fate of leaders and staff, are dependent on brief, data-driven inspections that take scant account of the totality of the education they provide. Some schools have responded with a disproportionate concentration on the teaching of English and mathematics in terms of time allocation, staff deployment, coaching and prolonged practice, and the extensive use of commercial materials, especially in the teaching of writing.

However, official recognition and acknowledgement of the potentially restrictive and adverse consequences for children's education and learning of this development has finally come.

In 2017, Ofsted's chief inspector, Amanda Spielman, commissioned a review into how the national curriculum is implemented in schools (Ofsted and Spielman, 2017). The review found that a significant consequence of a reduced understanding of the curriculum has been the narrowing of the primary curriculum in the final two years because of too great a focus on preparing for Key Stage 2 tests in English and mathematics. As a result, pupils were being deprived of lessons in subjects such as history, geography, languages, music, drama, computing, PE and art and design. She added that, as far back as 2001, there had been evidence of a restricted curriculum in primary schools, with the national literacy and numeracy strategies, along with increasingly demanding performance targets, adversely affecting the breadth of education provided.

Amanda Spielman went on to say that she had met many people who agreed that expertise in curriculum development and leadership had waned, with school leaders choosing to push curriculum development down their list of priorities. These leaders indicated that preparing staff to teach to the tougher assessment criteria for new SATs was more pressing.

She warned: 'Where school leaders and teachers have an overt focus on performance tables, this can lead to mistaking "badges and stickers" for learning and substance ... In addition, where there is little shared curriculum thinking among staff, it becomes increasingly difficult to moderate the influence of the test syllabus on primary curriculum design.' The chief inspector did, however, draw encouragement from the fact that 'many school leaders ... are already working to revitalise curriculum thinking to ensure that the content of young people's learning takes precedence over performance tables'.

In conclusion, she reiterated her determination that Ofsted would ensure that the curriculum received 'the proper attention it deserves' and, by implication, that the inspection process would be modified to achieve a proper review and acknowledgement of the nature and quality of primary curriculum, balanced against test outcomes and SATs attainment.

Not all are convinced or optimistic, however – including those whose scepticism derives from the failure by Ofsted to take practical account of their own concerns about the narrowing of the primary curriculum, raised more than 15 years ago.

The following comments are fairly representative of staffroom reactions:

Why do Ofsted think we teach only to the test?

Why is it, in Year 6, the children do almost exclusively maths and English? Is it because the teachers love maths and English and hate all the other subjects? Or is it because, during Ofsted inspections, the primary focus is the maths and English data, and progress in maths and English? No one ever went into a 'category' based on lack of progress in art!

So, Ofsted expect a broad and balanced curriculum, but still punish you if your results aren't up to scratch within a tightly defined list of subjects.

Schools cite as evidence of continued circumscribed inspection an article in the *TES* by Tim Brighouse (2016), which describes his survey of Ofsted reports from over 200 primary schools. He found that reference to curriculum content was confined to English/literacy and mathematics, with no comment – in any report – to any other subject in the national curriculum.

Anxiety has arisen that the narrowing of the curriculum may begin as early as the reception stage. A letter to *The Guardian* in January 2018 from more than 1,700 signatories – among them educationalists, parents and the IVF pioneer Lord Winston – expressed concern in response to an Ofsted report, *Bold Beginnings*, which called for a sharper focus on the teaching of literacy and numeracy at the reception stage.[1] The signatories of the letter took particular issue with the fact that the report effectively inferred that reception classes should be taught like those in Year 1, which, in turn, would mean a narrowing of the curriculum, a more formal teaching approach and less opportunity for play-based activity. The signatories also contested the assertion that schools deemed to be 'successful' already teach in this way – pointing out that the report was based on visits to less than 0.25% of schools, and suggesting therefore that Ofsted only visited schools where the teaching was congruent with the recommendations the report would ultimately make.

Last, but by no means of least concern to teachers and parents are reports from schools that pupils entering Year 6 are preoccupied with, and fearful of, their eventual achievement in the SATs, to the exclusion of any expectation of an inspirational or memorable final year in primary education.

Reclaiming the curriculum

Yet, for all of that, in recent years we have witnessed many schools resisting what they believe to be a mistaken belief in the security of a narrow curriculum and what, inevitably, would be a diminished learning experience for pupils. They have succeeded in providing a broad curriculum offer that enhances learning and maintains continuity and progression in pupils' attainment. These schools aim to nurture children's capacity to reflect on and evaluate their work and identify personal strategies for study and further learning. Interestingly, they can point to evidence that their retention of a deep and generous curriculum results in outcomes that do not merely satisfy requirements in relation to national standardised tests, but consistently exceed them. Many of the schools included in this book have been rated as 'outstanding' in all areas.

We are convinced about the value of the work in these schools and by the substance of their claims. We have been enthralled by much of what we have seen, and believe that

---

1   See https://www.theguardian.com/education/2018/jan/16/ofsteds-bold-beginnings-report-on-reception-class-curriculum-is-flawed.

the following chapters and case studies describe education of a transforming nature, which takes pupils into the realms of exploration, enquiry, learning and, very often, scholarship, and which enriches them beyond measure. These schools' pupils grow and thrive in developmental and human terms, and are often inspired to pursue a curiosity-driven quest for further investigation, research and knowledge. We would argue that it is the right of all children, whatever their circumstances in life, to have such an education.

In this book we share aspects of inspirational education and practice that we hope will enthuse colleagues in other schools. We hope that these accounts of initiatives – written by over 20 colleagues, each working within state-funded education – will encourage readers to reflect on, identify and esteem their own creative practice, and have faith in the worth of a full, relevant and content-rich primary curriculum.

The chapters describe – mostly in the words of head teachers, teachers and specialist coaches – exciting and creative learning. In the process, our colleagues refer to the beliefs, values, principles and philosophies that underpin and motivate their practice. They articulate their views of learning and how it is most effectively accomplished, the purpose and intentions that inspired the initiatives and projects they describe, and the ways in which these were resourced, realised, carried through and eventually evaluated.

At the beginning of each chapter, we briefly summarise our perceptions of the educational value of each initiative or long-standing example of curriculum development, the significance of specific aspects and the ways in which, it seems to us, they are likely to help maintain faith in, and commitment to, full and relevant learning. We believe the vision of each contributor, and what flows from that vision, represents a reclaiming of the curriculum and an enriched education for children.

Introduction

The primary debate

We believe it is necessary to review, however briefly, the decisive developments in primary education which, over time, have left no school untouched. We also consider the impact of the political intervention that has brought us to the current situation and the conflicting beliefs (still unresolved in important respects) about favoured and strongly advocated approaches to education.

Over the years, the primary sector has seen much discussion and disagreement, some of it damagingly divisive and conspicuously unhelpful, about appropriate philosophies, practice and approaches to the education of children, from birth to the pre-secondary phase. The debate continues around certain issues, not least the teaching of English.

One example of ill-informed and ultimately misleading argument, waged by those who cite the comprehensive and universal access to information through the extraordinary advances in digital technology, is that technology makes redundant the need for a knowledge-centred pedagogy and instead favours skills-based teaching and learning. We shall return to this issue later, since it has relevance, not only for our account of the work of the schools in this book, but more importantly for the meaning and purpose of education.

It is generally accepted that learning is central to our existence, to human development and to our capacity for thinking, decision-making and problem-solving. This helps us to manage; to ensure good, fulfilling and rewarding lives, often in the face of formidable difficulties and challenging situations; to maintain positive and life-enhancing relationships; to develop the intellectual capability and moral and spiritual sensibility that equips us to be part of, and contribute to, civilised communities; and to cherish what is best and most worthwhile in life.

There is also general agreement that, in the primary years, children typically learn in the following ways:

- They learn through being told things, having information and knowledge passed to them, having phenomena and skills demonstrated to them – hence the importance of the 'traditional' element of teaching.

1

■ They learn through language, their main instrument of enquiry. The more competently they can use speech, the more capable they will be as readers and writers, and the more effective and autonomous they will be as learners.

■ They learn through play and varied experience, often mediated by informed adults and peers.

■ They learn from negative knowledge – that is from trial and error; from determining why certain answers and solutions may be incorrect or flawed; why ideas, models and inventions might be improved upon, modified, refined or rejected altogether in favour of alternatives; and why it may be necessary to go back to the drawing board. Almost all human learning grows from, and harks back, to some extent, to ideas, hypotheses, notions, theories and beliefs that initially may have been wide of the mark. Such a process reflects the fate of all scientists, inventors, designers and artists.

■ They learn through a balance of what we will call performance and problem-solving: on the one hand, through the acquisition, mastery and development of a variety of vital skills; and on the other, through the resolution of meaningful, relevant and demanding problems to which these skills are applied.

■ They learn through regular experience of engagement with well-matched and meaningful learning tasks which are pitched, in cognitive terms, within reaching distance and the much quoted 'zone of proximal development' (Vygotsky, 1986).

■ They learn when they are inspired to pursue, individually and collectively, further lines of study and are equipped with the skills and resources to do so.

■ They learn when teachers and informed adults are available to support them through this process of venturing out into deeper water.

■ Crucially, children learn through talk.

Recent research has provided fresh evidence of the importance of talk, especially high quality dialogue, in children's development and learning (Alexander, 2017a). The Cambridge Primary Review (Alexander, 2009), for example, identified dialogue as being central to the aims of primary education.

Over the last decade, a growing number of primary schools have been implementing Robin Alexander's framework for dialogic teaching, which advocates a more extensive range of both teacher and pupil talk repertoires than those conventionally found in our classrooms, together with patterns of talk and classroom organisation that help teachers to more precisely diagnose pupils' needs, advance their learning and assess their progress.

Dialogue is about much more than oral exchanges in the classroom, however; it speaks to a particular stance on knowledge, learning and the curriculum. Alexander (2017b: 62) emphasises that dialogic teaching 'is as distinct from the question-answer and listen-tell routines of traditional teaching as it is from the casual conversation of informal discussion'. It requires:

- *interactions which encourage students to think, and to think in different ways;*
- *questions which invite much more than simple recall;*
- *answers which are justified, followed up and built upon rather than merely received;*
- *feedback which informs and leads thinking forward as well as encourages;*
- *contributions which are extended rather than fragmented;*
- *exchanges which chain together into coherent and deepening lines of enquiry;*
- *discussion and argumentation which probe and challenge, rather than unquestioningly accept;*
- *professional engagement with subject matter which liberates classroom discourse from the safe and conventional;*
- *classroom organisation, climate and relationships which are so disposed as to make all this possible. (Alexander, 2017a: 10)*

While broad agreement exists over such factors that contribute vitally to the learning process, a significant division endures over the most effective approach to the implementation of the learning process and how it can be most appropriately classified, managed and delivered.

For decades throughout the 20th century, theory relating to the education of young children was greatly influenced by so-called 'child-centred' approaches. The philosophy that underpinned these ideas had its genesis as far back as the 18th century in the work and beliefs of the Swiss philosopher Jean-Jacques Rousseau; the educator Johann Heinrich Pestalozzi and his great disciple, the German educationalist Friedrich Froebel, and the American educationalist John Dewey, whose views and theories substantially built on their work; Maria Montessori and Reggio Emilia's Loris Malaguzzi in Italy; and sisters Rachel and Margaret McMillan, and Susan Isaacs in the UK.

Much of the work of these educational pioneers was inspired by a belief that the child is a powerful, active participant in their own learning and cognitive development. In later years, it became fashionable to describe the child as the agent at the heart of their own learning. This was motivated by powerful evidence that children are inextricably and decisively involved in the learning process from birth, driven by an innate and insatiable curiosity, by their capacity to respond consciously, to think and deduce, and to come to conclusions, however tentative, based on observation and sensory engagement.

They were seen to engage in a constant process of making sense of their environment, and the questions and problems it posed. From the outset, this experience of their immediate world seemed to lead to conclusions and decisions that formed a basis for reflection, for further exploration and investigation, of constant effort to enlarge on and refine what they had already consciously absorbed.

Some observers likened the process to what is loosely referred to as a scientific mode of thinking: observation and involvement in aspects of experience, investigation and analysis of what is taking place, leading to the formulation of ideas and concepts, the sharing of findings and conclusions with others, the testing of outcomes and, eventually the re-examination and review of new evidence, leading to fresh attempts to refine the concepts that have been formed and to test further, and extend, the knowledge that has been acquired.

In practice, head teachers and staff in nursery and early years settings (and in some cases, in the first stages of primary education), inspired by the child-centred ideal, provided opportunities for children to engage in intensive exploratory investigation and experimentation with a range of selected and random materials within school and in the natural world. It was practice that, in time, came to be recognised and encouraged by school inspectors, writers and researchers. The movement, or at least some aspects of it, gradually took hold in increasing numbers of primary schools, and continued to develop in the post-war era and from the 1960s onwards, coinciding with the abolition of secondary selection in many areas.

As a concept of, and an approach to, the education of young children, it received what might be called its imprimatur in the great Plowden Report, *Children and their Primary Schools*. The report declared: 'At the heart of the educational process lies the child. No advances in policy, no acquisitions of new equipment have their desired effect ... unless they are fundamentally acceptable to him' (1967: 7).

Underpinning much of the thinking and practice of child-centred educationalists at this time, and thereafter, was the work of the Swiss developmental psychologist Jean Piaget.

His hugely influential and complex theory about the acquisition, construction and use of knowledge, as it applied to children in the first and early years of their lives and across the primary age range, is likely to have inclined some teachers to steer clear of what they perceived to be the danger of prematurely engaging them in abstract areas of learning and, by inference, to regard specialist teaching as dispensable before the secondary stage.

What followed in the couple of decades after Plowden came to be perceived as a golden age of child-centred education. There was certainly some outstanding educational practice inspired by its theories and principles. At its most assured, children were placed at the centre of learning, which was often initiated and instigated by the learners' own interests, pursuits and explorations, in environments and contexts structured and organised by teachers.

The following, witnessed by the authors, might be described as a classic example of such creative practice:

> Some years ago, Year 6 pupils at Mandeville Primary School in Hackney were studying aspects of flight. The teacher had selected the theme largely for the opportunity it afforded for work in mathematics, science and technology. The temptation offered by such a subject to draw everything possible into the study – art and geography, history and drama, and even, perhaps, music and dance – was strictly resisted. Aims and objectives were rigorously devised and ordered to promote significant learning, the acquisition of important knowledge, an understanding of concepts and ideas and the mastery of critical skills. The project was rounded off with a visit to the Science Museum. It was what happened there that caused the project, at the very end, to go beyond its meticulous and ordered boundaries into a new and unpredicted realm of experience, learning and rare achievement.
>
> In a remote corner of that museum, glittering with one marvel and revelation after another, the children came across a faded photograph of an aviator from a long-ago age, standing by a triplane, constructed it seemed from little more than wood, piano wire, string and sturdy brown paper. The aviator was A. V. Roe, with the flimsy aircraft he had designed and built alone, and in which, in 1908, he had made the first powered flight in Britain. The feat, an epic of lonely perseverance, imagination, courage and creative genius, was totally lost to memory a few weeks later when Louis Bleriot, encouraged and massively supported by the French government and accompanied by units of the French navy across the English Channel, made the first flight from France to Britain.

In a museum resplendent with exhibitions devoted to the achievements and glories of the great, Roe's modest little exhibit might well have gone unnoticed by pupils jaded at the end of an eventful day. But it was his photograph and the related information that transfixed them: for Roe had built the triplane underneath the railway arches on Walthamstow Marsh and made that historic flight in the clouds above the marshland, all within hailing distance of the children's school.

They were dazzled by the discovery, struggling perhaps to come to terms with the stark contrast between the bleak, desolate landscape of their environment and the marvellous transforming thing that had happened there, on a sunlit day, long ago.

When, next morning, ablaze with expectation, they ventured down to the arches, they found them deserted and overgrown. No single trace of that creation and flight remained. But their wonder and a kind of vicarious pride remained undiminished. It was as if some suggestion of the terror, the exhilaration and the glory of that venture into the unknown lingered still in the marsh air and touched their spirit.

It was they, not their teacher, who claimed there should be something at the site to commemorate what had happened there. It was he, the teacher, who led them gently from dreams of statues and pillars to think about the possibilities of a prestigious Greater London blue plaque.

And so began what seemed, at times, a hopeless quest – the putting together by the children of written appeals and submissions, of daunting oral presentations to authorities, politicians, historians and all the great and the good to secure a blue plaque for that derelict marshland arch. They persevered in the face of initial incomprehension, incredulity and even occasionally outright scepticism, with something of the irresistible determination that must have sustained the aviator/inventor himself.

Eventually, on a morning sunlit like the day of that first flight, and bearing their scrupulously constructed scale model of the triplane, the class marched across the marsh to the arches. There, watched by the surviving sons of Mr Roe and their families, who had travelled far for the occasion, the children of Mr Newland's class solemnly drew aside the velvet curtains and unveiled, on the old arch, a blue plaque in commemoration of the forgotten pioneer.

These Year 6 pupils were children to whom advantage, privilege and the things that come to the more fortunate in life were unknown and largely unattainable. But they were blessed to have encountered in their life a gifted teacher who took them into the realms of rich experience and to achievement that most would have thought beyond them. In the process, some, if not all of them, learned that they had within them the creative power and capacity to change their environment and to challenge and perhaps transform their circumstances.

What characterised this and similar inspirational work that we saw, whether it was the striking and spectacular or the low profile and unremarked, are certain prerequisites:

- Clear intentions about desired learning outcomes defined in specific aims and objectives.
- A transforming environment.
- A powerful narrative.
- Resources that inspire and support experimentation and invention.
- Encouragement of the scientific mode of enquiry.
- Access to high quality information.
- The involvement of teachers, informed adults and other specialists who intervene at crucial moments, so that 'what the child is able to do in collaboration today he will be able to do independently tomorrow' (Vygotsky, 1987 [1934]: 211).

At the same time, however, we saw other initiatives that were flawed in serious respects in terms of educational worth or value. Such shortcomings included:

- A marked limitation in the depth of learning achieved, due largely to the lack of teacher expertise in relation to important aspects of the study.
- Less than rigorous planning, leading to a lack of coherence in learning.
- A failure to fully or profitably engage some pupils to a degree that guaranteed deep learning.
- A temptation to include a range of subjects without fully identifying their relevance, or the value of the knowledge and learning they might yield.

The following episode, witnessed by the authors in the years immediately following Plowden, might be described as symptomatic of a lost learning opportunity for pupils, arising from teaching approaches limited by a lack of subject awareness and expertise.

Children in the infant department of an urban primary school had made a visit to a working windmill some miles away, and on their return, in classic learning fashion, had constructed a model of the windmill from a range of materials provided by their teachers. They talked, informedly and enthusiastically, to visitors about the construction, explaining that a windmill was a construction with sails driven by the wind. The sails, they explained, turned a great pole in the middle of the mill that, in turn, revolved a massive pair of stones at the bottom. The children insisted that the great revolving stones made bread, revealing in the process a hiatus in their conceptual understanding of the milling process.

A member of the class, a boy of 7, intervened to inform the listeners that, during the Second World War, the Dutch resistance regularly arranged the sails in ways that secretly communicated to the community information and advice. In the process, he was unconsciously signalling that he was one of those children with needs and capacities for whom teachers must plan and provide.

The positive outcome, and a reminder of the value of the school visit, was the children's achievements: having seen the phenomenon of a working windmill for the first time, they reconstructed it later in vivid style and commendable accuracy, and discussed some of its more obvious technical aspects with fluency.

A top junior class in the same school visited the windmill immediately afterwards and they too reconstructed it in model form. It was a superior creation in several respects – more correctly proportioned, the sails more secure and revolving more smoothly. What was missing, however, were any technical elements or working parts, any awareness or informed account of the workings of such a building, or any capability on their part to discuss the historic, economic or geographic reasons for the dominance of windmills in parts of the landscape of Britain, and why they had, in time, become largely obsolete.

There was little evidence in the response and understanding of pupils four years older of significant continuity and progression in their learning. For them, the educational visit and the activity that resulted from it might be said to be of severely limited value. And it was due, at least to some extent, to the fact that their teachers did not themselves possess the specialist knowledge and skills or the detailed curriculum maps that would have enabled them to challenge and enrich the pupils' understanding and take their knowledge further.

A further consequence of the absence of detailed curriculum definition and substance was practice in many primary schools, especially at the upper junior stage, which was concentrated on the 'creative' domain, with a particular emphasis on visual art. In most cases, such work, guided by teachers skilled and at ease in the subject, resulted in high quality outcomes and achievement. But the focus often tended to be extravagant in terms of the time committed, both by teachers and pupils, to the partial exclusion or diminution of other subjects, especially those of a more esoteric nature.

A typical example of this lack of balance in the curriculum was evident in a school that was nationally renowned for children's work in fine art, especially observational drawing and painting of outstanding quality. This village school was located not far from a major port, and long-distance lorries had found a shortcut through it to their destinations. A great mass of heavy traffic thundered constantly through the narrow roads, night and day, shaking the very foundations of the village and creating a serious hazard for pedestrians.

The children's glorious artwork often featured their local landscape, but when asked by an observer about the ever-present influence of the lorries in their community, they revealed no concept of their business or purpose. They didn't know where they had come from and where they were eventually destined, why they were so numerous, what was so precious and urgent about the cargo they carried or what incited them to such dangerous haste.

There was no evidence that the children were being made aware in their daily education of the great forces that were impinging on their lives to such a significant extent. Regularly passing by the school was traffic that belonged to a wider world, evidence of vital activity and business, of other languages and cultures, of other life systems that were, in effect, changing the nature of the children's environment and their mode of living. Yet, to them, they meant little or nothing. What, in fact, characterised the school, justifiably renowned for the art education it provided, was a lack of breadth, balance and, crucially, relevance in their children's learning.

In response to examples of this kind, concern about the nature and quality of much 'informal' child-centred education grew. It was tellingly conveyed by the distinguished educationalist Sir Alec Clegg (1909–1986), the chief education officer of the West Riding of Yorkshire County Council, which was renowned for the quality of its child-centred education. In a critique of contemporary national primary practice, Clegg suggested in the often-quoted phrase that too many teachers had 'climbed on the bandwagon but cannot play the instruments' (quoted in Alexander et al., 1992: 10).

At that time, schools and teachers had a considerable degree of autonomy in relation to the education they provided, as well as its substance and quality. One could visit schools a mile apart and see a significant difference between them in terms of the curriculum on offer. In some schools, children's learning experience could be replicated in successive years with little substantial progression in what they encountered or learned.

Curriculum guidelines

Peter Mortimer (1988) points out that about 40% of the schools sampled in his survey at that time furnished their staff with 'curriculum guidelines'. We are given no information other than this about the guidelines – nothing about which subjects or the extent and type of guidance they provided. The implication is that the other schools sampled offered no guidelines at all.

This is not to suggest that schools were negligent or took no account of continuity or progression. In most cases, teachers passed on the work the children had been doing to the colleagues responsible for the next stage of their education. There were general expectations of what the children should be achieving. Nevertheless, we suggest that for too many children education was a lottery; what they experienced in learning terms was heavily dependent on the school they attended.

It was not uncommon for teachers to unwittingly bias curriculum content according to personal preference and competence. The unbalanced project/topic – as distinct from the flight example described earlier – became symptomatic of the lack of curriculum coherence that characterised at least some primary practice in the decades succeeding the Plowden Report.

Some teachers took matters further and suggested that curriculum content was not of major significance; they perceived the learning process – in effect, teaching children to learn how to learn – as the truly critical issue. This state of affairs led to what was widely and derisively referred to as 'the dead greenfinch' curriculum, due to the probably apocryphal story of a teacher basing an exhaustive term-long project on a dead greenfinch discovered on his way to school. Though some schools provided inspired teaching and impressive attainment, especially in the visual arts, the doubts continued because there was no external national testing or assessment.

There was no requirement on schools to provide parents with evidence of their children's attainment and progress in comparative terms. While most parents were informed about their children's broad educational experience, it would not have been possible for them to know where they stood in terms of attainment in numeracy or literacy in a local or national context, simply because some schools might themselves not have known to any precise extent.

But an end was in sight. It was increasingly clear to a growing body of educationalists, among them HMI, that at least part of existing primary practice needed a radical review. There was a growing demand for:

■ A comprehensive mapping of the areas of essential knowledge, concepts and skills across every subject.

■ The creation of a balanced curriculum that established the central importance of subjects and their interrelatedness, and the decisive part they play in children's acquisition and mastery of skills, knowledge, concepts and attitudes.

■ A national monitoring instrument of individual school effectiveness.

■ Systems of assessment that measured children's attainment and progress in the areas of English, mathematics and science.

■ The need to consider the place and provision of specialist teaching in particular subjects at the upper end of the primary school – a development long flinched from by teachers and enshrined in the frequently quoted claim, 'We teach children, not subjects.'

In the end, decisive radical change was brought about by political intervention.

Curriculum intervention

The result was the national curriculum. The Education Reform Act 1988 introduced a national curriculum which applied to all pupils of compulsory school age. At Key Stages 1 and 2, it comprised the foundation subjects, three of which – English, mathematics and science – were defined as 'core subjects'. Children would leave primary school with end-of-key-stage level descriptors that would indicate very clearly the nature of their attainment and progress. These, in turn, were the elements to which Ofsted would attach increasing importance.

The aim of the national curriculum was to ensure a broad and balanced curriculum that would meet the needs of all pupils, enabling them to achieve their full educational potential. It would ensure that all children made progress in their learning, and would promote their good behaviour and safety and their spiritual, moral and cultural development.

The first national curriculum revolutionised primary education in England, and with it the business of schools, for the following reasons:

■ It represented a massive body of content in the broadest sense – of knowledge, ideas, concepts and skills, and a large range of subjects, packed with detailed objectives, that had to be accommodated within the existing timetable.

- It comprised sequenced levels of attainment which could be used by teachers as cognitive maps. These levels introduced an enhanced degree of intellectual emphasis and an overriding focus on pupil progression and achievement.

- It called for highly specialised knowledge of curriculum content on the part of teachers across a wide curriculum spectrum, especially at the upper end of Key Stage 2.

- It made assessment – formative, diagnostic and summative – an integral part of the teaching and learning process.

- It had immense implications for pedagogy, classroom management and teaching in general. This was reflected in the growing emphasis on the centrality of teaching and on how the curriculum was to be delivered and the learning organised.

However, the range and ambition of the revolution proved to be too much for many. The sheer weight of its detail, the daunting range of content, the myriad levels of attainment, the call for specialist provision in particular areas, the demands of the core strategies (especially in English) and the heavy time pressure threatened to be overwhelming. Primary teachers found themselves working in contexts that were new and often unfamiliar and at a pace they had rarely experienced. They recognised and acknowledged what was valuable in the national curriculum and welcomed the learning frameworks it provided, but they were struggling to survive.

Curriculum reviews

Responding to the need for change, over the following years successive governments initiated a series of reviews into the format and content of the curriculum which led to a radical reduction of previous content.

The current curriculum for Key Stages 1 and 2 was set out by the Department for Education in 2013. One is struck immediately by the contrast between the first and successive versions of the national curriculum and what the 2013 version appears to represent. Little more than a vestige of the detailed prescription that characterised the first national curriculum is left, but the strong emphasis on English and mathematics remains. Indeed, the whole content of the curriculum is heavily weighted in their favour. There can be no doubting the priority attached to them. The purpose of study and the aims and attainment targets sections are authoritative, clear and detailed. But the programmes of study are less detailed in terms of context.

Where, then, are teachers to turn for expert guidance in constructing detailed curriculum content for their pupils? How are they to provide what Ofsted's deputy director of schools Joanna Hall (2016: Slide 6) describes as: 'The broad and balanced curriculum [that] inspires pupils to learn. The range of subjects and courses [that] helps pupils acquire knowledge, understanding and skills in all aspects of their education, including the humanities and linguistic, mathematical, scientific, technical, social, physical and artistic learning.'

Such aspirations are easy to pronounce but represent a challenge when it comes to actually delivering adequate provision; so much so that Robin Alexander (2009) and his Cambridge Review colleagues deemed it to be the work of specialist experts. To accomplish it they urged the formation of accredited groups and training, and a rethink about the way schools are structured and managed.

In the long run, the challenge of curriculum design revolves almost wholly around the issue of content, and is inextricably bound up with the matter of subjects and subject knowledge. Down the years, some primary practitioners have been daunted by the challenge of providing breadth and depth of subject knowledge. There has been unhelpful polarisation between knowledge and skills, barely concealed antipathy to specialist teaching and an increasing tendency to dismiss the teaching of knowledge because it is so readily available from the Internet.

But content is so much more than that: it is at the very heart of what children must learn. Content is the substance through which vital skills, competences, perceptions and dispositions are taught and cultivated. They cannot be developed in a vacuum; they will not flower through an emphasis on process alone. It is vitally important that we define content precisely. Content is comprised of knowledge, ideas and concepts; areas for study, investigation and experimentation; and hard information – the latter certainly subject over time to change and development in line with the world it describes.

Specialist content is what subjects are comprised of. Unless we define it, map it and order it, the subjects, the areas of learning, the domains – however we group them or whatever we choose to call them – become meaningless.

Curriculum design and construction

We believe that the business of primary schools is to select what seems most appropriate for the education of the children they teach, to add to and enrich the basic substance of the national curriculum. Schools are in the business of negotiating and deciding what is desirable, useful and appropriate for their purposes. They must decide what is necessary for them to construct the curriculum that will further the learning they wish to nurture.

This work is based on the philosophy that the broader the curriculum, the wider the access to science and mathematics, to the creative and expressive arts, to environmental and geographical issues, to history and the humanities in general, the greater the chance of intellectual and cognitive growth and general development. They wish, through a reclaimed curriculum, to maximise the opportunities for children to be competent, to succeed and to respond and express themselves positively. Access to a full range of such learning experiences is likely to provide children with the best opportunity to emerge as complete personalities – aware of their potential, imbued with intellectual curiosity and a desire to learn more; spiritually, morally and socially secure; and confident in their environment and relationships.

The new national curriculum gives teachers flexibility and authority over the curriculum they choose to provide outside of the core subjects. There are those who will argue that such freedom and flexibility incur the risk of a return to the shortcomings and failures of exclusively child-centred education, which was often misunderstood and mismanaged and not adequately monitored. But we now have a different generation of educators. We believe the current generation of primary teachers herald a golden age of primary education for the following reasons:

- Many schools have been judged by Ofsted to be 'good' or 'outstanding'.

- Management styles in schools encourage distributed leadership and collegiality.

- Shared practice and pedagogy are at the heart of their education system.

- From an early stage in their career, teachers are asked to assume responsibility for leadership of colleagues in the formulation and delivery of areas of the curriculum where they have a particular expertise.

- Some schools are now better resourced than they were three decades ago. Many teachers are supported in their teaching and class management by highly competent teaching assistants and by developments in technology.

- Teachers' subject knowledge, their understanding of the learning process and the importance of continuity and progression, and how it may be ensured, is more substantial and well-founded than ever.

- Teachers are supported in their teaching (perhaps over-zealously, some might argue) by systems of assessment and evaluation.

The schools represented in this book are compelled by a determination that the children they teach and care for are educated in the fullest and truest sense to:

- Make sense of and deal creatively and positively with the circumstances of their lives, their current environment and the world at large.

- Command the major forms and features of language and use them readily and competently, across diverse genres, to serve their purpose.

- Think creatively and purposefully in the 'scientific mode' (i.e. observe critically, assemble evidence, analyse and reflect on what they have discovered, draw conclusions based on evidence and thought, test conclusions as far as possible, adapt and restructure these according to the outcomes of testing, communicate conclusions to others and hold them up to scrutiny and review in the light of discussion and informed commentary).

- Learn to think, respond and behave according to the form and conventions of major disciplines – that is, where necessary, to act as scientists, historians, geographers, technologists and mathematicians.

- Command IT skills and use digital technology to suit their learning purposes.

- Respond to the creative and expressive arts in a way that enlarges personal awareness and creative and learning potential, refines sensibility and sensitivity and provides for spiritual development.

- Be problem-solvers, who can engage with and bring reason and practical resources to bear on the challenges and problems of human existence.

- Master one other major language in addition to their native language.

- Go on learning in a progressive way, building on what they have acquired and mastered, impelled by an abiding sense of curiosity.

- Reflect on and analyse their own work to identify areas of success and progress.

- Recognise their growing acquisition of skills, competences and understanding, and the ways in which these can be used to take their learning forward.

- Be endowed with a strong moral and ethical sense and the capacity to relate sympathetically to others.

One example that encompasses at least some of the above comes from the head teacher of Riverside Primary School in Derby. The school has adopted an approach derived from the International Primary Curriculum (IPC) programme, which is founded on subject-based, personal and international-focused learning goals. They define what children might be expected to know and do, and the understandings they might develop as they move through school.

Year 1 had been working on the IPC theme 'holidays'. They had chosen to find out about Spain because of the input from our Comenius student who had been introducing the Spanish language and had shared information about her home in Seville. The children were becoming more and more excited about their learning and this culminated in them telling me one morning that they were genuinely going to Spain on a plane. I queried this, of course, and asked more about their visit. The children were full of enthusiasm and were sure they would be boarding a plane, something wholly outside their experience. They told me they had spent time carefully preparing passports and boarding cards and had discussed exactly what they would need to bring with them. Bags were packed and they were ready to go!

At this point I became a little worried. I had visions of a very disappointed Year 1 class who clearly believed they were going to Spain. The enthusiastic Year 1 team had done a very good job of convincing them, and I prepared for the worst.

However, what came next was a joy to watch. The children, passports in hand, arrived at the airport (the school hall) and sensibly went through to airport security (the first pair of hall doors). Their tickets were checked by a very astute member of airport staff (the Year 1 teaching assistant), and they were then led to the boarding gate. The excitement on the children's faces was wonderful to see as they talked about the planes they could see out of the airport lounge and when they might be allowed on the plane.

As they entered the plane (the second set of hall doors) and sat in their designated seats (on two wooden benches) the pilot introduced herself (the Year 1 teaching assistant again). The pilot then proceeded to ask them if they had spotted the Eiffel Tower as they flew over Paris, which was answered with a resounding 'Yes!' as all of Year 1 craned their necks to see out of the windows. After receiving their in-flight snack, they arrived at their destination and immediately began to practise their Spanish, greeting children they encountered with a confident 'Hola'.

Year 1 spent the day learning outside (the weather forecast was accurate and the sun was shining). They learned about Spanish culture and food and had fun.

Could they have learned the same facts in the classroom? Probably yes. But would they have enjoyed their learning and been involved in shaping their own learning and progress in such an exciting and meaningful way? Definitely not!

The chapters that follow offer further evidence of professional expertise, vision, ingenuity and inventiveness, and insights into teaching and learning that will be recognised by imaginative colleagues elsewhere. We are hopeful that these chapters will provide for other schools echoes of their own practice which is similarly wide ranging and creative.

Creativity in the curriculum

Creativity is a term frequently used in reference to notable primary practice. We believe our case study schools exemplify such creativity to a marked degree, and that it enables them to reclaim the curriculum.

Creativity in the learning process is one of the concerns of this book. We should, therefore, attempt to define what we mean by creativity in terms of pupils' learning, work and performance, and the pedagogy, curriculum and environment central to it.

However, to define creativity is a more complex and difficult matter than might be immediately apparent. We encounter the terms 'creative' and 'creativity' in everyday use. It is readily applied to those who display skill or capability in a diversity of activities: to musicians, dancers, actors, sports men and women, fashion designers, gardeners, chefs, disc jockeys, those who manage events and organisations and to numerous others who qualify by virtue of high competence and remarkable achievement.

What, then, is creativity? The following characteristics or aptitudes, which underpin creative instinct and behaviour, could equally well apply to the sciences as well as the arts:

■ Creativity is concerned always with actions designed or intended to achieve an outcome, with managing the challenging or the intractable, with making sense of things and with accomplishing something specific and new – however falteringly or tentatively.

- Creative expression or action is directed towards an achievement of some kind, whether it be a child struggling to improve the manipulative qualities of a puppet or an astrophysicist wrestling with a cosmological problem.

- To be judged creative, the action must be concluded and must satisfy the creator, after rigorous scrutiny, that it represents worthwhile improvement on, or enhancement of, previous effort or experimentation in relation to the same objective.

- It is probably safe to say that the creative act is never painless or facile, or free of setback, frustration, disappointment and perhaps even anguish. For example, it is common to hear Mozart's creativity described as effortless and his capacity to compose sublime music at an astonishingly early age as something almost magical – it happened inexplicably and was beyond his personal comprehension. Yet musicologists tell us that every note he composed, however readily it seemed to flow from his pen, reflected deep thought, intense reflection and clearly defined intention on his part. Albert Einstein, so often cited as the epitome of creativity, laboured constantly and exhaustively to the end of his days – interrogating, reviewing and, as he himself confessed, finding shortcomings in the things he had done, which have ultimately helped to shape our understanding of the world.

- The outcomes of creative effort, whatever its magnitude and wherever it stands on the spectrum from infancy to high maturity, must represent something notable or worthwhile to the neutral observer or analyst.

- Creative outcome or achievement should stimulate the creator to further effort or investigation in the same field of activity or a related area.

We believe that the work in schools described in this book demonstrates such creativity in action and exhibits the following characteristics and aptitudes:

- A sense of curiosity that feeds an irresistible need or urge to make sense of what is not clearly understood, and the capability to devise possible ways of arriving at such an understanding.

- A deliberate, thought-through and persistent attempt to arrive at an understanding of how functional objects are constructed, put together and work, whether it be a simple mechanical toy, a telescope, a beehive, a Roman ballista or a sports car designed to operate on a race track; and undertaking a course of action designed to learn, where possible, how to construct or replicate the object itself.

- A strong compulsion to make sense of natural phenomena – whether it be insects, animal life, growing things or the patterns of weather and their impact on the environment – through the framing of relevant questions, and by attempts at direct exploration and investigation. Essentially, a deliberate attempt to assimilate and accommodate what has been learned as part of acquired schema and to subsequently translate that into practice and further learning.

- A refusal to be readily satisfied with initial outcomes and solutions, whether it be an attempt to master a piece of music or make a raft, leading to further review, investigation and appraisal, and further effort that continues to require perseverance.

- A desire to make, compose, perform and create, and to do it well, across a range of experience and activities, individually or in cooperation with others.

A classic and frequently observed example of this is the readiness, indeed eagerness, of children to work untiringly with others and with intense concentration on an expanse of beach to build sandcastles. Here we can observe the resourceful use of found materials, the construction of artful defences against the sea, the damming and redirection of rivulets and channels for specific purposes (in the mode of those who build canals or drain the land to salvage it from the sea). During the activity, there will be the child who wearies of that occupation and goes off to skim stones or construct fragile craft from a piece of driftwood, and the passing parent or adult who brings additional expertise and fresh suggestion to the group. There may be painful, if resigned, acceptance of the ultimate fallibility of all their efforts and cunning ingenuity against the remorseless sea, and in the process, a developing ability to learn from experience and a growing understanding of natural phenomena. Yet, with all of that, there is a determination to return, to try again and make things better, not merely because the experience has been hugely pleasurable and rewarding but because they have a sense of something fully realised yet not wholly achieved.

Creativity in school

In any one day, in or outside the school, there will be evidence of children's capacity for such creative action, which may well go unnoticed simply because it seems no more than a commonplace preoccupation or an aspect of play, seemingly too fleeting or trivial to call for investigation.

The following examples, commonly observed across the whole primary age range, represent crucial elements of creativity and a capacity to devise complicated processes, the effective performance of which calls for a variety of skills and acute mental response:

- The seemingly spontaneous creation of complex variations on traditional games, with newly formulated rules and conventions.

- Adapting folk and fairy tales into improvised drama.

- Improving obstacles for a playground race.

- Constructing a bridge from random materials to cross a 'stream' constructed from carpet.

- Using blocks to build an archway, complete with keystone.

- Inventing and using a code to convey secret messages.

- Organising and running a 'hospital ward' to deal with the 'victims' of an accident.

There are other aspects of children's activity that regularly demonstrate creativity of a kind which is less readily recognised, but is nevertheless significant in terms of emotional maturity and the development of vital human qualities and capabilities, such as the ability to resolve conflict by conciliation without reference to adults, the willingness to take account of the views and opinions of others, and the readiness to comfort and sustain others in distress.

The work described in this book is largely concerned with the creative development of the learner, and the creative teachers, coaches and other experts who enable that creativity to flower in schools.

Creative teaching

Creativity, in any field of human endeavour, calls for a formidable range of skills, whether it be the scientist, physician or physiologist who achieves epoch-making breakthroughs in an area of medicine or pathology; the theatre director who brings about a transforming interpretation of a classic play; the civil engineer who dares to conceive of highways, tunnels and bridges that link what was hitherto thought impossible; the manager of an institution that provides high quality palliative care; the fashion designer whose creations enhance people's self-esteem and conception of themselves; the composer who writes an effective jingle; the cartoonist who satirises fallible politicians; or the botanist who discovers a plant that contributes to palliative medicine.

Where does the teacher stand, if at all, in the parade of such extraordinary, life-changing brilliance? In what possible ways might her work and her endeavours, day by day, over a period of time, be judged comparable to the aforementioned types of achievement? What are the qualities that entitle her to be described as creative in the truest sense?

Let us consider what might be considered as valid examples of creativity:

- Creative teachers are at the heart of children's education: as diagnostician identifying the pupil's learning capacity and needs, choreographing essential experiences and opportunities, and organising the environment and resources that will cater for those; bringing their comprehensive and expert understanding of the learning process to shape the individual child's development and the metacognition that will enable him or her to be an agent in their own progress.

- Creative teachers are motivated by a passion for, and a compelling enthusiasm about, existence and living – what they can take from it and learn from it, what it offers in terms of growth and enrichment, and how they can engage with and respond to it. They often bring their personal enthusiasms into the life of the school, offering children insight into and contact with (however fleeting it may be because of the pressure of time and circumstances) their world outside of school and the interests and pursuits that occupy, enrich and energise them – whether it be ballet, orienteering, archaeology, sailing, dancing or any of a host of others. In the process, they contribute to the broadening of horizons which is central to the creative curriculum.

- Creative teachers are informed by a comprehensive understanding of the learning process and its complexities, and manage the severe demands it makes in terms of provision, organisation and evaluation.

- Creative teachers command extensive subject knowledge – a critical and indispensable aspect of the learning process.

- Creative teachers seek out and secure, wherever possible, expertise from within and outside the school to enhance their work in particular projects or areas of teaching. Examples of such enterprise will be encountered in some of the following chapters.

- Creative teachers, without exception – whichever phase they may work in or whatever their subject responsibility or expertise – have an informed knowledge of significant aspects of literature, exemplified in their capacity to draw from it and bring to their teaching what is relevant, affective and inspiring. In the primary sector, such material will be drawn from folk and fairy tales, from sagas and myths and from the ever-expanding range of high quality literature and stories designed for children and young adults.

To those who might doubt the place, the value and the appropriateness of narrative in relation to other subject areas (apart from the contribution it makes to pupils' language), it may be worth considering the inspirational stories of scientists and engineers. Learning about the stories of the women and men who improved the lot of humanity, minimised pain and suffering and extended life expectancy by their endeavours, can be inspirational for younger generations, who are often awed to learn of the risks they took in their investigations and experiments, sometimes hazardous and life threatening. (One need look no further than the life and work of Marie Curie for an example of inspired genius and heroic perseverance and self-sacrifice which continues to benefit and sustain human life, or the scientists who devised anaesthetics, testing the drugs first on themselves, and made an immeasurable contribution to human survival and pain relief.)

To sum up, we would say that, at her best, the creative teacher engineers the transformation of children's lives for the richer and better.

Specialist teaching

Without adequate subject knowledge, educational practice can only be partially effective. This is a significant issue for teachers, especially those who work with pupils at the upper end of the junior stage. Few teachers feel wholly confident about providing satisfactorily, let alone creatively, for a cluster of subjects ranging across science, mathematics, linguistics, humanities, arts and sporting domains.

But it may not be too much to suggest that, in at least one of these subject areas, teachers should be equipped to teach effectively to the middle years of the secondary stage. It is this competence that ensures the maximum creative exploitation of a subject, that the best is taken from it to the benefit of pupils and there is the capacity to challenge and enable them to work and study at levels well above the average. In other words, to provide for differentiation at its most sophisticated. It is such knowledge and competence that enables teaches to act, in the fullest sense, on the Vygotskian principle that what children can manage at a particular time, with informed assistance, they can achieve soon after, with assurance, on their own (Vygotsky, 1986).

Teachers who command high subject expertise, and have the capacity to employ it creatively, fill the vital role of subject leaders or coordinators in schools, in which they furnish colleagues with the essential mapping of subject content and a range of detailed suggestions and pedagogical strategies, together with the practical support and mentoring that will help to ensure successful implementation.

But how can all schools, even small rural ones, provide such expertise across the broad range of national curriculum subjects, especially in areas such as languages and music?

In the case of certain subjects, some schools buy in expertise from outside sources or from neighbouring secondary schools, but this is not always feasible due to cost or timetable exigencies. Some schools are fortunate to have teachers specialising in more than one subject and provide for them to work exclusively in those areas. In many cases, schools are building up banks of lessons in various subjects that have proved to be notably successful in terms of pupils' learning. Of course, schools can also turn to the extensive body of materials available in reputable published programmes or on the Internet. At its best, this content is exhaustively mapped, chronologically organised and richly endowed with authoritative, practical and tested suggestions for teaching and learning.

Teachers with specialist expertise possess the insight, knowledge and skills to shape meaningful and captivating learning opportunities and experiences. But they recognise, too, when the parameters of a study might be richly extended by an unanticipated but potentially rewarding diversion or byway on the planning map. They can do so because they have the necessary confidence, capacity and creativity, as in the following brief example of creative and specialist teaching:

A Year 6 class in a London school had been set a formal, apparently limited task, arising from previous work in history. They were divided into groups of four, provided with a limited number of offcuts of card and invited to construct a bridge of any style and in any way they liked. The children were so interested in the challenge that the teacher took the project further, providing them with more elaborate materials and resources.

The task became a competition to find the most suitable bridge to fulfil a particular function. One bridge collapsed disastrously in the testing and, subsequently, some children who had researched the Tay Bridge disaster proposed that the group responsible should be 'tried for negligence'. Though somewhat uneasy at this turn of events, the teacher agreed – with the proviso that trial and investigation procedures should be thoroughly researched first.

As a result of the 'trial', the group responsible for the 'disaster' was instructed to redesign and submit a satisfactory model. The group requested permission to approach a parent for help. The teacher agreed, but suggested that the parent should come in and work in the classroom. The outcome was a suc-cessful construction of intricate design, accompanied by a presentation by the pupils, explaining its various refinements.

The study, investigation and work had eventually taken the pupils' learning significantly further than had been originally envisaged, due to the professional competence and creativity of the teacher in recognising and exploiting a valuable opportunity.

Wherever possible, to supplement their own knowledge and skills, teachers in the schools described in this book seek out and secure the engagement and collaboration of experts from within and outside the school to enhance their teaching.

To conclude, we have attempted to convey here a sense of an education of profound value – the inventive, creative and specialist teaching that promotes it and the rich curriculum that underpins and sustains it. We would like to thank all the contributors to the book and hope that you, the reader, may feel the same sense of celebration that they and their colleagues provoked in us.

Further reading

Alexander, R. (ed.) (2009). *Children, Their World, Their Education: Final Report and Recommendations of the Cambridge Primary Review*. Abingdon: Routledge.

Alexander, R. (2017a). Developing Dialogue: Process, Trial, Outcomes. Paper presented at the 17th EARLI International Conference, Tampere, Finland, 31 August. Available at: http://www. robinalexander.org.uk/wp-content/uploads/2017/08/EARLI-2017-paper-170825.pdf.

Alexander, R. (2017b). *Towards Dialogic Teaching: Rethinking Classroom Talk*, 5th edn. York: Dialogos.

Alexander, R., Rose, J. and Woodhead, C. (1992). *Curriculum Organisation and Classroom Practice in Primary Schools: A Discussion Paper* [Three Wise Men Report]. London: Department for Education and Science.

Brighouse, T. (2016). It's Time for Sir Michael to Sing Up About the Arts, *TES* (13 May). Available at: https://www.tes.com/news/tes-magazine/tes-magazine/its-time-sir-michael-sing-about-arts.

Department for Education (2013). The National Curriculum in England: Key Stages 1 and 2 Framework Document. Available at: https://www.gov.uk/government/uploads/system/uploads/attachment_data/file/425601/PRIMARY_national_curriculum.pdf.

Dweck, C. (2012). *Mindset: How You Can Fulfil Your Potential*. London: Robinson.

Hall, J. (2016). A Broad and Balanced Curriculum: Key Findings from Ofsted [PowerPoint presentation] (27 September). Available at: http://www.insidegovernment.co.uk/uploads/2016/09/joannahall-1.pdf.

Mortimer, P. (1988). *School Matters: The Junior Years*. London: Paul Chapman.

Ofsted (2017). *Bold Beginnings: The Reception Curriculum in a Sample of Good and Outstanding Primary Schools*. Ref: 170045. Available at: https://www.gov.uk/government/publications/reception-curriculum-in-good-and-outstanding-primary-schools-bold-beginnings.

Ofsted and Spielman, A. (2017). HMCI's Commentary: Recent Primary and Secondary Curriculum Research (11 October). Available at: https://www.gov.uk/government/speeches/hmcis-commentary-october-2017.

Plowden, B. (ed.) (1967). *Children and Their Primary Schools: A Report of the Control Advisory Council for Education (England)* [Plowden Report]. London: Her Majesty's Stationery Office. Available at: http://www.educationengland.org.uk/documents/plowden/plowden1967-1.html.

Stoll, L., Fink, D. and Earl, L. (2002). *It's About Learning (and It's About Time): What's in it for Schools?* London: RoutledgeFalmer.

Stoll, L. and Louis, K. S. (2007). *Professional Learning Communities: Divergence, Depth and Dilemmas*. London/New York: Open University Press/McGraw Hill.

Vygotsky, L. S. (1962). *Thought and Language*. Cambridge, MA: MIT Press.

Vygotsky, L. S. (1986). *Thought and Language* (rev. edn), ed. A. Kozulin. Cambridge, MA: MIT Press.

Vygotsky, L. S. (1987 [1934]). Thinking and Speech, tr. N. Minick. In R. W. Rieber and A. S. Carton (eds), *The Collected Works of L. S. Vygotsky*. Vol. 1: *Problems of General Psychology*. New York: Plenum Press, pp. 39–285.

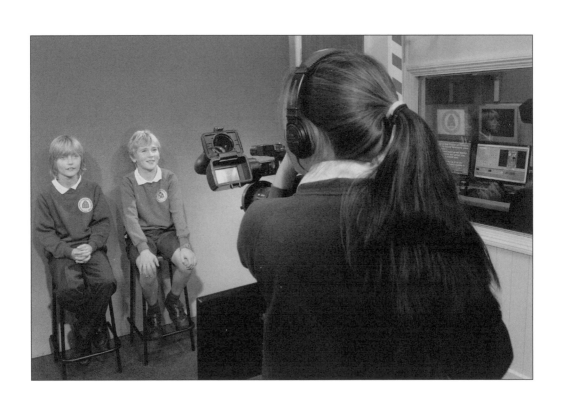

Chapter 1

Learning With and Through Nature

Sue Stokoe, head teacher, Boldon Nursery School – Outdoor Nursery, South Tyneside

Boldon Nursery School – Outdoor Nursery is a unique institution in that it is the only local authority maintained nursery school in the country that operates out of doors for 85% of the time – 'all day, every day, whatever the weather'. It puts into practice an approach to the education of children in the early years that some consider unduly daring and unorthodox, even revolutionary. It certainly represents a significant departure from the commonly held view of what would be traditionally referred to as 'nursery practice'.

The nature and structure of the children's education, and the organisation of the school designed to ensure its provision, are based on the philosophy and belief of the head teacher and staff that children learn more deeply and effectively when they are engaged in, and motivated through, play-based opportunities. It is a belief grounded in intensive research and close observation, and is inspired by a comprehensive understanding of the work of renowned thinkers and pioneers in the field of early years education.

At Boldon, the entire range of children's activities and experience are scrupulously structured, and the whole environment – indoors and outdoors – is creatively organised and resourced to realise the aims, principles and objectives of the school, while ensuring outstanding achievement in relation to educational outcomes.

The terms 'specialism' and 'specialist' are more commonly encountered in relation to the education of pupils at the upper end of the primary stage and throughout the secondary sector. Yet it is specialist teaching of the most comprehensively informed and of the most proficient nature that takes place at the remarkable Boldon Nursery School.

As a model or initiative, Boldon's commitment to the importance of nature as being central to children's development and education can provide inspiration for other early years providers who wish to move towards a more creative and specialised approach to the curriculum.

In 2016, the school won the *TES*' 'Early Years Setting of the Year' award as well as its most prestigious award, 'Overall School of the Year'.

Background

Boldon Nursery School – Outdoor Nursery is a local authority maintained nursery school in South Tyneside. The school has 94 children aged between 2 and 5 years. There are six teaching staff, including the head teacher, teacher and a senior educator, and five of the six staff have a Level 5 or above nursery qualification.

The school is set in an area of deprivation, supporting children from a mixture of workless households, low-income households and working households. A children's centre for families, run by the local council, was built on the site in 2006.

Walking through the area on my way to view the school for the first time, I quickly grasped its potential and felt the desire to create a more unique provision for the families it serves.

I really wanted to be at Boldon, believing I could make a substantial difference for this community and – with the right team – change lives, aspirations and attitudes.

I came to the school in February 2006. It was typical of a nursery school of its time. The school had previously been awarded Beacon status and had been given an 'outstanding' judgement from Ofsted in 2000. The school was deemed to be successful by both the pupils' families and the local authority. The environment featured lots of different brightly coloured walls and displays, defined areas for sand and water play, and a safety surface in an enclosed outer area which housed a climbing frame for all weathers. This supported a very traditional early years curriculum, but the children played outside with wheeled toys only while the inside space was being tidied up for lunch to be served.

There are distinct differences between our approach and the more conventional approach to the delivery of the Early Years Foundation Stage (EYFS) curriculum. Traditionally, adults plan activities for the children, with most of them taking place inside. Quite possibly, the children may be allowed outside for only a limited time or not at all in very cold or wet weather. They may be stopped in their play to be brought inside for a story, or for some phonics or number work. This can restrict the children's ability to lead their own learning and to consolidate deeper levels of learning.

The traditional nursery typically contains workshop areas, including the home corner for role play, writing, building, dressing up, computing, maths, arts and crafts, and may also feature sand and water trays. Activity areas outside might include an area for gardening, using wheeled toys, water trays and possibly a mud kitchen. The use of tools, fire, climbing and any work with nature is usually carried out within a Forest School framework, where a small group of children access the programme over six weeks until it is the turn of another group.

Important as these experiences can be, at Boldon we believe that this model of planning can restrict the children's opportunity to be learning with and in nature every day, for most of the day.

What convinced me of the need for change and development at Boldon Nursery was an Ofsted judgement of 'satisfactory' during an inspection that took place during my first four days as head. My vision for improvement came from my previous experience in the early years and from recent research into the value of outdoor play. Nina Morris of OPENspace Research had already identified the impact that urban spaces can have on children's life chances (2003). She has also explored the impact of outdoor provision on speech and language development and, more specifically, on life skills, health and well-being. This triggered my desire and determination to change the way learning for our youngest children was approached and facilitated.

Nowadays, at Boldon, the children access the outdoors in free-flow situations where they can go out or in whenever they want during the session.

Moving outdoors

From my first year at Boldon, we observed children more closely and introduced free-flow from inside to outside during the whole day session. This raised numerous issues with staff, many of which will be familiar to colleagues in their own settings: 'We can't be outside all the time. How will the children learn what they need to learn?' was the initial response from parents and some colleagues!

The understanding and motivation of parents and staff is crucial to any success in a school. We had to devise our seasonal curriculum notes and share these with parents and others. (These are available on our website.) Doubts continued to rumble: 'Well, we can't be outside in the cold, it's not right for the children.' 'Children suffering with a cold can't be outside – they need to be warm and snug indoors.' But we pressed on (in any case, flu and cold germs germinate in indoor heat and spread quickly).

We spent a lot of time and money finding the right clothing to withstand the showers, wind and heavy rain we get in the North East, and we soon had the evidence to justify our approach: we had parents commenting on how healthy their children were for being outside, and we could also demonstrate impact in terms of the progress the children were making, which is verified in our last two Ofsted reports.

Between 2006 and 2009, time was invested in trying to create and implement a vision for early years care and education at Boldon (including the children's centre), which resulted in many changes for our staff. We changed the school's name in September 2012 to incorporate its very unique practice: Boldon Nursery School – Outdoor Nursery.

Motivation

From experience, research and observation, I believe that children learn better and deeper and have more transferable skills when they are active, engaged and motivated through play-based opportunities. As a child, I did all the things that are quite possibly deemed to be dangerous nowadays: I climbed trees and structures (yes, I broke my arm!);

made campfires, dens and trails; and mixed potions with flowers and plants from the garden without anyone 'risk assessing' them beforehand. I played away from home, often taking a picnic with me to share with friends. I had an active and imaginative childhood. I recall the feeling of freedom and the sense of power in making decisions and being allowed to find things out for myself.

My journey into and through education drew me to the pioneers of childhood development and learning. I saw myself as an advocate for childhood and set out to prove that, as a school, we can promote learning through play and still produce excellent results for our children. We have achieved this, with two 'outstanding' Ofsted inspections in 2011 and 2015, both of which cited the curriculum as innovative and stimulating:

> The curriculum is extremely stimulating, incorporating a broad range of rich, inspiring, varied and creative experiences. The statement, 'the best classroom and richest cupboard is roofed only by the sky', underpins the school's ethos and drive to use nature and the seasons to stimulate children's curiosity and enhance their learning. This includes in their early reading, writing and mathematical work.

> The inspirational and forward-thinking headteacher inspires a highly effective staff team who ensure that all children are provided with rich and interesting learning experiences. The highest levels of achievement are maintained because senior leaders have a crystal-clear vision, are highly ambitious and have high expectations of both children and staff. (Ofsted, 2015: 1, 4)

A visit from HMI in February 2013 confirmed our innovations as inspiring. The resulting report, *Getting It Right First Time* (Ofsted, 2013), sets out the features of strong leadership and the ways in which strong leaders develop and sustain high quality provision.

Colleagues, visitors and inspectors often describe me as someone who isn't afraid to let go of the reins or veer from the norm. I believe I am giving children what they have a right to: a truly play-based and mostly child-initiated curriculum which includes a great amount of time spent outside exploring, being creative and motivated and becoming knowledgeable.

By supporting this with highly experienced, informed adults who are secure in their own learning and who have a genuine interest in children, we ensure the learning moves on and the children achieve. It is not the easiest teaching model, but it is the most rewarding for both the children and adults here at Boldon.

Inspiration

The practitioners who have most inspired me on my journey, particularly when I became a head teacher, are Susan Isaacs and Rachel and Margaret McMillan.

Susan Isaacs promoted the nursery school movement and it is her description of an early years setting that I aspire to provide: 'a place that should both mirror the family through love and warmth, as well as offering new and exciting opportunities and resources that might not be available at home, providing social experiences and friendships that are vital to a child's development' (Isaacs, 1952: 31). She clearly helped parents and practitioners to develop a greater understanding of the child's developmental needs. Her planning of the Malting House School was done carefully to best facilitate the children's development. Our garden has been designed to support whatever schema (the patterns of repeated behaviour which allow children to explore and express developing ideas and thoughts through their play and exploration) a child is demonstrating. For example, a child displaying the positioning schema (constantly stacking, lining and balancing objects – and themselves) may use a climbing tree, fallen leaves or sticks and branches to support their thinking and learning.

The McMillan sisters, Rachel and Margaret, were pioneers of health before turning to education. They opened the first open-air nursery school, which still flourishes today. The sisters believed that children needed fresh air to maintain good health. Much research has now been carried out to confirm their ideas. A study from the University of Derby reported on the UK's first month-long nature challenge, which asked people to engage with nature every day for a month (Richardson et al., 2016). The study identified the positive impact of nature on health and well-being, and the increased self-esteem for children, along with increased creativity, risk-taking and discovery.

Margaret McMillan's famous quote, 'The best kept classroom and richest cupboard are roofed only by the sky', is our motto and the frame for our curriculum provision. Our philosophy is to provide outdoor learning where the curriculum is derived from nature, the seasons and the elements. By being outside, children's communication skills and language development are inspired by the natural world. A significant proportion of our 2-, 3- and 4-year-olds come to us with extremely poor speech and language skills, many may still have dummies and bottles, and a few don't yet have a bedtime routine and still sleep in their parents' beds.

From our own action research (carried out in 2010–2011), we know that when we took our children off-site to the 'Beach and Burn' (a local park with a stream), they played and communicated very differently. Being in the outdoors meant they played more imaginatively and cooperatively and developed their capacity for creativity, problem-solving, communication and intellectual development. Resources were often on a bigger scale (e.g. boulders at the beach), which required planning in order to move and use them. This meant they had to talk to each other! This was a great motivator for moving our learning to predominantly outdoor contexts. We have seen a vast improvement in the children's communication and language development by the time they leave us, and this is also confirmed by the feeder primary schools that the children later attend.

Best practice – play-based early years education

We know that children learn best when they are interested and engaged, and the characteristics of learning documented in the EYFS curriculum highlight this (Department for Education, 2017). Using children's interests as the basis for our curriculum helps to ensure that learning is not only interesting, but it is also meaningful, first-hand and relevant. The EYFS statutory framework states that we need to consider the child's individual needs and interests and use this information to plan interesting and challenging environments and opportunities. We also know from our own observations that most children choose to be outside. Quite often it is the adults – both teachers and parents – who choose not to be outside for whatever reason.

At Boldon, we have combined children's interests with nature to develop our unique curriculum. We focus on teaching life skills, and believe the children will retain, perfect, trial and use these skills as they go through their own lives. Children at 3 and 4 years old are confident and capable learners who will tackle almost anything.

Setting up learning areas

To enable us to provide the best indoor and outdoor areas, we invested a great deal of time as a team on research. Moving from a very traditional indoor and outdoor nursery environment had to be planned extremely carefully. Our parents and local authority officers were the ones who had doubts and asked lots of questions, so as a team we had to be prepared to be true to our vision and explain what our philosophy meant and why we were adopting it. As with any new initiative, it is important to first understand the reason for it and then have an implementation plan that will be adjusted along the way.

Our outdoor environment was only a little better than basic. As a team, for our continuing professional development (CPD), we spent a year meeting every Wednesday after school for an hour to discuss our observations of the children's use of the outdoors, and identified what was missing. We were particularly interested in our provision for boys, who tend to use active learning modes more than girls. National data for EYFS points to girls achieving better than boys. The Primary National Strategy document *Confident, Capable and Creative: Supporting Boys' Achievements* (Department for Children, Schools and Families, 2007) formed a basis for our own action research into gender differences and the challenge of raising boys' development. As a starting point, we revisited learning styles, children's schemas and how individual children learn. This became our baseline for building the outdoor provision. We had to ask ourselves: if children are going to be outside for most of the session, how can we ensure that there is enough challenge for them?

Once we began to unpick the nature-based/outdoor curriculum, we could identify the level of challenge. For example, when harvesting and collecting sticks for the fire to keep us warm in winter, we can introduce sorting according to size – big/little, fat/thin, long/short. We can move on to counting how many sticks we need, and solve the problem of a fire going out too quickly by adding one more to make the fire burn longer. Using and applying mathematical skills for real purposes can motivate and interest children.

Every season brings its own challenges, the need to solve problems, and opportunities for children to learn and develop in response to the world around them – at a time and pace that are relevant to them and their own experiences, and not because that is what the planning sheet says for that week!

Most importantly, the children need to have faith in the adults and trust that they understand their thinking. The adults need to be prepared to act on the children's behalf at all times and to go on a journey with them to find out more, how and why. If it takes us 12 weeks to figure out how the water that comes from the clouds not only feeds our spring bulbs, but flows down the drains and back into our sink in the bathroom, then that is how long it takes. The learning is deep, embedded and meaningful.

We can spend a whole morning, maybe a week, collecting and measuring rainfall and watching it trickle away into the unknown, because during that time complex thought processes arise and our senses are stimulated. We are interested, and we are staying with this group of friends until we find the answer. Along the way we may just dip into how the sunshine dries our springtime puddles and why, despite our rainfall gauge telling us that it didn't rain during the night, the grass is wet. We stand in the heavy downpour, with our mouths wide open, wondering if this water is really what we drink at the dining room table at lunchtime, and ponder over how those huge grey clouds suddenly begin to part and almost disappear. When was the last time we saw blue sky, and what is blue sky?

Time and space to reflect, completely immersed in the seasons and elements, helps us to answer our questions and creates more questions to pursue and find answers to. In measuring rainfall we are mathematicians; in recording imaginative stories about the power of clouds we are writers; in concocting mixtures of sand, mud and water on the wettest of days we are sculptors or scientists; and in all of this we are the best of friends, working and discovering together and dependent upon one another.

Nature as a learning arena

Outdoors, we have trees to climb for strength, balance and perseverance, and we have a hide to support under-and-over schema – as well as being a lovely place for bird watching! We also have mud and water in abundance due to the climate of the North East.

An information station in the grounds houses plentiful research materials, including charts, photos of wildlife and plants in the garden. Magnifiers, bug jars, clipboards and other equipment enable the children to have all they may need outdoors to help them consolidate a find, go on a journey or identify and name a bug they find in the long grass.

Our mud kitchen is a place where recipes come to life and the ingredients are real – but the stories to go with our creations push our imaginations to the limit. We gather at the fire house to keep warm or share food. Being together is important, but if we want to be alone, a place to hide and feel enclosed can always be found in the wild.

Inside is our home from home

We have taken a very unique approach to setting out the indoor learning areas at Boldon. These replicate a home from home, to provide the love and warmth that Susan Isaacs (1952) talks about. The inside space also supports the learning that happens outdoors. It took the team a long time to get to where we are today: with lots of discussion between ourselves, and with children and parents; through observation and tweaking to get it right; and being prepared to continuously adapt our planning according to the cohort's needs.

Inside you will find a flow of spaces that adhere to the thoughts of the child across their day: 'I need to rest, so where will I go?' or 'I'm feeling hungry, where do I eat?' No longer are the spaces defined by adults and their ideas of what a child would like to play with or see in their environment that day. Instead, there is a permanent home for objects, materials and equipment that reflects the children's lives outside of the nursery walls.

They can rest in the lounge space on the sofa by the (electric) log burner, stretching out and watching the animals and children in the allotment. They can eat in the dining room at the adult-sized tables and chairs, while chatting with friends and satisfying their hunger. And it will be this way until the children leave the nursery, because that is how they become independent and feel truly at home in the environment.

We constantly have discussions about the child-height cooker in the kitchen space, as well as other potential health and safety issues and risk assessments. Obviously, these matters need to be considered carefully, but we usually conclude that the benefit of the activity/resource is greater and worth the controlled risk. Our children's kitchen would be incomplete without shelves filled with ingredients stored in glass jars and canisters, or without the cooker to bake our ingredients. Our passion for children having real experiences, without being hidden from everyday life for fear of it not being 'safe', and allowing them to make links to their world is what drives our unique provision and innovative thinking.

We have learned a lot from Tim Gill (2007), who describes risk management in play contexts as being different from the workplace because a degree of risk is often beneficial, if not essential. We regularly discuss and value the specific, positive things that children gain through the play opportunities that we are assessing.

To enable us to provide the indoor and outdoor areas we have today, we have invested a great deal of time as a team through our own CPD and an action research enquiry about risk with parents. We have drawn from the ideas of the 'forest kindergartens' in Denmark, the 'nature kindergartens' in Scotland and the environments of pre-schools in Reggio Emilia, Italy. In pairs, the six staff have visited one each. These have influenced our creative curriculum, both inside and outside, in terms of access to nature without boundaries, the use of real objects (from crockery, cutlery, glasses and jars to animals and plants) and the time and space we devote to working through a nature-based pedagogy.

How the learning and creativity arises

When our new children start with us in September, they have already visited the nursery and have established a relationship with their key person and with the outdoors. The first 'resource' the children meet as they move to the outdoors is our playground 'beach'. The beach is something they are all familiar with as it is part of the culture here in South Tyneside, where we have some of the most beautiful coastlines. Our children already recognise and feel secure playing with sand and water on a bigger scale. This confidence supports the children to move out much sooner into the wider, larger, open space beyond.

One example of how learning and creativity arise and develop is through our lighthouse. The children recognise the lighthouse we have at our playground beach as a replica of Souter Lighthouse in the village of Marsden. As their curiosity grows, a group who are interested will visit the real lighthouse. They may, after a few visits, have the stamina to climb to the top and learn that it has 76 steps. They may develop an interest in the lights – how they work and who works them – and whether there are any other lighthouses in the country.

Their enquiries may inspire drawing, painting, clay modelling, storytelling, writing or an interest in ships, boats and the sea. The potential for learning for both the adult and child is relevant, real, motivational, inspiring and interesting. Responses to the children's interests often result in smaller learning groups (i.e. children who have a common interest), and possible lines of direction can result in a project that is documented visually from start to finish, making the learning evident.

Using natural resources

We try to be in tune with the current season, so cooking may start with very simple foods that don't even need to go in an oven. In September, apples are on the trees and blackberries are on the bushes. We harvest the fruits and use them – one of our very first dishes will be a crumble or pie made from apples and blackberries. We aim to ensure that the fruit picking, peeling, cooking and eating all happen in the same session in order to consolidate the learning for the children. They experience the planting, growing, harvesting, cooking and eating, which means they learn and understand the nature of the entire process.

We give our children time and space for learning and creativity. They can cut down some willow wands from the garden, and peel and then bake them in a tin on the fire that they have lit and is now smouldering. When the sticks have cooled they have made their own charcoal: name me a child who wouldn't want to write with a pencil they have made themselves!

Any visitor to the nursery can immediately see that we use natural, open-ended resources that are abundant in the locality. These beautiful materials offer the children the opportunity to be creative in their play, to cooperate with each other and to design and test ideas. Our children develop profound respect for the natural world and the materials they can gather freely from natural habitats.

How our team works

As educators, we have a responsibility to provide opportunities for children that enrich their lives and equip them with lifelong skills. Changing a lifestyle for a family, through partnerships that support them to see the importance of childhood (and what impact they can have on their child's ability to cope in the real world), is what empowers our team to make a difference.

As with any team, each staff member at Boldon has their own passions and strengths, and often this is what drives our provision. If the staff are in a space where they feel confident and happy, using materials they are inspired by, then the children will feel and develop these traits too. Alongside this runs a skill set which is unique to each adult; they might be very creative, or a good tree climber, or an allotment lover (we are lucky to have all of these!), and from these skill sets the quality of the practice flows.

Over a prolonged period, the team have developed relationships that are open and honest, and as a result are very productive when working in a more challenging way. The team are in a place where they can support each other often, challenge each other always and ensure that what they do each day is confidently part of the woven fabric of the place, knowing why and what impact it has for the children with whom they are working.

The adults work with groups of children for lengthy periods of time – gone are the days of rotas and swapping areas to make it 'fair'. Instead, fair at Boldon is staying in a place you love, having real ownership over a project or idea and seeing it through to the end, no matter how long that takes. To facilitate such a philosophy, the team needs to communicate often and about everything.

With leadership and management strategies which encourage the team to question and evaluate constantly, effective decisions are made daily and are always made in response to the wants, needs and ideas of the children – first and foremost around their fascinations and interests. Through carefully looking at their own practice and pedagogy, the staff have been on a journey of self-reflection which has underpinned the changes at Boldon over the years, frequently agreeing to innovative ideas and trying things that are outside their comfort zone.

Daily, this is reflection. Weekly, this is planning with the children in the moment. Monthly, this is assessing the children and ensuring the challenge and support is always there, but always in line with what they love. There is also considerable documenting and sharing with parents. 'Flexible' is a word we use often, and being considerate is an essential trait. Trust in each other is what allows this to happen, and respect for each other makes it work.

Conclusion

At Boldon Nursery we support the child's innate need to be outside whatever the weather. One staff member will support learning in the indoor studio space and, in the early days, toileting. The rest of us are outdoors – supporting, consolidating and bringing new learning to their world. From registration to going home, a child may, if they choose, never enter the indoor space. They may even choose to eat lunch outside around the fire.

When we unpick the impact of our teaching and learning model by looking at the progress data, our outdoors provision clearly supports the holistic development of the child. For the past five years, we have seen consistently high rates of learning and progress made by all our pupils. Vulnerable groups make similar rates of progress and most catch up with their peers. Working in the way we do allows the child to have a childhood, to learn and make outstanding progress, to be healthy (which raises attendance) and to develop speech and language at an astounding rate, which reduces the need for interventions.

The benefits for the pupils are evident, and those for the school have also been exceptional. As well as being awarded *TES*' 'Overall School of the Year' award in 2016, we are now involved in a European project with three other countries – Scotland, Norway and the Czech Republic – looking at nature as a powerful learning arena. We have been asked to host study tours from delegates across the globe, including Australia and New Zealand, who are interested in what we are doing. By approaching children's learning a little differently and more creatively, we can all make sure that we give our young children the richest opportunities to develop holistically and become creative and independent learners.

Further reading and useful links

Constable, K. (2014). *The Outdoor Classroom in Practice, Ages 3–7: A Month-by-Month Guide to Forest School Provision*. London: David Fulton.

Department for Children, Schools and Families (2007). *Confident, Capable and Creative: Supporting Boys' Achievements. Guidance for Practitioners in the Early Years Foundation Stage*. Nottingham: DCSF. Available at: https://www.foundationyears.org.uk/wp-content/uploads/2011/10/Confident_Capable_Boys.pdf.

Department for Education (2017). *Statutory Framework for the Early Years Foundation Stage: Setting the Standards for Learning, Development and Care for Children from Birth to Five*. Available at: https://www.foundationyears.org.uk/files/2017/03/EYFS_STATUTORY_FRAMEWORK_2017.pdf.

Gill, T. (2007). *No Fear: Growing Up in a Risk Averse Society*. London: Calouste Gulbenkian Foundation.

Isaacs, S. (1952). *The Educational Value of a Nursery School*. London: British Association for Early Childhood Education.

McMillan, M. (2008). *Early Childhood Education: A Series of Classic Readings* (11 vols). New Delhi: Cosmo Publications.

Moore, R. and Wong, H. (1997). *Natural Learning: Rediscovering Nature's Way of Teaching*. Berkeley, CA: MIG Communications.

Morris, N. (2003). *Health, Well-Being and Open Space Literature Review*. Edinburgh: Edinburgh College of Art and Heriot-Watt University.

Ofsted (2013). *Achieving and Maintaining High Quality Early Years Provision: Getting It Right First Time* (3 July). Available at: https://www.gov.uk/government/publications/achieving-and-maintaining-high-quality-early-years-provision-getting-it-right-first-time.

Ofsted (2015). School Report: Boldon Nursery School (3–4 March). Available at: https://reports.ofsted.gov.uk/inspection-reports/find-inspection-report/provider/ELS/108665.

Richardson, M., Cormack, A., McRobert, L. and Underhill, R. (2016). 30 Days Wild: Development and Evaluation of a Large-Scale Nature Engagement Campaign to Improve Well-Being, *PLOS One* (18 February). https://doi.org/10.1371/journal.pone.0149777.

Robb, M., Mew, V. and Richardson, A. (2015). *Learning with Nature: A How-To Guide to Inspiring Children Through Outdoor Games and Activities*. Cambridge: Green Books.

Santer, J. and Griffiths, C. with Goodall, D. (2007). *Free Play in Early Childhood: A Literature Review*. London: Play England/National Children's Bureau. Available at: http://www.playengland.org.uk/media/120426/free-play-in-early-childhood.pdf.

Forest Kindergartens in Scotland: http://www.owlscotland.org/local-options/forest-kindergarten

Forest Schools in Denmark: http://denmark.dk/en/meet-the-danes/forest-preschools

Reggio Emilia Approach: http://www.reggiochildren.it/identita/reggio-emilia-approach/?lang=en

About the contributor

Sue Stokoe

After graduating with a BEd in primary education, Sue Stokoe started her career as a reception teacher in a large primary, before going on to support visually impaired children and opening a nursery class in an infant school. Later, she was seconded to the local authority to work within the early years team, and, in 2006, was appointed head teacher at Boldon.

Chapter 2
The Window

Bertie Hornibrook, head teacher,
Chadlington CE Primary School, Oxfordshire

Chadlington CE Primary School engages its pupils in a wide range of learning activities, individual, group and class-based, across a broad curriculum. Among the activities, two in particular stand out for the brilliance of their invention and the high quality of their execution: making a sophisticated animated film based on a folk tale, and designing and planning a stained-glass window for the school hall, with a range of children's proposals and sketches for the commissioned artist.

A particular feature of all the learning activities at the school is the degree of intense research and investigation that underpins them and, on the part of the pupils, an informed awareness of the purpose and the significance of what they are doing, enthusiastically and authoritatively conveyed when explaining the processes in which they are engaged.

Typical of this was the comment of a Year 6 girl who, during an assured account, paused to say about a particular fact, 'Perhaps I should check that for confirmation,' and turned to the Internet to do so. After a few moments of intense concentration, she turned back to smile and say, 'I thought I'd got it right!'

A few months later, at a well-attended gathering to mark the unveiling and dedication of the window, we witnessed again the assured competence of the pupils. They talked not only of what had inspired that great initiative and how it had been brought to a conclusion, but also of many other examples of notable learning outcomes throughout the school. As we left, we could not help wondering how few, passing by that little school along a quiet country road, would guess at the admirable things that were happening there, in the widest educational terms.

Background

Chadlington is a small village school set in a rural landscape. It is a Church of England voluntary controlled school for just over a hundred pupils aged from 4 to 11. The school has achieved the Gold Artsmark and has been approved to deliver the Arts Award. Through the inclusive music programme, all pupils have the opportunity to learn an instrument and play in the brass orchestra.

On entering the school, all pupils are automatically enrolled into the Little Acorn Film Company. By providing a rich film-making curriculum, the pupils are encouraged to become collaborative learners, expressing their own ideas with confidence and developing empathy for others.

A creative project

The aim of this project was to create a stained-glass window; not the tissue paper kind that stains your fingers all the colours of the rainbow and leaves you peeling away a second skin of glue from your hands, but the real kind that breathes life into a building and withstands the passing of time to both delight its makers and intrigue future generations.

Tissue paper stained-glass windows evoke memories of my own primary education in the 1970s when the notion of 'creativity' was synonymous with 'art and craft'. Now, in the 21st century, with the Internet putting the world at our fingertips, we can easily open up a truly creative curriculum that encompasses all areas of learning. In this age of global communication, ideas grow exponentially. If our children are to keep pace, and continue adapting to the rapidly changing world in which we live, we must help them to become innovators, problem-solvers and collaborators, and for this they need to develop creativity. Creativity is the realisation of our original ideas and imagination in some form of tangible outcome. Our stained-glass window project serves to illustrate this process.

Leading the creative curriculum

Developing a creative curriculum that is holistic in nature inevitably has implications for the planning process. Strong leadership is required in weaving together the multidisciplinary elements of the primary curriculum, giving learning direction and a strong sense of purpose. A deep knowledge of the curriculum and an awareness of the needs of the learning community that the task requires make this a job for an experienced teacher. As a head teacher, I consider leading learning – *what* we learn and *how* we learn it – to be my core purpose, so I lead the curriculum: orchestrating large-scale projects, ensuring the curriculum remains relevant and topical, scaffolding objectives in response to any shifts in learning needs indicated by our assessment and monitoring systems, and providing for the changing interests and talents of the school community.

I have found that there are many benefits to retaining curriculum leadership. The role gives me a strong understanding of the learning that is taking place in school, allowing me to maintain an up-to-date awareness of the progress that children make – from their entry into the Early Years Foundation Stage (EYFS) to their exit at the end of Year 6. I have more freedom to monitor the delivery of the curriculum and observe its impact than a teacher with a full-time class commitment would have. This allows me to identify good practice that we can build on to improve the school further and to support colleagues in developing the confidence to deliver the full breadth of the curriculum. Through the planning process, I scaffold learning, helping less experienced teachers to provide effective differentiation. I plan challenging projects that will feed into continuing professional development, encouraging teachers to move beyond their comfort zone and creating an ongoing dialogue about learning that unifies the team.

Think big

Learning, like a journey, should begin with an end goal in mind, and just like the final destination of a journey, that has to be a place worth getting to. It should be a challenging goal because we value the things that we strive for, and our sense of achievement and pride in what we do is usually proportionate to the effort invested in reaching our goal. When I sit down to plan the next project, these are the things that I bear in mind. Much like planning a journey, I begin by building up a picture of the destination: what will it look like? Will it inspire everybody involved? Is it something that will live on in school folklore, creating a shared experience and sense of pride? Aiming to achieve a worthwhile end goal is very different from conceding to the demands of a results-driven curriculum and has a much greater impact on raising standards.

At the 'blue sky thinking' stage of designing the project, I draw on my existing knowledge, trawl the Internet for relevant information and ideas, and talk to anybody and everybody about what I am planning to do. Acknowledging this 'thinking time' is significant because we have to afford the same opportunities to our children if we want them to engage with the creative process. The excitement of problem-solving together gives a project impetus and keeps everybody coming back for more. This period of information gathering can be lengthy but it is never without reward. In the past, for example, it has led us to find a rocket scientist in our local community and launch a science experiment to the edge of space from the school playground, to build a green-powered kit car and race it against other young engineers, and to screen a film festival in our local theatre.

The plan to create a stained-glass window stemmed from my thinking while planning the teaching of light and shadow. I began to research shadow puppets as a way to engage the children's interest in developing their scientific knowledge of physical processes. This led me to explore the work of Lotte Reiniger, a German film director and pioneer of silhouette animation, whose first films were delighting audiences nearly 100 years ago. Struck by the intricate beauty of her work, I watched several of her films and was inspired by her developing use of colour, achieved by using translucent layers in the set design.

I decided to work with the children to make an animated film called *The Window* – a modern-day fairy tale. Pursuing the idea of light coming through a window, I began to look into artists who had designed stained glass, and from this came the idea of creating a stained-glass window that would express the values of the school: 'Let your light shine: imagine, believe, achieve'.

Feasibility

Once I have a project goal firmly in mind, I begin to consider whether the project is viable before I share it with others. The procedural thinkers on the team will always want to know how the project is going to be achieved before they feel ready to engage with it. In planning the creation of a stained-glass window, I asked a number of questions to ascertain the feasibility of the idea: was there a suitable window that we could replace? What size would the design need to be, and how would this affect the cost? Where would the window be made, and how would the children be involved in the design and making of it?

To find answers, I searched the Internet, looking for stained-glass artists who had already worked successfully with children in schools. As a result, I came across a very talented artist called Claire Williams. When I spoke to Claire, I discovered that all of the 100 children in our school could be involved in the project and that they would have their own unique design incorporated into the finished window. I looked at costing and potential sources of finance and put together a proposal. With the proposal agreed by governors and our Church Trust, we were ready to go ahead. With the practicalities assured, I turned my attention to the educational value of the project by mapping out the creative process.

Phase 1: Imagine

Imagination is more important than knowledge. Knowledge is limited. Imagination encircles the world.

Albert Einstein

The first phase of the creative process, imagine, refers to the thought processes and assimilation of experiences that lead to the incubation of viable ideas, enabling creative thinking. We might see creativity as the result of a spark of inspiration, a light-bulb moment, but this can only occur if we have acquired a wide enough base of relevant knowledge and understanding through our prior learning to relate ideas and extend our thinking in innovative ways.

To help the children make links between their learning and life in the real world, our topics are designed around different careers and jobs, rather than subjects. This also creates greater flexibility, allowing us to adapt projects to meet changing curriculum needs. The window project began with a topic entitled 'We are artists', which encouraged learners to explore the work of successful stained-glass artists, from the romantic imagery of the Pre-Raphaelite artist Sir Edward Burne-Jones to the more abstract designs of John Piper.

The artists were chosen for their different styles in order to encourage learners to relate ideas, comparing and contrasting the work of these different artists and exploring the historical contexts that shaped their thinking. Part of the richness of our curriculum is derived from a strong commitment to experiential learning.

Wherever possible, we provide the children with access to learning beyond the classroom. Pupils visited the Ashmolean Museum, in Oxford, and took part in a workshop interpreting Pre-Raphaelite paintings. This enabled them to gain a basic understanding of symbolism which they developed in their study of Pre-Raphaelite poetry. Pupils also studied *The Light of the World*, by Holman Hunt, using the opportunity to explore the religious symbolism of light and to gather imagery which they would later be able to draw on when developing their own design ideas.

The next step in the process of the window design was to take children to see original stained-glass designs of Burne-Jones and Piper in their architectural context. Pupils in Key Stage 2 were taken to see these in Coventry Cathedral and Christ Church Cathedral, in Oxford. Key Stage 1 pupils visited St Mary's Church, in Fairford – home to the most complete set of stained-glass windows in the country, surviving from medieval times.

The visits to these hauntingly beautiful places of worship allowed the children to further deepen their understanding of symbolism, most poignantly through the journey of reconciliation and resurrection embodied in the architectural design of Coventry Cathedral. The children took part in workshops at both cathedrals. They explored the effect of various shapes and colours in the design of the windows and talked about how these combine to evoke different thoughts and emotions in observers, providing a language to describe spiritual experience.

Prior to the visits, the children started a new topic called 'We are film-makers'. They were asked to tell the story of the windows in a documentary to be screened to families at our school film festival in Chipping Norton Theatre. Encouraging the children to identify as members of a film team always inspires their focus and collaboration on a school visit. The pupils recorded their experiences using tablets, a DSLR camera (offering a higher quality picture for the larger cinema screen) and a small hand-held microphone. Their ideas and images were later used to structure and inspire documentary screenwriting.

While visiting Christ Church Cathedral, we took the opportunity to investigate local architecture and track historical changes through time. The children explored how the changing design of the windows reflected life during different historical periods – for example, they drew comparisons between the narrow slit windows of Oxford Castle, representative of the architecture of warfare, and the much larger windows of today's more outward-looking society.

Following this accumulation of learning experiences, we set the children the challenge of designing a stained-glass window to replace the large window in our school hall and reflect our values: 'Let your light shine: imagine, believe, achieve'. What might *imagine*, *believe* and *achieve* look like, for example, if they were personified as angels in the style of Burne-Jones? What symbolism could be used to express their meaning? The pupils discussed their ideas in depth, drawing from the skills, knowledge and understanding they had acquired over the course of their topics as film-makers and artists. They drew their own versions of these figures and worked together to create a short animated film about the creation of a stained-glass window.

Phase 2: Believe

Watch your thoughts, they become words; watch your words, they become actions; watch your actions, they become habits; watch your habits, they become character; watch your character, for it becomes your destiny.

Frank Outlaw

Chadlington is a Church of England voluntary controlled school and, as such, Christian values underpin all that we do. However, we refer to belief in its broadest sense, encompassing trust and confidence as well as faith.

As educators, we know that both a child's self-belief and her ability to believe in others will profoundly influence her ability to develop as a learner. Without such trust, she will be afraid of making mistakes and lack the confidence to take risks, which in turn will inhibit her ability to learn. When I discuss obstacles to learning with children, time and time again they tell me that they are frightened to get things wrong and worry about what other people will say. If we want to encourage children to invest in the experiences that we offer, we need to reward risk-taking by focusing on the process of learning over time and using praise to reward pupils' growth as learners, rather than depending on a largely results-driven curriculum which measures learners' success by judging each piece of work that they produce. Instead, these pieces of work should serve as indicators of a child's developing knowledge, understanding and skills in their learning journey. This focus on the process of learning is not at odds with the idea of achieving an exciting and challenging end goal, which will bring its own reward through the sense of pride that pupils will gain from their creative achievements.

In the classroom, pupils are encouraged to develop self-belief by recognising each small step that they take towards mastering a particular skill or developing their knowledge and understanding. We engage pupils in ongoing dialogue about their learning, using an online tracker called Pupil Asset. Essentially, Pupil Asset provides us with a real-time 'mark book' that can be accessed anywhere, by any teacher, using a computer, tablet or smartphone. The mark book takes the form of a national curriculum tick-list that can be adapted to meet the school's own needs. Achieved objectives are coloured using the equivalent of a traffic light system. The formative data that we gather feeds into summative assessments and the results of each cohort are summarised in a tracking sheet. 'DNA' rows – mapping the curriculum objectives that pupils achieve each term – help us to track pupils' individual rates of progress over the year and flag up the need to provide interventions or step up the level of challenge.

From a management point of view, the system effectively generates reports on attainment and progress, allowing leaders to evaluate the achievement of different cohorts and groups. Although, from a classroom management perspective, perhaps the most useful tool is the 'achievement summary' tab, which allows teachers to see instantly which pupils in the class have achieved an objective, are working towards it or are not yet ready to begin working on it. This allows teaching to be precisely targeted, using dynamic pupil grouping and avoiding over-reliance on organising the class into fixed ability groups. With starting points clearly established, assessment information is then used to address misconceptions and feed forward. A series of 'next steps' helps pupils to understand how they can achieve their next objective by breaking down the learning journey into a chain of smaller and more manageable goals. Of course, the size of these steps depends on the learning ability of individual pupils. Sharing these steps with pupils at the beginning of a unit is extremely beneficial in helping them to see the path they need to travel and to develop belief in their own ability to reach their goal.

Just as important in the development of pupils' self-belief is the role of the teacher in destigmatising mistakes. Some children are so anxious about being seen to get things wrong that they will go to great lengths to avoid this; we all recognise the child with the tummy ache, the child who screws up her work, the child that won't even begin a task, the child who disappears to the toilet at every opportunity – the list goes on! Valuing mistakes as part of the learning process, and creating a culture where this is seen as the norm, is the quickest way I know to help children develop a 'give it a go' attitude to tricky tasks. Likewise, the skilled use of differentiation in response to informative ongoing assessment procedures ensures that children of *all* abilities experience the acquisition of learning goals as something that is just within reach, if they are willing to strive for them. This levels the playing field because all learners are having to struggle to reach their goal. These high expectations across the board not only help children to value effort, made by themselves and others, but also allow them to experience that success is the result of hard work sustained over time, and not about instant reward. Our curriculum is enquiry based, allowing everybody to access it at his or her own level.

We can also encourage learners to develop self-belief by helping them to understand that expertise can be developed with practice – that it is perspiration and not inspiration that leads most of us to achieve. Successful learning calls for effort, determination, resilience and commitment. Hattie and Yates (2013) discuss the correlation between the development of expertise and the time invested in developing skills, knowledge and understanding in a particular field. Knowing that others have struggled before us, and gone on to achieve exceptional results, is extremely encouraging to learners at the beginning of their journey. Children instinctively look for role models and we should provide them by creating a curriculum that explores the work of others – not just 'the greats' such as Burne-Jones and Piper, but people who are working successfully in their field today. Meeting a role model, such as our artist, Claire, helps learners to develop belief in the achievability of a goal.

Our stained-glass window project presented pupils with opportunities to learn about faith through their exploration of the significance of light. Children visited Stonehenge and the nearby Rollright Stones, exploring different theories about the purpose of their construction and weighing up related evidence. The visit to Great Rollright also inspired some impromptu drama and creative writing while enjoying the atmosphere of the stone circle on an idyllic summer's day.

Throughout the year, the children continued to explore the symbolism of light in faith, going on to compare Diwali and Christingle celebrations, identifying similarities and differences. This led them to consider how our values could be expressed in the design of our window in a manner that would be inclusive to different beliefs. They discussed their own responses to our school motto, both in relation to the biblical imagery in Matthew 5:16, 'Let your light so shine before men, that they may see your good works, and glorify your Father which is in heaven', and as an expression of the importance of using and celebrating our own talents.

Phase 3: Achieve

I am always doing what I can't do yet in order to learn how to do it.

Vincent Van Gogh

Everybody plays their part in achieving the challenging goals that we aim for. We all learn together, adults and children alike. The more we challenge ourselves, the more we expect to succeed because we have found that by working as a team, we always do. Leading a small school is a job with many challenges: the small number of personnel, for example, and the need for staff to wear many hats at the same time. However, it is a job that I have found deeply rewarding over the years, not least because of the creative freedom that it offers and the rich possibilities for collaborative learning that life in a close-knit community provides.

I can't overstate the importance of collaboration in achieving large-scale creative projects, and this works at all levels. At an adult level, shared experiences not only bind the team together but also allow us to model good practice, to work strategically together in leading school development and to manage workload. There are just four classes in our school and the equivalent of four full-time teachers. As a teaching head, I am also part of this mix. All teachers contribute to our 'collaborative leadership team', working to implement agreed development strategies, rather than carrying individual subject leadership responsibilities. This management structure is the key to our creative success as we all pull in the same direction and support each other.

By operating in this way, and by all playing our part in carrying out a creative project, we also model effective teamwork to our pupils on a daily basis. They, in turn, grow to understand the importance of collaboration in undertaking challenging creative projects. Taking a collaborative approach to creativity allows us to capitalise on research into how we learn. Hattie and Yates (2013) explore research on the limitations of cognitive load. Their conclusion, that we are able to process information more effectively by sharing cognitive load, is certainly consistent with observed outcomes from the projects that we have undertaken in school.

Through the experience of creating a stained-glass window, the pupils covered a wide range of learning objectives in English, maths, science, art and design, history and RE, making meaningful links across subjects by taking a multidisciplinary approach to learning. Before we began to make the window, the pupils carried out research to find out how glass is made. They discovered how materials change state; how these changes occur at different temperatures, depending on what the material is and whether the change is reversible or not; and that the temperature needed to make glass can be reduced by adding sodium carbonate. The children explored how the materials used in a stained-glass window are chosen for their particular properties: glass lets light through but not water, and it is rigid enough to hold its shape; lead is soft enough to bend and to provide support for the individual pieces of glass within the window; and the addition of iron oxide, for example, changes the colour of the glass, creating a greenish-blue colour.

Older pupils also researched how glass can be formed when lightning strikes some types of sand, making fulgurites. In order to bring the making of glass within a classroom environment, teachers made sugar glass to demonstrate how stunt glass is made: children observed the changing states, examining the resulting pane with wide-eyed wonder. Lower Key Stage 2 pupils explored whether light can travel through all materials and older pupils designed a test to find out whether the colour of glass affects the amount of light that passes through it, measuring and recording their results with an electronic light meter.

This knowledge was then developed further through the pupils' creation of sets and puppets for their animated film, *The Window*, providing them with many more opportunities to apply their scientific understanding to problem-solving within a real-life context. In my experience, children achieve at a much higher level when they can see the purpose of what they are doing, so we need to provide them with real and relevant contexts for learning. In making their shadow puppets, the children experimented with a range of materials and different light sources, choosing translucent tissue paper to animate a dragon's eye, painting on transparent acetate layered over a light box to create a cloud ship and using opaque black card over a tissue paper window to make a silhouette of pigeons. In creating their animations, the children repeatedly explored the various shadows formed when materials are held at different distances from a light source.

Having acquired a wide range of prior learning experiences, the pupils were ready to begin work on the window. The project was carefully designed to ensure that all children could contribute at their own level. Although they had all designed their own version of the window, we relied on Claire's expertise to create a stained-glass window of which we could all be proud. Having consulted with the school, Claire took our 'values' brief and the image of the acorn from our school badge to develop her design. We wanted the words 'imagine', 'believe' and 'achieve' to feed into the roots of an oak tree, and rays of sunlight to symbolise 'Let your light shine'.

The design process

The children were fascinated by the detail, vibrant colour and movement in the design and were eager to participate in the workshop that would lead them through the process of creating their own piece of artwork, to be incorporated into the finished window. Rich discussions ensued about the symbolism in the composition, with many children now demonstrating the ability to make links between their different learning experiences, relating and extending ideas at a much deeper level. This is the benefit of the creative curriculum; it layers learning like an onion skin through an accumulation of experiences, and it is this depth of learning that allows the children to assimilate and accommodate ideas, thereby enabling them to develop their own creative capacity.

Claire began her stained-glass workshop by explaining the design process that she goes through when she is making a window. She then worked with different age groups to create the children's individual pieces. She explored the idea of texture with our youngest pupils in EYFS – the children went outside and made bark rubbings for the glass to be used in the oak tree; pupils in Key Stage 1 drew living things that grow in the earth, using a range of reference books and visual sources for inspiration; and children in lower Key Stage 2 drew flying insects to decorate the sky. All of the images they created were taken back to Claire's studio to be scanned into her computer to create decals for the glass.

The oldest pupils, in upper Key Stage 2, worked with glass. They each covered a small pane of glass with wallpaper paste and arranged a pattern of oak leaves over its surface, before shaking a layer of coloured powdered glass across it, using a tea strainer to ensure even coverage. Finally, they peeled off the leaves, leaving their imprint in the glass. Needless to say, the teachers joined in! Claire fired the finished pieces and cut the glass to form the foliage of the tree. Children in Year 6 also designed the lettering for the school motto, including a braille version, which was typed by one of our pupils, a blind child.

With the children's artwork complete, Claire pieced together the window in her workshop, keeping us up to date with her progress by sending a series of photographs. Back at school, the pupils mapped out the measurements of each pane and worked out how much glass she would need.

Conclusion

Our curriculum is designed to provide authentic experiences in all subject areas, allowing the children to repeat learning within different contexts, building depth and breadth of understanding and providing pupils with numerous opportunities both to develop and demonstrate mastery. Links between learning experiences are made explicit. The use of SOLO (structure of observed learning outcomes) taxonomy (see also Chapter 16) provides a helpful framework for considering pupils' development as creative thinkers, moving through the prestructural, unistructural, multistructural and relational stages of knowledge acquisition, before developing extended abstract thinking. Children need to travel through each of these stages to be able to work at a deeper level and produce creative outcomes that are truly innovative. The creative curriculum is now more relevant than ever in helping them to develop mastery across a wide range of subjects.

In the finished result – in this case, the installation of a large stained-glass window – it is easy to see that the creative curriculum brings its own rewards. In living out our values in the way that we learn, we are able to make learning irresistible. Even the most reluctant learners want to be involved because by working collaboratively, scaffolding learning and valuing all areas of the curriculum, everybody is able to experience success and play to their strengths.

The fascination on the children's faces when the finished window was revealed was a testament to the success of a truly creative curriculum, and was duly praised by Ofsted and Statutory Inspection of Anglican and Methodist Schools inspection teams.

For me, the enduring memory will be of the open evening at which the window was unveiled and dedicated by the Bishop of Dorchester. The children proudly and confidently presented all of the work they had put into the project, clearly articulating their learning. The event was so well attended that we had to open the hall windows so that some parents could look in from outside because there was no room left in the building. When we can create this kind of buzz about learning, we know that we must be doing something right.

Further reading and useful links

Hattie, J. (2012). *Visible Learning for Teachers: Maximizing Impact on Learning*. Abingdon and New York: Routledge.

Hattie, J. and Yates, G. (2013). *Visible Learning and the Science of How We Learn*. Abingdon and New York: Routledge.

Pupil Asset: https://www.pupilasset.com

SOLO: http://www.johnbiggs.com.au/academic/solo-taxonomy/

About the contributor

Bertie Hornibrook

Bertie Hornibrook has been the head teacher of Chadlington CE Primary School for more than a decade and, over the course of 25 years, has developed curriculum expertise through her work in a varied range of primary schools. She is passionate about film and established the Little Acorn Film Company, which is run by children. She worked with talented animator Jim Parkyn (originally a puppet-maker for Aardman) to create two lively animated films: *The Big Blue Thing on the Hill* (narrated by former Prime Minister David Cameron) and *The Window*. Bertie is currently working on developing visual literacy and inspiring writing through film.

Chapter 3

A STEAM Curriculum Initiative

Helen Bruckdorfer, head teacher, and Susan Bush, curriculum development consultant, Torriano School, Camden

Torriano School might have contributed a chapter on several different themes. It is a UNICEF Rights Respecting School and an Ashoka Changemaker School, with children's rights and active citizenship placed at the core of its ethos and values. The school is committed to the United Nations Convention on the Rights of the Child being the framework for all they do as a school community. The school is also committed to global learning as an Expert Centre for the Global Learning Programme. Recently, it has formed a new partnership with the United Nations Regional Information Centre for Western Europe through the school's advocacy of the Sustainable Development Goals (SDGs).

The school offers its pupils a broad curriculum, and makes effective use of its London location and all of the learning opportunities the capital city affords its schools, especially within the arts. Many schools are familiar with STEM initiatives, but Torriano and the London Borough of Camden have been working on projects which also incorporate the arts: STEAM is the acronym for science, technology, engineering, arts and mathematics. The head teacher's conviction is that creativity (A for arts) is integral to work on other STEM subjects. This requires an interdisciplinary approach, one in which arts and STEM subjects combine as a valid proposition.

The STEAM curriculum initiative described in this chapter encompasses learning, genuine scholarship and investigative and creative activities of exceptional quality and high attainment across the whole primary range. The term-long project brings together:

- An interdisciplinary study centred on STEAM.

- The school's ongoing focus on the SDGs, commonly referred to as the Global Goals, and on ways of making them a reality.

- The school's commitment to the education of children – and the community – for global awareness and competence.

Teaching and learning throughout the project involves constant interaction with other areas of the curriculum, most notably in English and the creative and expressive arts. The whole learning experience is enriched and illuminated by visits to, and work with, institutions such as the Royal Observatory, Greenwich, and the input and expertise of noted scholars and researchers in lectures, demonstrations and seminars.

The pupils curated a STEAM exhibition, displaying all aspects of the study and investigation, and the outcomes arising from them, centring on what is described as 'the fundamental question': 'In what ways must we adjust and change our behaviour to sustain our future on Earth?'

Background

Torriano School is situated in north-west London. The school has 447 pupils on roll and serves a diverse community in an area of significant deprivation, with the proportion of pupils eligible for the pupil premium significantly above the national average. The proportion of pupils from minority ethnic groups and those who speak English as an additional language is also significantly above the national average, with over 40 languages spoken in the school. In addition to the mainstream provision, the school has a language resource base supporting children with severe language impairment and social communication disorder, with provision for 16 pupils from the Early Years Foundation Stage (EYFS) to Key Stage 2.

Genesis and inspiration

At Torriano, we believe that schools can encourage STEAM fusion by creating a context that allows pupils to use creativity as a prism through which to view all STEAM subjects – using art not as a specific subject but rather as a creative process in which to experiment with, among others, digital and scientific skills.

Torriano is an inclusive school community with an ethnically and socio-economically diverse community – in effect, a global microcosm. We therefore seek to educate our children and the community for 'global competence', which is a crucial step in the lifelong process of developing a global outlook. This global competence involves a combination of knowledge and understanding, cognitive and socio-emotional skills, and values and attitudes. We aim to provide opportunities, of which STEAM is one, for our school community to understand its place in the local, national and global context. In effect, this is creativity with a cause, and we encourage everyone to participate in taking action for our collective well-being and sustainability.

The genesis and inspiration of the STEAM project came from a long-standing commitment to disciplined curriculum innovation developed through involvement in the RSA and UCL Institute of Education's Grand Curriculum Designs project and participation at a local level in Camden's Cultural Commissioning group and Primary Careers conferences. We have developed partnerships with a range of cultural organisations, businesses, community organisations and non-governmental organisations (NGOs) to design bespoke interdisciplinary learning experiences which promote skills for the 21st century. Some have evolved because of our enduring dedication to careers education. The school is part of the London Enterprise Ambassador scheme, which has supported the development of these links, helping us to explore this sector through the Founders4Schools organisation and INSPIRE.

As a result, teachers are required to collaborate with a wide range of experts, supporting colleagues and the community in a symbiotic way. A STEAM team has been created, which comprises of senior leaders, subject leaders, a designated governor, the performing arts leader and an artist-in-residence. These adults work with a taskforce of appointed children who collaborate annually to co-create the project activities.

The global dimension

The key to achieving our aims for STEAM is to embed it within whole-school themes and community events which take place throughout the year. One vital long-term ambition we promote across our curriculum is for pupils to develop an entrepreneurial skill set, take risks and communicate well, but also be able to contribute to highly skilled, knowledgeable teams. Partly because of this ambition, the STEAM initiative has focused on computer science and computational thinking in mathematics and science. The global learning dimension of the curriculum necessitates projects having a strong emphasis on sustainability and innovation with the ultimate aim of reducing global inequalities, promoting action on climate change and seeking ways to end poverty.

In the academic year 2016–2017, the school maintained its curriculum focus on the SDGs, or Global Goals. The 17 SDGs pledge to end poverty by 2030, and apply universally. In line with our vision and values, we aim to increase our community's awareness of the aims and objectives of the SDGs and to advocate ways to make them a reality. The whole-school theme 'Making Connections, Making Changes' featured cross-curricular learning activities to develop the children's ability to advocate effectively through acquiring and improving their global learning knowledge, understanding, skills and values.

Our STEAM timeline

In the spring term, themes are viewed through the prism of STEAM. The project scopes across both key stages (including EYFS) and has an intensive whole-term focus. Our annual project approach begins by researching some of the theme-relevant resources available and devising strategies for possible learning sequences for each year group, incorporating both the school's planning and the national curriculum. This results in further discussion and development by the STEAM team, with the final recommended outcomes agreed by senior leadership. During a staff INSET, the formulated project action plan is presented and the staff are asked to support its development, aided by the curriculum development lead, curriculum coordinators and external partners.

In 2017, for example, for the STEAM exhibition, the children explored ways to change our behaviour to sustain the planet. This aligned with our approach to encourage children to consider that many futures are possible, and to give them a voice in advocating one which will most benefit the common good.

Setting the context, purpose and ignition

To introduce the STEAM focus question in a way that enthused and engaged the Torriano community, the school began by celebrating UN World Wildlife Day, hosting a range of specialist speakers on animal habitats and conservation. In addition to sharing their knowledge and expertise, they explicitly informed the children about the STEAM skills that they utilised every day in performing their jobs.

This was exemplified during a visit by the award-winning documentary maker Patrick Morris, who has filmed in remote areas and collaborated with experts from many disciplines, including scientists and engineers, and whose films require both technical and teamwork skills. He shared information with the children about the natural habitats of some extraordinary animals, which helped them to understand causation and the significance of the deleterious effects of human activity on the planet, specifically on natural habitats.

Other contributors to this launch event day included the Orangutan Foundation and the Eagle Heights Wildlife Foundation, with whom the children were able to observe birds of prey and were informed by their handler about their diet and habitat adaptations which allow them to survive in an ever-changing environment.

To build on the interest generated at the launch, further events were organised for community participation. Principal among these was a visit to the school by Dr Emily Grossman, an expert in molecular biology and genetics, who is also a passionate advocate for gender equality and diversity in science. She conducted workshops for parents and children across the school, with her key focus (the role of the science communicator) having been predetermined in discussion with the STEAM team.

A common key skill identified for all the year groups had been the 'scientist as communicator'. The children were explicitly taught communication skills, and eight from each year group were given the role of STEAM communicators during the exhibition itself. This complemented the school's concurrent action research project on the explicit teaching of vocabulary. Teachers used strategies from the Voice 21 framework to develop the children's linguistic, cognitive and oracy skills. The children undertook coaching, practising their role as a science communicator and learning subject-specific vocabulary and questioning and presentational speaking skills.

Following the launch, year groups embarked on specific projects linked to the science national curriculum – with a common focus on the different skills required to be a scientist (as defined by the British Science Association) – while the exhibition projects were also linked with the relevant SDGs throughout. The arts focus in STEAM was maintained and monitored by the school's artist-in-residence, Jack Cornell, whose contributions were integral to the design and implementation of the creative element of the project.

In summary, whole-school preparation for the exhibition allowed for deep learning, real-world contexts and the inclusion of a range of partnership expertise.

The STEAM exhibition

The whole-school preparation culminated in the STEAM exhibition, 'The Elements of Change'. The exhibition event day allowed the children to creatively demonstrate and articulate their knowledge and understanding about the key issues which were covered in the teaching and learning sequence and highlighted in visits to and by our project partners. The children mastered diverse media to communicate their ambitions for our future – essentially, a respectful and sustainable coexistence with the natural world.

Visitors were taken on a journey by the children through alternative sustainable futures, made possible by a combination of technology, imagination and creativity. Key Stage 2 children shared their learning about sustainable cities, biochemistry and eliminating waste in space, and those in Key Stage 1 explored habitats and climate change. There were opportunities for parents and other visitors to have 'big conversations', raise 'big questions' and sustain themselves throughout with produce from the Torriano Waste Cafe.

Work and learning outcomes

The work and learning outcomes were made evident through key learning experiences. Assessment and evaluation of the children's learning was conducted by the science leader and other curriculum subject leaders. This involved a combination of collective reviews with year group staff and both questionnaires and discussions with pupils. In addition, science enquiry skills were assessed against the national curriculum and recorded through a formative assessment framework.

Impact was also directly evidenced in the school's Key Stage 1 and 2 science teacher assessments in 2017, in which the children significantly outperformed the national average. These STEAM learning experiences also illustrate the degree to which the pupils are involved in their organisation, in advocacy activities and in exercising the opportunity to develop their own experiences.

Some specific examples of work and learning outcomes included the following activities.

EYFS: don't waste the waste!

The youngest children prepared for STEAM by finding out how, why and where the community recycled its waste, which resulted in an appreciation of the importance of reusing and recycling. This linked to SDG 12: 'responsible consumption and production'. Their investigation culminated in a walk to the recycling bins across Torriano Avenue to recycle their milk cartons and unusable paper. Putting the arts into STEAM, they presented their learning creatively by constructing an installation made from recycled materials which conveyed their message 'Don't waste the waste!' The installation featured a large-scale world map highlighting the volume of plastic in the oceans, and the message was further conveyed by the children performing with shadow puppets and creating illustrated posters.

Cross-phase collaboration

Year 2 and 4 collaborated on the 2017 STEAM exhibition in a joint project on natural habitats throughout the world. They considered the survival adaptations of different animals in these varying biospheres. Human impact, notably climate change, was a factor in their learning, so they considered how these habitats are changing and how this adversely affects the animals' ability to survive and thrive. Learning was enhanced by visits to partners such as the Grant Museum of Zoology and London Zoo.

The learning outcomes were creatively expressed in their own dioramas of these habitats, which included representations of the animals and their survival adaptations. Throughout, links were expressly made to SDGs 14 and 15: 'life below water' and 'life on land'. To express their findings and reactions creatively, the children constructed a map of the world and made blocks of coloured ice, which they melted onto the areas affected by climate change. The children also made fact cards about the animals living in these varied habitats to further convey their knowledge and understanding. They concluded that this would illustrate to everyone how we need to look after our planet.

In keeping with the focus on key vocabulary, the children were able to demonstrate their knowledge through the use of subject-specific terms such as ice, melting, freezing and deforestation. Others created models of giant fossils of animals that are now extinct or critically endangered to illustrate the imperative need to ensure a future where habitats are conserved and protected.

The cross-curricular nature of the project was demonstrated through English lessons, in which the children wrote non-chronological texts about habitats, adaptation and the negative effects of human impact.

Partnership working: space – who's going to clean that up?

In our national curriculum science unit on space, the planning for Year 5 incorporated SDG 9: 'industry, innovation and infrastructure', and the scientist's communicator skills were those of the developer and the regulator. The enquiry which developed these links within the STEAM theme was the dilemma of space debris, which allowed the children to explore the impact that humans are already having in space. This incorporated an investigation of human exploration of other planets as an alternative home to Earth and the resulting abandoned materials that are accumulating in space. The children considered how humans could ensure that space exploration is conducted sustainably, thinking about practical solutions and the need for regulation.

Their enquiry was launched with the aid of the astronomy programmes and courses offered by the Royal Observatory, Greenwich. The children were given the opportunity to discuss the planets and new solar system discoveries with astronomers, to experience simulated life in space and to attend a screening of *Star Trek V: The Final Frontier* in the planetarium. A visual journey of exoplanets and the strange new worlds which astronomers are discovering – including NASA's most recent discovery of seven Earth-sized planets orbiting TRAPPIST-1 – was another highlight.

As always in our STEAM projects, Year 5 children communicated their response to their learning through the expressive arts in conjunction with The Place, a contemporary dance school in Camden. They devised their own performance piece conveying the characteristics of planets through movement and dance, which was showcased at our STEAM exhibition.

Both Year 5 classes collaborated to create a musical composition called 'Algo-Rhythm', which took its inspiration from the American artist Sol LeWitt, who created a series of conceptual works consisting of a set of instructions executed by draughtsmen, rather than by the artist himself. The children used this concept to create their own compositions using Logic Pro X, which enabled them to appreciate the synthesis of computer science, music, geometry, biology and several other STEAM subjects. The exhibition featured an interactive display for visitors to engage with and create their own algorithms.

Children's enquiry: do robots have a useful place in a sustainable society?

In Year 6, the children researched the most efficient sustainable energy sources, including some still in development, as part of their focus on SDG 11: 'sustainable cities and communities'. They assessed the advantages and disadvantages of these innovative technologies and the scientific skills needed to develop them.

Some children in the sustainable city team decided to follow their own line of enquiry inspired by two exhibitions in London, 'Robots' at the Science Museum and 'Electricity: The Spark of Life' at the Wellcome Collection. They analysed the roles of robots in society and considered the range of possible futures for humanity. They identified the ethical dimension as key, posing the question: 'Are robots sustainable?'

A series of robots were constructed and devised, exploring possible functions and the engineering involved in assembling and programming them. The children created a film about their project and visitors to the exhibition were invited to code instructions for the robots during their visit.

Parental and community engagement

The success of this creative STEAM project, culminating in the exhibition, depends upon parental engagement and local enterprise involvement. The exhibition was open to parents and the wider community for two full days, with the children and science communicators acting as their guides.

The children involved their parents from the project's inception, including setting homework tasks for them – notably a popular periodic table quiz. Parent visitors to the exhibition were keen to demonstrate their learning by taking part in a follow-up activity – the periodic table orienteering course. Their progress through the course was accompanied by a soundtrack of the children performing their periodic table song.

The Torriano Waste Cafe, now an established part of the exhibition, was inaugurated at STEAM 2016 with a focus on reducing food waste and meat consumption as part of the children's advocacy activities relating to climate change issues. Partnerships have since been consolidated with local restaurants which have supported the Waste Cafe initiative by providing chefs and a pizzaiolo to cook pizzas, which were topped with waste ingredients donated by the school community. The children staffed the Waste Cafe throughout the exhibition, with help from parents and professional partners, to both educate and feed customers with specialities – including their very own cricket brownies!

Full STEAM ahead: plans for further development

Camden Council, in partnership with the Knowledge Quarter, has launched a STEAM Commission to bring together the borough's businesses, schools and other key institutions. It seeks to improve career opportunities for young people and ensure that businesses can benefit from the range of talent in the borough. Peter Dudley, the director of education in Camden, said, 'I was knocked out by your STEAM event. The children were incredibly eloquent and knowledgeable about all the areas of study across the school – irrespective of their actual age.'

As head teacher, I contributed to the subsequent Camden STEAM Commission report (2017), which advocated the importance of the arts in STEAM and promoted an interdisciplinary curriculum design approach. Other committee recommendations include developing a STEAM hub in the borough, with the additional remit to tackle under-representation and provide all of Camden's young people with access to the opportunities in its thriving STEAM economy. Torriano joined this hub as a partner school in 2018 with the specific aim of disseminating our practice and expertise in this area.

The school's emphasis on the arts in its curriculum has been recognised, in that we now provide training for other local schools in support of their application for the Artsmark award, sponsored by the British Council. The award provides a clear framework for teachers to plan, develop and evaluate arts, culture and creativity across the school curriculum. In assuming this advisory role, Torriano will look to achieve the coveted Platinum Artsmark award, which in turn will reinforce its strong partnerships with cultural organisations.

Equally, Torriano will continue to play a significant role in advocating for global citizenship and sustainable development education to be key drivers in schools' curriculum development. Future curriculum policy development at the school is determined by all staff in partnership. An added dimension is that of cooperation and collaboration with international colleagues, NGOs, civil society organisations and academic institutions to promote sustainable education as a key element of initial teacher training programmes.

Conclusion

Torriano colleagues were proud to read this quote in a recent issue of *AD Magazine* (produced by the National Society for Education in Art and Design) from our creative collaborator, Cornelia Parker: 'They do an incredible show at the end of the year, one involving STEAM (Science, Technology, Engineering, Art and Mathematics). Pupils have made extraordinary installations and videos about climate change – they seem so incredibly well informed.' (Leach, 2017: 5).

None of us can predict what the future holds for our children, but this parent's comments suggest that they feel optimistic about the ways in which their children may be able to contribute to the world of STEAM: 'So impressed with the learning, understanding and hard work right across the school! … Hopefully these wonderful children will grow up to lead us in the future!'

At Torriano, we believe that outward-looking and innovative learning organisations are best placed to spread outstanding practice. As a result, we encourage our staff to build a professional learning community that is focused on continuous improvement of teaching and learning which leads to a culture of high achievement for all.

Further reading and useful links

Camden STEAM Commission (2017). *Creating Camden's 21st Century Talent: Report and Recommendations of the Camden STEAM Commission*. Available at: http://camden.gov.uk/ccm/cms-service/stream/asset/?asset_id=3595910&.

Leach, S. (2017). Interview: Cornelia Parker in Conversation. *AD Magazine*, 20 (Autumn): 2–6.

Ashoka Changemaker Schools: https://www.ashoka.org/en/program/changemaker-schools

National Society for Education in Art and Design (NSEAD): http://www.nsead.org/primary/education

STEM Learning: https://www.stem.org.uk/audience/primary

Sustainable Development Goals (SDGs), or the Global Goals: http://www.un.org/sustainabledevelopment/sustainable-development-goals/

UNICEF's Rights Respecting School Awards programme: https://www.unicef.org.uk/rights-respecting-schools/

Voice 21: https://www.voice21.org

Wellcome Trust: https://wellcome.ac.uk/what-we-do

About the contributors

Helen Bruckdorfer

Helen Bruckdorfer is the head teacher of Torriano School, where she has been involved in the development of the school's ethos and vision for the past 11 years. Before headship, she was a national literacy consultant for Ealing, with an additional remit for developing the use of IT to support teaching. Her core belief that education has a crucial role to play in changing and influencing the life chances of every child was instilled from an early age, with both parents having high profile careers in education. Following in their footsteps, teaching was always Helen's first choice of career, and her passion to improve every child's opportunities to achieve the best they can remains at the forefront of her thinking, whatever challenge is involved.

Susan Bush

Susan Bush is currently curriculum development consultant at Torriano, where she was a full-time member of staff for 17 years prior to retiring. Her expertise in curriculum innovation was recognised by the National College for School Leadership, for whom she became a primary curriculum advocate. She now works ad hoc at Torriano, assisting staff to develop whole-school themes, including SDG-related initiatives. Susan was the school's expert centre coordinator during the Global Learning Programme pilot phase, and took a lead role both in attaining Torriano's Ashoka Changemaker and Rights Respecting School status and in orchestrating its involvement in the RSA and UCL Institute of Education's Grand Curriculum Designs project.

Chapter 4

The Broad and Balanced Curriculum Enriched by IT

Jonathan Bishop, head teacher, Broadclyst Community Primary School (Cornerstone Academy Trust), Exeter

A single, intensive day spent at Broadclyst Community Primary School (BCPS) is probably sufficient to leave the visitor with the firm impression that pupils are experiencing the sort of education that will develop the skills and knowledge they need to carry into the future. The journey takes one from a nursery setting – immediately recognisable for its high quality early years practice which is enhanced by touch-screen technology – to a mud kitchen. Through Key Stages 1 and 2, there is evidence of the educational journey the pupils are making from those early years.

The school's commitment to project-based learning (PBL) is clear. It aims to find balance and richness in all subjects, with creativity and personalisation underpinning the learning. This was evident in a maths lesson where pupils were solving carefully differentiated problems in a purpose-built computer lab large enough for two classes, with a computer terminal for each pupil. It was also evident in an art class where a specialist teacher was working with textiles, and a PE session where pupils were timing themselves and trying to achieve a personal best in various athletics-based activities.

In the school's TV studio, four Year 6 pupils were totally absorbed in making a film about national policy on the funding of school lunches, which they would be sending, by way of protest, to the prime minister. They had interviewed members of staff and fellow pupils and were nearly ready to edit their footage. During lunch, another informative and motivational film made by pupils, about lunchtime issues, was being shown while 'miked up' teachers on duty ensured that older pupils were looking out for younger ones, and all were enjoying their meal.

From the Forest School to the library, the school provides carefully structured, imaginative, relevant and challenging teaching and learning, all within a broad curriculum. But at BCPS, the learning experience is strengthened and shaped by the application of sophisticated digital technology.

This chapter provides an insight into the rationale, implementation and outcomes of the major IT and global developments which the school makes central to the pupils' education. Thanks to these, and to the school's ongoing success with its Global Enterprise Challenge (GEC), which head teacher Jonathan Bishop launched in 2014 in partnership with Microsoft, it is difficult to resist the conclusion that, in this rural school, one is given a glimpse into the innovative and technology-centred practice of the next decade and beyond.

Background

BCPS has two-form entry and over 440 pupils, aged from 2 to 11. It is set in rural Devon, near Exeter, and is a member of the Cornerstone Academy Trust, a multi-academy trust that provides education across several schools. It also oversees professional teacher training through the Cornerstone Teaching School, based at BCPS, which was awarded teaching school status in 2013. Teaching schools are outstanding schools that work with others to provide high quality training and development to new and experienced school staff.

The Cornerstone Teaching School's strategic board includes local secondary and primary schools, the University of Exeter and Microsoft. Thanks to its connections with Microsoft, BCPS has a national and international reputation for the innovative use of IT to deliver both high standards of pupil achievement and school-to-school collaboration within the UK and overseas.

The school is committed to supporting children to feel confident to try new things, take risks and reach their full potential. This is realised through:

- ■ Freedom: encouraging individuality, responsibility and community.

- ■ Forward thinking: embracing technology, trying new things, preparing for the future.

- ■ Feeling valued: promoting self-esteem, friendship, respect, listening, kindness, safety and accepting differences.

A broad, balanced and personalised curriculum

As successive governments worked to raise educational standards, UK schools began to put a narrow emphasis on literacy and numeracy, so losing breadth and balance in the curriculum. This was the unintended consequence of focusing on activities that are easy to test and measure.

In a speech at the Festival of Education on 23 June 2017, Ofsted's Chief Inspector Amanda Spielman talked about a review of the national curriculum and the need for schools to move away from a focus on literacy and numeracy purely to enhance their league table status. She said that 'all children should study a broad and rich curriculum' (Ofsted and Spielman, 2017).

This is an approach that I implemented here at BCPS some years ago. As our multi-academy trust has grown, all our schools have sustained the offer of a broad, balanced and personalised curriculum, underpinned by a whole-school approach to technology.

There is a tension in every curriculum plan between what could be perceived as child-centred ideology that looks at stage (not age); between creativity and discovery learning, and what could be seen as a philosophy of knowledge development and assessment. The child-centred approach can be deemed random, chaotic and look less likely to result in the acquisition of the required basic skills and knowledge. However, when teachers have detailed subject skills and knowledge, and high quality resources that enable them to deliver the curriculum in a more structured way, children can learn all the things that every 'educated' person should know.

We are told that teaching must occur within age-expected norms and that children are not only required to achieve their personal best, but also to excel when benchmarked against others. But most educators recognise that the two approaches (the so-called child-centred and the assessment/outcomes-focused) are not mutually exclusive, but finding the balance is key.

Skills and knowledge

When there is a breadth within the curriculum, there is a danger that it won't be deep enough. It is clear that core skills can open the door to deep, enquiry-based learning, but what do we really mean by breadth and balance? Is that breadth within a day? Is the curriculum balanced over a week? Or over a term? By the time we have taken out assembly, lunch, PE and an hour dedicated to literacy and numeracy, there is very little time for the other eleven subjects in a broad curriculum. And in a curriculum that is designed to equip children with skills for the 21st century – creative thinking, problem-solving, communication and social interaction – achieving a balance is extremely hard.

In the recent past, this problem has been addressed by covering the basics at primary level and introducing breadth with depth during secondary education. However, doing the basics just leaves us with the basics. Schools need also to develop children's language, character, personality, thinking and problem-solving skills. The challenge for teachers is that those skills are hard to test, measure and put into league tables.

Painting by numbers

We have found that academically gifted and intellectually capable children can often become uninspired, under-challenged and ultimately disengaged in an assessment-based curriculum, while some of the most behaviourally challenging children use their innate capabilities to undermine formal education and then find themselves excluded.

The relevance of a broad and balanced curriculum is that it is equipping the child not just with the basic core skills but also with the chance to develop their creativity and express their feelings and ideas. All too often the creative and performing arts become marginalised subjects, yet we may recall that Mozart was composing at the age of 4 and

Picasso was drawing skilfully at a similar age. It may be that a rigid curriculum, designed to benchmark schools, simply doesn't allow for prodigies or even the very capable.

It is probably safe to claim that most, if not all, parents, teachers, schools and, indeed, governments would wish for children a broad, relevant and balanced curriculum designed to provide for their educational development and the realisation of their full potential.

However, the current disproportionate emphasis on the teaching of the core subjects, influenced, we believe, to a significant extent by government expectations, seems to suggest that this is the only approach likely to achieve the required standards of attainment. Yet intellectual awareness and comprehension, creativity, understanding and problem-solving capacities are not assuredly and effectively realised by a limited curriculum.

In fact, the recent narrowing of the goalposts creates unhelpful anxiety and a lack of confidence in the pupils who are being pressurised and in the teachers we are driving to achieve the results we want. Approaches to the teaching of reading, writing and maths that are excessively focused on meeting limited levels of attainment are, in a sense, akin to 'painting by numbers'. Creativity, problem-solving and debating difficult topics cannot be taught through a closed and exclusively didactic approach.

There are five key areas where we see a closed approach leading to the potential for conflict in relation to the development of our pupils:

1. **Cognitive ability.** There is the danger of a narrowing of perspective and of expectations. Expected levels of attainment can become glass ceilings and lead to a general lowering of challenge. A broad and balanced framework must work to support the talents of each child, whether athletic, musical or academic. It must uncover and understand their enthusiasms and innate capabilities and give them choice with high expectations and no glass ceilings.

2. **Attitude.** Grit and determination, a growth mindset, knowing how to deal with others, empathy and competitiveness are all necessary qualities to develop in a child, but league tables and the need to foster both equality and competition can lead to a climate of anxiety and impossible expectations, creating stress. As a result of the government driving up standards at the cost of individual personalities, we are seeing children with mental health issues at an early age.

3. **Assessment.** In a target-driven world, with ever-moving goalposts of impossibility, assessment has become increasingly formulaic. A disproportionate concentration on data-driven attainment in certain areas takes insufficient account of

children's achievement in other, critical areas of their development. We are so fixated on 'data drops' that we are not allowing children to flourish within a broad curriculum. There is a danger that we may ignore their emotional state, engagement, home circumstances and personality.

4. **Marking.** Marking is often done only so that parents, or Ofsted, can see that each child is being tracked in detail. We need to address this myth: education is now being seen as the neatness and quality shown in a child's exercise book, and schools have invented complex, multi-coloured marking systems that don't actually have the desired effect of improving pupil achievement, but nevertheless demonstrate to Ofsted that their teachers are being diligent in terms of monitoring, assessment and pupil feedback.

5. **Teacher disillusionment.** The teachers we need are people who question, think creatively, solve problems and share their skills with the children. But these kinds of teachers may, by nature, be non-conformists when it comes to the timetable or curriculum. They go into the profession because it is a vocation, but they end up being limited, measured and sometimes disillusioned.

PBL across the school

The key to all these issues is the broad and balanced curriculum. However, until schools debate and appreciate what this means, we will never move beyond the 'tussle' between measurability and the need for children to be taught little more than the basics at primary level.

At Broadclyst, we focus on the provision of a broad, rich, relevant and balanced curriculum, using the most up-to-date technologies available to us in order to prepare pupils for a fast-changing world. But how do we achieve a broad and balanced curriculum if there is so little time? For us, PBL provides the key to creative curriculum design.

PBL is a way of creating real-world, purposeful, outcome-driven learning. More than just topics, this is a vehicle that enables educators to bring together skills and knowledge. We have introduced a Global Communities Project that provides PBL with international collaboration for every year group. We are working to bring communities together, as our children use technology to work with their peers around the world. This brings an international dimension and cultural diversity to their learning, as well as a clear purpose to develop their core skills.

Here are some recent examples of our PBL projects:

- A Year 1 project was science based – with the children planting seeds, taking time-lapse videos, studying the diversity of weather patterns and discussing with their peers around the world the differences between their various countries.

- Year 2 developed a music project, creating, recording, listening and performing and comparing their musical styles with others around the world.

- Year 3 studied a specific artist and created virtual art galleries, Skyping with their peers in other countries.

- A Year 4 project involved taking photos of people in a diversity of activities and occupations within their community and sharing their galleries internationally.

- Year 5 created documentaries, using our TV studio, to engage in investigative journalism, sharing videos with our worldwide community of schools.

- For the last decade, each Year 6 cohort has been involved with our longest-standing PBL project: a business enterprise called the Global Enterprise Challenge, which now involves hundreds of students and teams who collaborate across at least 20 countries. Hugely motivational for the children, and exciting for the teachers, it incorporates business skills including product design, market research, manufacturing and marketing. It encompasses many different elements of the curriculum, putting the children's learning into a real-life context. The approach is to give them the skills and knowledge with which to achieve a successful business: with this clear focus, STEM subjects are brought together to create an output.

PBL across the curriculum

Naturally, PBL can extend beyond STEM. We can bring together other subjects in PBL, too, such as the creative arts. A drama performance starts with the literacy skills needed to analyse texts and write a play script. Then the collaborative element of PBL comes into its own, as the children work as a team to create different characters and build a plot, because the project encompasses art, design and technology, music and dance.

There are other humanities-based PBL opportunities. At BCPS, we involve the children in producing historical re-enactments, in which they research (as analytical historians) a day in history and the period that it sits within, to recreate and tell a story. The additional skills required include literacy, drama and performance. The children are also grappling with the challenges of taking their place in society, so we could have a discrete personal, social, health and economic (PSHE) education lesson once a week or we can engage them in PBL.

Another PBL approach we use is the production of video documentaries by the children (see page 80 for more on this). These are all about cultural awareness and the global dimension – for example, 'attitudes to smoking and e-cigarettes' or 'sustainability of travel and global climate issues'. Building an ethos and culture is not just about engagement within school, but ensuring that we're developing the human qualities of empathy, tolerance and respect. These are often seen as formulaic values, recited in assembly, but they don't necessarily create a thinker out of a child and could be perceived as a form of indoctrination. The world has massive cultural diversity, and tolerance comes from an understanding of different viewpoints which need to be woven throughout the teaching, affecting every single subject, and should be the responsibility of everyone in the school.

PBL gives a real-world relevance to education in tandem with the knowledge we need to apply to different subjects, rather than simply giving timetable priority to STEM subjects. It helps to build the ethos and values of the school community, getting the children engaged in discussion, debate and the celebration of moments. If we want to develop responsible, mature young adults who are learning to take their place in society, education has to be seen as a whole, not the sum of the individual subjects taught at the ring of a bell. Every time, it comes back to more than the application of knowledge and a timetable.

By creating a curriculum encompassing different projects with end goals to be achieved within specific deadlines, we also encourage grit and determination in the children, as well as a growth mindset, bringing both skill and knowledge into the curriculum. The approach creates opportunities for relevant and worthwhile work in writing, reading and the application of maths, which achieves higher order thinking, learning and outcomes. And yet, we can still – if we design our curriculum with the right project at the right time – deliver the right subject skill and knowledge, and hence save time.

Being able to design a curriculum that can deliver high quality learning in an efficient and effective way is the most important skill of a good teacher.

The importance of IT to successful PBL

In a world where technology underpins everything – from our cars, shopping and banking to our homes and the environment – the compartmentalisation of IT into a subject (and the argument that it is too costly for schools so we should only teach traditional basics) must be contested. By giving children the tools to access the wider world, we enable them to collaborate and communicate beyond the narrow confines of their locality and culture. We cannot deny our children the opportunity to embrace the developments they need to make them successful citizens in a global world. It is vital that we utilise the power of technology to support the efficient and effective quality of education afforded by PBL in the curriculum.

So many schools seem to be in state of denial about IT and shelter behind the barriers of limitations on resource and time. But, just like a pen, pencil, ruler or book, a computer is another tool in the modern teacher/learner toolkit. To allow for learning to go beyond the lesson, IT needs to empower learners today, providing them with the tools to research, study, create, share, collaborate and express their views in a modern world. The effective use of digital technologies ensures that learning is extended beyond the school day and the school building.

The Global Enterprise Challenge

Background

In 2014, I took the Broadclyst enterprise project concept to the Microsoft in Education Global Forum. In a *Dragon's Den* style pitch in competition with ideas from schools from around the world, I put forward the idea of making the project into a global challenge, connecting schools and children aged between 9 and 12 across the world using Office 365 technology. This was the winning pitch, and we won an award of a staggering US$25,000 to make the GEC a reality.

The money was used to provide start-up funding for schools around the world to join the Challenge in the first year, but one of the rules was that all participating schools must return that funding to BCPS at the end of the project to allow it to run in future years.

In the first year, 31 schools from 20 countries collaborated in creating business enterprise teams and developing their small companies, pitching their ideas to a 'Dragon's Den' of their teachers, and then designing, manufacturing, marketing and selling a range of 10 products including bookmarks, phone cases, key rings, smoothies and muffins. And they made a profit!

Ongoing developments

The Dragon's Den is a key component of the GEC, as this experience helps the Year 6 pupils develop many of the key skills needed in later life. To present their ideas and reports clearly, the children need to develop literacy skills. To carry out effective product and market research, and build a prototype, they need science and technology as well as problem-solving, creative and thinking skills. To trade successfully, they need numeracy skills to keep accounts and calculate profit and loss.

Now in its fourth year, the GEC has expanded to involve children from both primary and secondary age groups. Schools receive online support throughout the project as they share and communicate with one another. Every teacher and child has an individual account in a dedicated Office 365 setup, a Skype for Business account and a collaborative workspace. They are also given access to download a copy of Microsoft Office. Through the Challenge, the children gain a knowledge of world markets and currencies, as well as honing their entrepreneurial skills and developing an understanding of cultural diversity and creativity through the use of IT.

The tools offered by Office 365 have powered this purposeful collaboration and creativity among the children, who have made group conference calls with Skype, presented ideas with the digital storytelling app Sway, and shared and voted on them using Yammer instant messaging.

This challenge is truly unique in its emphasis on collaboration, and in the past three years we have been proud and encouraged to see children from more than 45 schools in 30 different countries working together so productively towards a common aim and purpose. The sharing of ideas, discussion and feedback transcends distance, culture and economic situation, and sets positive values and skills for their futures as global citizens.

What the teachers say

Lebanon: Rana Sabbidine Osta, principal of Makassed Khalil Shehab Primary School, emphasises the importance of Microsoft technology in providing learning platforms for the children: 'With SharePoint, they can share their biographies and tasks with their peers. This rich platform helps students understand the business development and management concept by enabling them to organise, manage and access their work. It facilitates team communication while creating a professional-looking website for their company.

'OneNote helps them organise their ideas, and has become a very important tool for documentation, planning, presentation and evaluation because they can see everything in one place. We assign different tasks for every child, so their access to the entire structure of the work with OneNote is crucial.

'Skype makes learning and exchanging ideas very real for the children. We share lessons with other schools, and we share with the parents too. It connects people together and makes distances non-existent.'

The Netherlands: Bertjan ten Donkelaar, head teacher of Daltonschool Elserike, observed that his students preferred Yammer: 'Getting in contact with children from all over the world is exciting and a bit frightening as well. Direct contact via Skype is the scariest part for some of them. With a message board like Yammer, when they are not sure about a word or sentence, they can always ask their teammates or teachers before sending it. Yammer is easy to use for exchanging ideas and gives a nice overview of the work from all the different teams.'

What the children say

Nine-year-old Briana from Allman Town Primary School in Kingston, Jamaica, participated in the 2016/2017 GEC: 'The technology in our school has helped me to receive information about the products we are making, like ideas about how they could look, and how to make them. When we use Skype, I also get to see other children from other countries, and to see what they are doing and what their classrooms look like. They also get to see how well we work as students in Jamaica. This is exciting to me. We get to share information about our Jamaican culture and especially our school.'

Another 2016/2017 participant was Reina (13), at Al-Makassed Omar Bin Al-Khattab College, Beirut, Lebanon: 'Participating in the project has taught me business skills and terms used in selling, buying, trading and manufacturing products. GEC has given us a global perspective of business development. Moreover, my teammates have become independent and have taken ownership of our enterprise. We have realised the importance of teamwork. We are working as a team, with a team leader, yet each member has a distinct role ... We have also recognised the importance of the ICT skills that we are using in different stages of the challenge.'

Whole-school approach to IT

BCPS is a Microsoft Showcase School and has two Microsoft Innovative Educator Experts (MIEEs) on its teaching team. The MIEE programme was created to recognise global educator visionaries who are using technology to pave the way for their peers in the effective use of technology for better learning and improved pupil outcomes.

Around the world, there are over 6,000 educators who have been selected as MIEEs for their excellence in teaching and learning. These educators spark creativity among their students and inspire their peers as they find innovative ways to incorporate 21st century learning into their classrooms. Broadclyst's two MIEEs run a rolling programme of parent training to increase parental engagement with learning by providing them with a practical understanding of the school's electronic resourcing – a level of transparency that has pleased parents.

We have embedded technology throughout the school and have found that it has enhanced the sense of community through collaboration between teachers, children and parents. Even in early years education, children use face recognition software to log in to devices and digital signage is embedded within their environment.

Our strategy is underpinned by leadership and the understanding that IT is as fundamental a service within the school as stationery, staffing, energy and catering. It is a core service and a central part of the school's ethos, underpinning the teaching and learning of every subject. It requires constant research and development, with the trial and evaluation of new technologies to inform our vision and seize the opportunities that they provide.

Our central focus also includes the recruitment, retention and development of highly skilled teachers who embrace the latest digital tools, remain at the forefront of our drive for innovation and are also part of our ongoing research and development processes.

The whole-school approach to technology has transformed the learning environment, providing a new way for both teaching and learning. The tools that enable this collaborative learning space are both physical and cloud-based.

In physical terms, a wireless projection system is used across the school. Instead of using a whiteboard variant, teachers project from Surface Pro 4 tablets. This allows them to move freely around the classroom, using digital ink to draw diagrams and write notes while still interacting with the children. In addition, Microsoft's Surface devices are deployed to the children on a one-to-one basis. The teachers' notes sync in real time to these devices and the children can wirelessly project their own screens to share their work with the class. This allows a seamless transition between the very traditional concept of pen and paper, digital inking and the power, mobility and flexibility of tablet and laptop use in an endless variety of situations and environments.

These physical tools are coupled with the powerful range of cloud-based tools available through Office 365, accessed on any device and in any location, so providing the rich functionality of desktop productivity tools such as Word, Excel and Publisher.

In the world of work, it is standard process to have many drafts and iterations in the multi-authoring of work, to ensure that collaborative efforts not only achieve a good outcome but also enable people to learn from one another. The school models the adult world of work by using Office 365 tools. Using these to work collaboratively is an improvement on giving children an exercise book to work on in isolation, with the possibility of teacher feedback confined only to the work's surface features and not to the content and meaning that the child is trying to express.

Collaboration and problem-solving in IT

At Broadclyst, we use OneNote, a key application within Office 365. This collaborative tool helps the school to break down the barrier between learning at school and learning at home. Each class's OneNote class notebook is organised in such a way that children and their parents can find and access the materials and resources that were used in the classroom on a particular day. Students have personal areas that act as portfolios for electronic work, as well as providing a way for them to organise their learning targets, watch video feedback and update their to-do lists.

OneNote has become the teachers' whiteboard. Using digital inking, they can write directly on screen and then not only project this to screens around the classroom, but also sync it to the children's desktop devices *and* any device accessing the lesson through the cloud (including parents' devices). All curriculum resources for teaching and learning are placed in OneNote – for example, there may be a PowerPoint presentation, a video streamed to the page and web-links to guide children to the right resources. With instant access via the cloud, students and their parents can track and chart lessons and projects as they evolve over the school year.

We use OneNote to deliver specific assignments to individuals or groups, allowing for dialogue between teachers and children to track, target and feed back. It allows for the 'flipping' of learning, where children access resources in advance, so the focus of their lessons becomes learning rather than watching a teacher's presentation. Similarly, it enables children to embark upon extended projects and activities that they can carry on at home.

The school has discovered that using the power of OneNote to engage the learner to continue activity at home is much more effective than homework. This is because the issuing of homework to children has unintended consequences. When a child needs help, whose homework is it – the child's or the parents'? Homework can cause family dissent (unwittingly created by the school!) as well as adding an unnecessary workload for teachers who subsequently must mark and support each individual child, thereby reducing curriculum time.

In OneNote, however, work is collated digitally (even work in the physical world is captured in the OneNote pages) so that teachers can annotate using digital ink and commenting tools and record their own verbal feedback, without ever 'defacing' the children's work or wasting time expecting students to respond to the marking rather than improve their work.

While OneNote is the central pillar of the school's PBL tools, there are many others that add value to the mix. Forms is a tool that enables the creation of surveys, quizzes and polls, with instant results, while Yammer is a private social network that the children use both within the school and with their peers across the world to discuss ideas and compare cultures. A new addition to the Office 365 suite, Teams, brings together OneNote, email, Skype and a calendar in a hub to further facilitate teamwork.

The power of video

Video as a tool for teaching and learning, for the communication and presentation of ideas within a PBL environment, is massively empowering. It is crucial that children can articulate their thought processes through the spoken word, expressing their opinions and hearing the views of others.

BCPS has a dedicated TV studio, in which the children are taught to express their views and present them with clarity. It gives them a voice and a presence. Starting with the question 'Who is my audience?', the children go through the tasks of researching, storyboarding, scriptwriting, editing, presentation, feedback and dialogue. TV brings together a multitude of skills including structuring, planning, sequencing and writing; great literacy teaching stems from oracy.

For the teachers, too, video is invaluable. They can record their lessons and feedback so that children can re-watch an explanation or remind themselves of a lesson when the face-to-face teaching session has ended.

To bring high quality videos into a child's learning, the teachers use ClickView, a video learning application that allows teachers and students to access curriculum-related video material in a similar way to YouTube. By cropping and sharing video clips in OneNote with quizzes embedded into them, the teachers can observe the children's interactions and challenge and assess their understanding.

Video as communication is intrinsic to the school's teaching and learning. The children can connect with people outside of the school through conference calling and Skype, bringing in knowledge, experience and expertise (including parents or colleagues) in meetings or presentations, or collaborating across the globe on a daily basis. The making of video documentaries in Year 5 and the GEC are typical examples.

Conclusion

All teachers have a responsibility to embrace the technology available to them, allowing children to access resources before a lesson and continue collaboratively beyond the school day. This is the way to create lifelong, independent learners who don't have the 'school's out' culture, but instead have views they can express and the support of friends, peers and teachers in developing their talent and skills for the world in which they will grow up.

We must empower professional teachers to create rich learning opportunities, using all the tools we have at our disposal. In Finland, educators are striving to eradicate subjects and use PBL entirely. But here in the UK, we are too often drawn back to excessive and crude testing that limits our children's potential and places time-consuming and irrelevant workloads on our teachers, all of which leads to a wasteful stunting of our children's creativity.

Further reading and useful links

Atherton, P. (2018). *50 Ways to Use Technology Enhanced Learning in the Classroom: Practical Strategies for Teaching*. London: Learning Matters.

Beetham, H. and Sharpe, R. (eds) (2013). *Rethinking Pedagogy for a Digital Age: Designing for 21st Century Learning*. Abingdon and New York: Routledge.

Ofsted and Spielman, A. (2017). Amanda Spielman's Speech at the Festival of Education (23 June). Available at: https://www.gov.uk/government/speeches/amanda-spielmans-speech-at-the-festival-of-education.

ClickView: http://www.clickview.co.uk

Global Enterprise Challenge (GEC): http://globalenterprisechallenge.education/

MIEEs: https://educationblog.microsoft.com/2017/08/new-2017-2018-microsoft-innovative-educator-experts-showcase-schools/#U4aGX8fjqO4AmxIt.99

Office 365: https://products.office.com/en-gb/student/office-in-education

Yammer: https://www.yammer.com/

About the contributor

Jonathan Bishop

Jonathan Bishop has pioneered the way in developing media-rich digital classrooms, home-access systems and collaborative and creative online learning spaces and in establishing working partnerships with schools and companies around the world. As a national leader of education (NLE), with his experience of a creative curriculum and the integration of digital technology in the classroom, he is a regular speaker at education conferences.

As chief executive of the Cornerstone Academy Trust, Jonathan is building a multi-academy trust which includes a teaching school and Broadclyst and Westclyst Community Primary Schools, which also provide nursery provision from 2 years upwards.

Chapter 5

An Enriched and International Curriculum

Marion Mills, head teacher, Blewbury Endowed CE Primary School, Didcot

This chapter describes Blewbury Endowed CE Primary School's deep commitment, maintained over many years, to the provision of a broad curriculum designed to develop and enhance children's knowledge and understanding of the world beyond the local and national, to enrich their learning and to furnish them with skills and attitudes that will enable them to thrive.

Marion Mills begins by describing the wide range of learning activities and projects related to four elements identified by the school as being fundamental to human life. But the chapter is largely concerned with the education provided by the school in relation to the 'international dimension' and the development of the pupils as global citizens. She also outlines the many ways in which the ambitious and visionary initiatives have been achieved, highlights the educational outcomes and offers encouragement for schools that are contemplating similar developments.

The school's international programmes have involved teachers, children and, in certain cases, parents in active and creative partnerships and links with schools in Europe and beyond, which could be justifiably described as transformational in a creative and enriching sense.

Background

Blewbury Endowed CE Primary School was established in 1707 on Lady Day, 25 March, through the endowment of William Malthus, who was a rich merchant born in the village. The school was set up for 50 poor children and provided them with clothing and an apprenticeship scheme for local trades. The children received £1 a year for clothing at the rate of 1d (old penny) a day, six days a week, for 40 weeks of the year.

Nowadays, it is still a small school (approximately 165 on roll) with just six classes. The latest Ofsted report (2015) highlighted a key feature of the school: 'The innovative curriculum engages pupils. [Parents and pupils] say teachers make learning fun and they are very enthusiastic about the broad range of educational visits that support their learning.'

Blewbury's curriculum

Our curriculum is organised so that the whole school is working on a common theme. This enables the children to study in a holistic way, which develops knowledge across history, geography, design and technology as well as art and science. The curriculum for each class is appropriate to the age group and covers prescribed points in the national curriculum. This means that a child will not repeat elements of the national curriculum unless they are relevant or help to connect or reinforce new learning.

While there are objectives to be met in English and mathematics at each age group, these all build on the previous year's work and progress should really be thought of as a continuum. In any class, regardless of the age mix, we believe that it is imperative to consider each individual to support them all with their next steps for progression and learning.

At Blewbury, we use fluid grouping within classes so the children can be grouped to work with an adult in order to reinforce a piece of knowledge or a skill, rather than just because it is a particular day of the week or the children have at some point been assessed to be at roughly the same level.

As teachers, we are uniquely privileged to provide the kind of education that will enrich children's learning, enhance their self-esteem and confidence, broaden their capabilities and equip them with the skills that will enable them to flourish in an increasingly global world.

We recognise the inestimable benefit of a broad and challenging curriculum, and for over 17 years our school's focus on the international dimension has been a defining element of what our children experience. The whole-school curriculum is underpinned by constant reference to four universal elements that we have identified as essential to human life and its sustainability, development and progress: communication (interaction), survival (climate), exploration (settlement) and innovation (shelter).

The following examples illustrate some of the ways in which these elements are translated into learning activities that involve the pupils engaging in a wide curriculum and expanding their awareness of international issues. It is important to stress that our teachers pay scrupulous attention to the balance of subjects in their planning, not only within individual projects but also in the contribution they make to an enriched curriculum.

Communication/interaction

One year, the communication element inspired work on the science of the radio, thanks to the school managing to secure the services of a university graduate who had studied radio production. He developed a radio magazine with older pupils and taught them about the major technical aspects and the skills and capacities associated with them, including the art of interviewing. The pupils produced news reports, debates and discussions, interviews, fashion updates and programmes of wide-ranging interest.

A group wrote a play which they recorded, requiring the training of technical directors, voice rehearsals for the cast and the manufacturing of sound effects. As the work progressed over the period of a week, further programmes were developed, edited and taken to a recording studio in Gloucester. A group of pupils spent a day at the studio, recording programme music, advertisements and jingles.

A few days later, all the pupils who had been involved congregated in the school hall to listen to the radio magazine they had produced, streamed live from the studio in Gloucester. Parents listened at home or at work and the file was added to the school website.

Survival/climate

Further learning comes from the survival element. For example, Year 3 children selected a temperate climate zone for their study. They considered what the implications of this would be for produce ripening in the autumn. On local walks they identified and picked blackberries, damsons, wild plums and crab apples, and were guided and assisted by parents in the making of jams, chutneys and juices.

The process involved them in the mathematics of weighing, ratios, timings and the costing of additives, as well as issues of hygiene and health and safety. They documented and illustrated the process, recording recipes, preparations and cooking instructions. They preserved the products, labelled bottles and jars, which were accompanied by written descriptions of the ingredients, and sold them for a profit at a market which they organised and managed.

Exploration/settlement

This topic requires the pupils to study some of the ways that Anglo-Saxon settlements were built and the reason for their placement. One year, Years 5 and 6 decided that a model of the landscape in which such a settlement was likely to be located should be a central focus of the study. They researched intensively before they began their construction of the model. They learned about the significance of marshes, lowland floodplains and oxbow lakes, constantly adding to their understanding of the elements that were essential or might contribute to the siting of an ideal settlement. One parent, an expert in mining, talked with them and identified the critical issues in terms of excavation and construction.

From their studies they discovered that early Anglo-Saxon communities often made important tribal decisions in group councils or moots, so the pupils decided their own planning should be worked out in a similar fashion.

Guided by their investigations, they concluded that the settlement should be: located within reach of the coast; close to a river since much of their travelling for business was done by water; convenient to woodland for the availability of timber for a variety of building and construction purposes; in an area likely to be rich in animal and bird life that could be hunted and trapped for meat, fur and skins for clothing; and within the reach of mountains or hills that might be mined for stone for building materials.

With their extensive research concluded and recorded, the pupils set about the construction of a scale model that incorporated as near an authentic replica as possible of every significant element of the village: buildings, watermill, farming plots, animal enclosures, workshops, river craft and inhabitants. Care was given to the representation of defences against attack, but the inevitable attack from Viking marauders was played out and the successful defence of the settlement inspired some dramatic writing.

Innovation/shelter

The final term is focused on shelter. One group of pupils attempted to approach the theme from a global perspective, studying homes in various regions of the world which are subject to extreme climatic conditions such as earthquakes, hurricanes, monsoons and tornadoes. They looked into the ways in which the location, the materials used and the types of construction employed were interdependent. They then replicated the structures in small models.

The pupils' research had brought home to them that, often in the case of sudden disasters and emergencies, populations had to live in hastily constructed and makeshift shelters. In the middle of their investigations the Gorkha earthquake in Nepal occurred, and they witnessed – in vivid detail on TV – the horror of what was happening and the devastation inflicted on the area and its people.

They explored ways in which they could respond to such a disaster in terms of the shelters they might construct. To enable them to carry out their planning they were provided with long bamboo canes, tarpaulins, string and clips. As they built their shelters – which varied widely in style – on the school field, the area took on the appearance of a refugee camp. In response to urgent requests on their part, it was agreed by the school and parents that they would 'trial' the shelters by sleeping on the site on a Friday night. They were fed (certainly more substantially than the unfortunate people whose plight they were simulating) and sat round campfires before settling down for the night.

Inspiration days: holistic learning

Another way we broaden the curriculum is through termly 'inspiration days'. We believe that these events, involving the whole school working together and informed by specialist input, generate very valuable teaching and learning outcomes.

Examples of our inspiration days include:

■ A Sports Exploration Day centred around rugby. One parent, an expert in the sport, ran practical workshops designed to explain the basic rules and clarify the less complex features of the game – the notion of attack and defence, the value of critical skills, the importance of teamwork. All of the pupils (working in their age range) played short, non-contact games, enabling them to gain some broad concept of the features of rugby, including important skills such as passing, decision-making, striving for openings in attack, securing cover in defence and retrieving possession.

Workshops involved:

● The designing of rugby club strips and the construction of rugby balls in various pliable materials.

● An exploration of the benefits of the game for healthy physical development and an emphasis on safe, fair play.

● A talk on women's rugby by a parent involved in this rapidly developing area of the sport.

■ A Philosophy Day based around a visit from a well-known local female explorer who described her intriguing and creative approach to life. She explained her compelling need to learn and discover all she could about the extraordinary and irresistible wonder of the world. She described her experiences and adventures, some occasionally daunting, that her search had involved her in, what inspired it and compared what she did to the explorations of people in the worlds of science, medicine, invention and innovation.

She conveyed to the pupils what she meant by a philosophy – a driving force in her life – and the determination needed to carry out explorations.

Seminars involved:

● Particular aspects of her exploration and travel, aided by reference to visual material and maps.

- Whether there was a possibility that what she did might have made unfair demands on others, perhaps even involving them in difficulties or dangers.

■ An Engineering and Construction Day, where we invited a commercial company to work with the children – challenging, guiding and inspiring them to create the most extraordinary range of durable and, in some cases, architecturally arresting structures made from an extensive range of simple materials, such as canes, rods and elastic bands.

Workshops involved:

- Mastery of intricate skills.

- Teamwork, with the children sharing ideas to achieve a collective outcome.

- Designing and planning from their blueprints and constructing their own structures, where possible, for specific purposes.

Residential visits at the heart of character building

While many teachers are familiar with the benefits of residential visits, at Blewbury we have found them a great opportunity for character building. They serve as a way of exploring the curriculum outside of the classroom while also developing certain characteristics, and these have greatly helped when developing our international opportunities.

These include:

■ Perseverance and resilience.

■ Confidence and risk-taking.

■ Community spirit.

■ Tolerance and integrity.

■ Curiosity and problem-solving.

The international dimension: becoming global citizens

The international dimension is the element that sets Blewbury apart from many other schools, and is quickly embraced by most of our teachers. Many have been able to widen their personal and professional horizons and some of our experiences have changed and enriched the lives of both adults and children.

The school has regularly hosted teachers from Germany and Switzerland who need to enhance their qualifications by completing time in an English-speaking school. We have hosted an Italian language assistant and, on three occasions, Japanese teaching assistants for six months each. More recently, we have had students from German universities visit for sustained periods as part of their training and professional development. Their contribution to school life has benefited our pupils and teachers by providing a wider perspective, sharing different approaches to teaching and demonstrating their linguistic awareness and expertise.

There are four sections to the international dimension in our school, which are interrelated but can also stand separately.

1. International School Award

Blewbury is the only school in the country to have received the British Council's International School Award every three years since its conception in 1999 – that is, six times in total. An action plan is submitted in the autumn, the actions are completed during the school year and then an evaluation is sent to the British Council for assessment in July.

To receive the award, schools must be committed to developing an international dimension throughout the whole school, have an international coordinator, ensure this work is in the school development plan and then promote seven curriculum-based and internationally minded activities which will take place during the year. Three of these activities should involve the sharing of educational practice in other countries and partner schools, and one of the activities must have a language basis.

This may sound daunting, but it should be noted that there are foundation and intermediate certificates which are more easily attainable for some schools. The first of these requires just one activity and a clear intention to find a partner school overseas, while the latter needs three curriculum activities, one of which involves collaboration with a partner.

To achieve and maintain this award it is important to embrace international work at all times, not just in the year when an application is being made. At Blewbury, we do this through the books we choose to share with the children, the harvest festival, the organisation of our curriculum and the ways in which we work with our partner schools. We also participate in a local Partnership International Day.

Take One Picture

One of the most innovative ways of integrating international work into the curriculum was when we embraced one of the National Gallery's Take One Picture themes. We were confronted with a 17th century painting by Willem Kalf, *Still Life with Drinking-Horn*, which shows a red lobster on a table with a peeled lemon. There is a drinking horn and a glass, all laid out on a luxurious Persian rug. The image triggered a cross-curricular adventure because each object led us to a different part of the world where people experience specific extreme weather events.

Via a series of clues, we sent the children on a 'Great Global Extreme Weather Scavenge Hunt' – for example, the United States has buffalo horns, but also tornadoes; and Mexico has a strong association with silver, but is also linked with hurricanes. Gradually, the pupils worked their way around the world, through the doldrums, to find lobsters in New Zealand and sandstorms in Syria and Iraq while hunting down a Persian carpet. We found lemons in Italy as well as snow blizzards. We did not show the children the complete image until the end of the project, so that they enjoyed the final revelation of the links between the objects in the painting and appreciated why they had been searching for them.

A global harvest

As part of our theme on innovation during the autumn term, we consider 'farm to fork' – that is, how wheat is harvested, how flour is produced and how different breads are made around the world. The children taste, cook, research, explore and invent. We involve visiting Italian and Spanish teachers in our learning through making gnocchi and churros. We also find out about the bread in our link schools in Germany, Spain, Finland and India.

Later in the school year, we look at the way water has been stored and used in the past. We extend this to the innovative ways that water is currently harvested and used around the world. Further examples of the type of activities that we include are around shelters and work on climates, which links with our Indian partner school.

2. Linking with other schools

First exploits into Europe

At the same time as being introduced to the International School Award, we learned about the British Council Comenius programme. A visit for teachers from our part of Oxfordshire was organised to a town in Sweden where we would be hosted in different schools.

This was in October, and by January we found ourselves hosting not only two Swedish teachers but also two Greek teachers from Athens, and attending a meeting where we set about applying for a Comenius grant. Unfortunately, the Swedish school had to leave the project after the first year, so the next year we linked with an Italian school from Turin instead.

The project lasted for three years, inspiring work by the children on storybooks, a joint calendar, pictorial dictionary pages and much more.

Extending to Uganda

East wasn't the only direction in which we were travelling. Through the local authority, another link was formed with a school in Uganda. We all met in the capital Kampala, and Blewbury, with 165 pupils, was linked with Butagaya Primary School, near Jinja, which had 1,500 pupils.

My memories are of a sea of yellow uniforms and so many smiles. All the children had walked several kilometres to school, and virtually none of them had shoes. The welcome was of a kind I had never experienced before. My adaptation to deep-drop toilets and washing my hands in a bowl was minimal compared to the contrast when the Ugandan head teachers came and stayed in our homes. Three meals a day, flushing toilets, running water, electricity, new cars which weren't tied together and nobody walking for miles along the sides of the roads were just some of the contrasts they witnessed.

Finding a joint project was interesting because our classroom environments were so different; all the Ugandan classrooms had between 80 and 120 pupils. However, they had an abundance of land and were making some attempts at gardening, so we agreed that sustainability would be our shared goal. We started to cultivate an area of our school as a garden so that we could compare and contrast.

We raised funds so the Ugandan school could buy tree seedlings which would help towards their sustainability. Some trees provided fruit, others shelter and shade and some could be used as firewood or sold as telegraph poles; our intention was that the money raised would be reinvested. Later, three of Blewbury's teachers returned to Uganda to find that the children had planted 'Marion's avocado tree'.

The following summer, a local secondary school used our Ugandan partner school as the site for their World Challenge and built a chicken house. Our next task was to sponsor their chicks and raise money for maize, and these rich experiences had the added benefit of being easy to feed back into the curriculum.

Another summer and another project: the parents at school had taken our link to their hearts and two of them ran the New York City Marathon, gaining sponsorship for

Butagaya. A group from Oxfordshire went to the school and some set about helping to build the Blewbury-sponsored kitchen. The distinctive design used much less wood and had chimneys to facilitate smokeless cooking. For the first time, staff had the facility to cook for all the children at lunchtime; until then many had survived on chewing sugar cane.

More reciprocal visits followed. We did not see the need to use anywhere else in our study of a comparative village in a non-western culture; we had such a rich resource with so much first-hand experience. The seedlings had grown into 'Marion's tree lot'!

Other African links

Visits to sub-Saharan Africa and many other countries are currently possible through the British Council's Connecting Classrooms project.

For several years we had visits from choirs of children from Nigeria and South Africa, who sang in the village. The South Africans demonstrated the gumboot dance, which is performed by dancers wearing wellington boots. This was a rich experience for our children which they embraced fully. On the first visit, we found that our pupils had taken off their shoes and were playing football in their socks because the visitors were playing barefooted!

Cost has prohibited more visits. However, we shared our welly dance with parents and collected donations in a wellington boot, which went towards pop-up schools in South Africa.

3. Travelling with children

Comenius Key Action 2 projects

This three-year project involved us with schools from Poland, Sweden, France, Spain and the Czech Republic. Our project was called 'Fit for the Future' and had distinct themes each year: year one was about healthy exercise, healthy food and healthy mind – preparing yourself; year two was knowing about your own locality, landscape and traditions; and year three was about sustainability for the future – a global view.

The most progressive element of this project was the decision to travel with children. Knowing the other adults involved is essential because you have to trust the host school and the parents they select to host your children. Our decision was that the children would travel in pairs and that we would take six or eight children with us.

We had met in England to plan the project before applying, so our first official meeting was in France – where we engaged in work about physical activity and exercise and learned about a game played in the Bordeaux region. Next, we were off to Spain and sharing work on healthy snacks and producing a recipe book. The final meeting that year was in the Czech Republic – our first with the children. We took eight children and focused on retelling stories from picture books. We removed the words from a picture book from each country and then encouraged the children to tell the stories in their own language. Later, we shared the original versions and considered how they compared.

The next year saw an adult-only meeting in Sweden, where we developed a website, prepared for our collective work in England and, very importantly, discussed what we had discovered from our earlier visits. We learned traditional games and dances from each other, and shared our herbariums and weather reports. We studied important people from each country and created PowerPoint presentations to share. We agreed on a festival day which would be the same in each country, and took recordings of these to our next meeting in Poland, which was in June.

The final year of the project was very memorable. We started in France with all the schools having to come up with five ideas to go towards an eco-charter. We held a council meeting with the children and by a process of voting we agreed six elements for our joint eco-charter. These included reducing waste at lunchtime and wearing extra clothing before turning up the heating among other pledges, which all the children signed. We also had a practical day working alongside several classes doing a beach clean-up.

Having had an adult-only meeting in the Czech Republic, we met with children in Sweden to put on a big exhibition about each school and our work in the project. To finish, the children all signed a declaration that they had designed themselves saying that although the project had ended, they pledged to persevere with the eco-charter in their schools and lives.

Our next project was 'My Way, Your Way, Euroway', with schools from Germany and Italy and, later, Poland. We created a large picture which had as a watercolour background the three skylines, and in the foreground houses from the different countries. These were linked with digitally produced pictures of all the children taking part in the workshop. Each school now has a copy of this huge picture.

Erasmus+ Key Action 1 projects

Since 2014, it has been possible to apply through the British Council for Erasmus+ Key Action 1 grants. These have been set up so that schools incorporate them into a European development plan. Schools can apply for funding to visit partner schools, job shadow or attend courses run by various organisations across Europe. This could be focused so as to develop language teaching, but it could equally be about developing entrepreneurship, creativity, the use of ICT or any other related areas. Applications must be made in the early spring term and schools can apply for one- or two-year programmes.

Our teachers had previous experience of travelling to European schools as part of our curriculum-based school-to-school projects, but this was largely for their own professional development. Visiting other schools, whether in England or another country, always raises issues about methodology and can give rise to some deep pedagogic discussion. Sometimes it helps to clarify our philosophical approach and remind us of a purpose beyond Ofsted and SATs results, bringing us back to forgotten theory which once might have contributed to our own practice. For the younger members of the profession, it can awaken a desire to learn more and recognise the nature and quality of teacher training in other countries.

Some areas that we set out to improve or investigate included:

- The ability to teach languages within our primary school: developing staff language skills.

- Teacher knowledge of other European educational systems: raising awareness and developing views and ideas about varying pedagogical approaches.

- Appropriate attitudes to learning in young learners and setting the lifelong learning mindset: giving confidence to teaching staff to share and validate their own practice as well as learn from others.

- New learning methodologies which will help to prepare pupils for 21st century life, equipping them with the skills to flourish in a changing environment which is not just knowledge based: adapting creative approaches to teaching and learning which encourage engagement and independence.

- Technology to enhance student and teacher cooperation across Europe: incorporating European cultural aspects into our curriculum.

The British Council has a website area, 'schools online', which can best be described as a European 'dating agency' for schools. Any schools that wish to take part in a school-to-school project, are interested in job shadowing or feel they have something to offer can set up a profile. Messages are on a secure platform unless you decide to correspond further with a teacher representing another school, and then direct email can be used.

Another useful platform is eTwinning, which allows staff to interact with schools in other European countries without travelling. This is an excellent way to start building up the international dimension in a school, and is a good place to start exploring and collaborating.

Erasmus+ Key Action 2 projects

In 2014 the European Union changed its funding, meaning all the funding streams for schools, universities and sports clubs – which previously came through the Comenius Lifelong Learning programme – now came through Erasmus+.

We worked with our German partners, the school from Spain and one from Finland that we had visited during Key Action 1. Our theme was 'Communication, Cooperation and Collaboration for All Together'. Each project meeting lasted from a Tuesday to a Sunday and involved workshops for the children on the Thursday and Friday. Teachers engaged in discussion and training during the workshops. The children, as usual, stayed in pairs in host families.

Our children travelled to Finland, where the focus was mathematics. The children dealt well with a language which was extremely different, and with the all-night daylight and tales of wolves in the woods around the remote village in which they stayed. They greeted us if they saw us, but just got on with relating to their host family children, talking to each other and enjoying being children in another country. They embraced the fact that we had lunch at 10.30 a.m., finished school at 1 p.m. and could play in the woods. Most of the children even tried a sauna.

We found that the children from Spain and Germany were less relaxed than ours, and wondered why. Everyone had a word bank book and everyone had been communicating with their host family by email and photos, but in discussion it transpired that the greatest difference was that our children had been going on residential visits since they were 7 years old. This meant that for some of them the trip to Finland could have been their eighth time away with the school. As a result, our children respond creatively to new experiences and cooperate, are willing to try new experiences and be open to ideas, are used to discussion and are not afraid to express their opinions.

During the 10 years since 2007, when we took part in our first visit with children, 110 children have travelled with the school. Fifteen different adults have been involved as well as many more who were part of our hosting group. The best analogy of the effect when you act as a host school is that of a stone being thrown into a pond, with many ripples emanating from the centre.

4. Global Learning Programme

Our most recent international venture has been to become a hub school for the Global Learning Programme, which is a government initiative operated with support from Pearson Publishing.

As a hub school, we are called on to encourage others to join our network and then deliver a series of free continuing professional development sessions according to a prescribed programme. Each school is eligible to choose training opportunities from a wide range of providers through a voucher system. As a school, we had the confidence to adopt this training role thanks to our previous global work and projects.

The training themes are challenging but can fit into many aspects of the curriculum – for example:

- Globalisation and interdependence.
- Images and perception.
- Poverty, development and sustainability.
- Global learning through real-world maths and stories.
- Critical thinking and global learning.

The children are challenged to find out about the sources of commonly bought food or the constituent parts of mobile phones, and what implications this has for long-term sustainability. Their research helps to raise awareness of the United Nations' Sustainable Development Goals which we are challenged to meet by 2030 – when our very youngest children won't even have started higher education!

Conclusion

Through the design and development of our whole-school curriculum, we help children to build relationships with each other, to understand the rich texture of their learning and to develop their knowledge of the wider world. They are encouraged to see links between subjects and to recognise the links that comprise their learning.

We are fostering an ongoing desire to find out, to question, to take risks, to solve problems and to try innovative approaches. Hopefully, we are helping to create children with a growth mindset (Dweck, 2006). By challenging them, we hope to develop the emotional resilience that they can carry into their adult lives and become responsible adults who will take with them the fundamentals of reasoning, empathy and consideration.

Through our internationally minded global projects, we aim to ensure that our children understand their own worth and the worth of others, both near and far. We aim to encourage our children to feel part of a global community, which is working towards the development of a united world.

Further reading and useful links

Dweck, C. (2006). *Mindset: The New Psychology of Success*. New York: Random House.

Ofsted (2015). Blewbury Endowed Church of England Primary School Report (3 June). Available at: https://reports.ofsted.gov.uk/inspection-reports/find-inspection-report/provider/ELS/123167.

British Council: https://schoolsonline.britishcouncil.org/international-learning/international-school-award

Erasmus+: https://www.erasmusplus.org.uk/

eTwinning: https://www.etwinning.net/en/pub/index.htm

European Union Education Gateway: https://www.schooleducationgateway.eu/en/pub/index.htm

Global Learning Programme: http://glp.globaldimension.org.uk/

National Gallery – Take One Picture: https://www.nationalgallery.org.uk/learning/teachers-and-schools/take-one-picture

Sustainable Development Goals: http://www.un.org/sustainabledevelopment/sustainable-development-goals/

About the contributor

Marion Mills

Marion Mills started at Culham College of Education in 1970, studying maths and science. Her three-year certificate of education course turned into a four-year BEd (Oxon.) in applied plant science and psychology of education. Twenty years after her first graduation she gained an MEd, again through Oxford University, so a second trip to the Sheldonian theatre! She has taught in four different schools in Oxfordshire, and has been head teacher of Blewbury Endowed CE Primary School for 21 years.

Chapter 6
Learning Outside the Classroom

Colette Morris, head teacher, and Susan Perry, head of outdoor learning, Christ Church CE Primary School, Battersea

This chapter describes the transformation of a piece of urban wasteland into an extraordinary, multifaceted and lavish garden with the aim of creating an educational environment that is profoundly affecting and beneficial for children. The vision that inspired it and the ambition that carried it through are breathtaking. It has involved large-scale external and community involvement as well as the input of professional experts.

Christ Church CE Primary School was the first school in London to achieve LOtC Mark (Gold) accreditation for Learning Outside the Classroom. The head teacher and her staff believe that their outdoor learning approach not only enhances children's learning across the curriculum (e.g. in science, environment study, mathematics, language development, writing and the visual arts), but also their spiritual, mental, emotional and physical well-being, teaching them kindness, respect for all life and the responsibility to care for and shape their environment. The school's radical approach to children's learning has some resonance with the work of Boldon Nursery School – Outdoor Nursery (see Chapter 1).

In recent years, as a result of their work on the school's outdoor environment, the children have been guests at the Chelsea Flower Show, exhibited regularly at the Royal Horticultural Society (RHS) Harvest Festival Show, had their work published and discussed their garden with members of a visiting all-parliamentary group.

Colette Morris and Susan Perry provide a vivid sense of how the staff and pupils have created, over time, a special and spectacular environment. They describe the learning which the gardens can inspire but, perhaps, for a full appreciation of what is taking place, a guided tour may be called for ...

Background

Christ Church CE Primary in London is a smaller than average primary school with a nursery class. Nearly 90% of the pupils are from minority ethnic heritages, with the largest proportions being Black African and Black Caribbean. The proportion of pupils who speak English as an additional language (EAL) and who are not fluent in English when they enter the school is triple the national average, the proportion eligible for free school meals is three times higher than the national average, and the proportion of disabled pupils and those with special educational needs (SEN) are also above the national average. Their main needs are moderate learning difficulties and emotional and behavioural problems. The school exceeds the government's current floor standards which set the minimum expectations for pupils' attainment and progress.

The vast majority of pupils have no access to an outdoor play space or garden at home. Many pupils have limited understanding of how food grows or where it comes from.

The beginning

Visit Christ Church CE Primary on any day of the week and you will find children learning both inside and outside the classroom. We have four gardens where the children learn throughout the year. They repot plants, prune trees, draw from nature, work out mathematical problems and write creatively and scientifically.

This may lead you to think that we are a suburban or rural school. However, we are in fact located in a forbidding urban environment in the heart of Battersea. We have created and developed our outdoor space to add to the layers of learning that all children need to experience in order to learn and thrive. Like our garden, this expansion of our curriculum has grown organically over the past eight years.

The spaces between the old national curriculum and the new one gave us an opportunity to decide our own direction in 2009. We had already introduced learning outdoors and decided that we needed to expand our curriculum further to consolidate indoor learning through outdoor experiences. For example, if you are learning about tens and ones in the morning, then you could be counting and putting the pots into groups of ten in the afternoon, so we know how many we have and how many we need to buy.

There were several reasons for this. We knew from research about the benefits of outdoor learning, and we wanted the children to have access to the health and academic benefits that this kind of learning offers. The children loved being outside and learning outside, but they did not get much opportunity for this because of the built-up environment in which they live.

Several opportunities presented themselves, and because they fitted with our vision for outdoor learning, we took them:

- A former governor of the school with a landscaping company built the school a garden on-site. The timber was donated by a local company.

- The local Falcon Estate Residents' Association was considering how to develop a piece of land, and the outcome of this was that the school took on the lease of an overgrown piece of land about 200 metres from the school.

- We applied and were accepted to be an RHS partner school so that we could learn from experts.

- St Luke's, a local church, encouraged us by giving us a donation for developing the garden.

- Various individuals, such as Elizabeth Johnston, the clerk to the governors, supported us both with financial donations as well as insightful ideas.

We knew that if we were to get the children outdoors, then we would have to promote and develop outdoor learning rapidly to keep the momentum going. Colette, the head teacher, answered every email that involved helping schools with outdoor projects. This included: Battersea fire station, who cut down the trees and bushes that engulfed the garden; a local business (Wates), who gave us a corporate day and cleared the ground; the Prince's Trust, who took out all the tree stumps; and Wandsworth Young Conservatives, who cleared some very tangled undergrowth. We have since had help from Good Gym, Lend Lease, Vibe teaching agency, the RHS and many other corporate groups. All this help cost us nothing.

While engaged in these tasks, we were all learning from the RHS London adviser for schools, Jim Bliss. He taught us about growing plants successfully from seed for our school garden and inspired us to keep going. To stimulate interest and mystery, we held a 'Secret Garden' opening for our new space, even though it was so overgrown at that point that no one could get into it! We wanted to keep our profile high and keep the community interested in what we were doing. An all-parliamentary group came to look at our patch of bare ground and the children met them and talked to them about why they liked learning outside. This kept the story going.

With the groundwork underway, Colette turned her attention to the staff. If we were to continue to flourish, then everyone needed to be part of it. Growing sessions were put into our staff training and Colette began to take Year 6 once a week for outdoor learning to better understand what it would look like. The RHS invited us to the Chelsea Flower Show in 2010. Not only did we go but we were allowed into the M&G Garden to meet the garden's designer, Bunny Guinness. The children were fascinated by her knowledge of plants and talked to her about their garden. Inspired by them, she asked the garden's sponsors, M&G Investments, whether they would donate the garden to our school and they said yes.

So, a couple of lorry journeys and some help from local teenagers later, the flower beds were sitting in the Secret Garden ready to be installed. This was a huge opportunity to drive the momentum forward, because if the beds were fitted we would be able to start growing much sooner than we had anticipated.

Soon after, the parents and the local community planted espaliers and fruit trees. Teachers and support staff sowed vegetable seeds with the children and planted the seedlings out in the garden in the spring. The result was a fantastic harvest of organic produce which was weighed, measured, cooked, sold and eaten. We were successful in our bid to the National Lottery Awards for All and built a greenhouse and a log cabin with the funding we received.

We began to feature in publications: the RHS' *The Garden* magazine, the *Guardian*'s 'Eye-witness' pages, local newspapers and even *Farming Monthly* when the London Orchard Project helped us to plant a mini orchard at the end of the Secret Garden. We have exhibited our produce every year at the RHS Harvest Festival Show. The children inspire people's interest as they clearly 'own' the outdoor learning so completely and are so enthusiastic about what they are doing.

Roehampton University were offering a master's in education sponsored by Lend Lease, and Colette took the opportunity to develop her own understanding of the project by registering and working on a dissertation entitled 'Horticulture as a Vehicle for Learning: A Case Study of an Urban One-Form Entry Primary School'. This gave us the opportunity to have focus groups of children and adults analyse their responses to outdoor learning to obtain a better understanding of the project. It also provided evidence to present to governors on the benefits of this way of working in our setting.

As the project grew so did the need for staff who were interested in developing outdoor learning. We had worked predominantly in Key Stage 2 so far. Now, however, we were fortunate to employ a head of outdoor learning, Susan Perry, who was passionate about outdoor learning as well as having a wealth of experience in outdoor settings. This was the key that opened so many doors and started the beginning of a new phase of more strategic development.

Funding

Many parts of our project were achieved through donations from people who wanted to support the development of outdoor learning. As well as the Awards for All grant, we have also obtained funding from the DM Thomas Foundation for Young People, Metropolitan Public Gardens Association, Wandsworth Eco Fund, St Luke's Church and Battersea Rotary Club. It is important to look for and connect with groups who are dedicated to supporting such work.

As our work has an impact on children's outcomes, we used some of our pupil premium funding to support parts of our outdoor learning programme. For example, our writing project funds a local author to work with pupils on their creative writing using the garden for inspiration.

Getting started

We sat in the garden, looked around and asked ourselves: what might outdoor learning look like in this school? We were clear that we wanted to create an interactive space for children and adults in which the learning would be facilitated to encourage real-life problem-solving and personal development.

Most of our children live in flats in local tower blocks. We wanted our school garden to be a space that they felt they could own. We wanted to grow vegetables and flowers, to collect seeds from our own plants (including chard, broad beans, sunflowers and others), to understand lifecycles and nature, and to create a sustainable (and inexpensive!) garden.

One of the first things we did was to consider what resources we needed. We came up with a simple list:

- Watering cans
- Pots, plant labels, seeds
- Compost
- Mypex membrane and woodchip for groundcover
- Gardening tools: trowels, forks, spades, dibbers, secateurs
- Lots of gardening gloves!
- Signage and interpretation to give a voice to the garden

We also considered the areas that we wished to develop and create with the children:

- Potting area
- Orchard
- Seating area for a whole class
- Large fixed whiteboard
- Pond
- Ramped access to enable us to take wheelbarrows up and down the stepped entrance

The wish list became our 'blue sky thinking' document, so we gave ourselves permission to think big. Our ideas sowed the seeds for an outdoor learning strategy and implementation plan that considered a range of questions:

- What outdoor learning research had already been done, and what was the best way to evidence the value of this investment of staff time and energy?

- How do we communicate with and engage staff, pupils, families and the local community?

- How do we link outdoor learning to the school curriculum?

- How much will it cost? Who could help us make it happen?

Each action on the implementation plan was prioritised as being short, medium or long term. It was great putting the short-term actions into place quickly as we felt that we were making progress.

We consulted with staff and conducted a survey to establish what gardening expertise and outdoor learning skills we already had in the school. We also identified which staff were less confident and might need extra support. We researched sources of funding for individual projects – for example, creating a perfume garden, making planters out of recycled tyres, building a pond, making raised beds and benches and running a gardening project in the summer holidays.

One of our long-term aims was to secure accreditation that would acknowledge the quality of our work and help to keep us on track. Our head of outdoor learning started to collect evidence to apply for the gold-level Learning Outside the Classroom (LOtC) quality mark, using the scheme's application criteria as a helpful checklist. Our focus was enhanced by creating a small steering group consisting of the head teacher, head of outdoor learning and school business manager.

Staffing structure

Governor support was vital. If we were to focus on outcomes using outdoor learning as a vehicle for our curriculum, the school governors needed to be fully informed so they could mentor and support this area of school development – particularly as we realised (a little late) that our project had reached capacity and could not develop further without restructuring our staff team.

The governors' finance committee members were very supportive during this process. It involved us writing new job descriptions that would help us to secure the outcomes we wanted for the children, families and community for whom we work. The restructuring enabled us to secure the dedication and commitment of well-trained staff who believe in what they are doing and the impact it will have on pupils.

With a staffing restructure the whole-school work was enabled. We now had a team dedicated to learning outdoors which worked untiringly to teach and inspire both children and adults. Expert support was brought in from our gardening adviser, Jim Bliss, who was now working independently (as Bliss Landscapes), and he provided vital knowledge and skills that we could not do without.

We also work with volunteers whenever possible to complete tasks that our children can't do. For example, we needed to remove a huge ivy root that was stopping our grapevine growing and had to enlist some help. Sometimes these are corporate groups who volunteer for a day, or groups like Good Gym who come for an hour with about 30 people.

With all this in place we were able to plan for whole-school teaching and learning.

What we do and how we do it

Schools are busy places, so an almost immediate challenge was to consider how best to share the garden tasks to ensure that the living outdoor space for plants and creatures was cared for.

Without doubt, our most willing volunteers are the children. At lunchtimes, they volunteer to do gardening jobs – watering the corridor plants, weeding, watering the fruit trees, washing pots, planting seeds, cutting back stinging nettles and a whole lot more. At first this work needed close supervision, but now, as the pupils have become more experienced, the older pupils supervise the younger children. We also have a garden leader scheme so that our young gardeners can earn special privileges to work more independently.

The school's team of three outdoor learning staff also work with small groups in the afternoons. Class teachers refer pupils for a variety of reasons including bereavement, emotional upheaval (connected to domestic violence), speech and language development, disability, mental health and/or behaviour issues. We work in a very focused way with small groups (from one-to-one sessions to groups of up to eight or ten children, but mostly with about four children in each group) to address issues such as anger management, social skills, teamwork, confidence building and so on.

Colleagues involved with our outdoor learning programme have good horticultural skills and are confident when working in the garden. They also work across the curriculum and support class teachers to deliver whole-class outdoor learning that includes problem-solving, maths, literacy, ICT (especially filming using tablets), science, art, cookery and topic work.

The outdoor team also conduct one-to-one sessions if a situation arises where a pupil needs space to talk about challenging school or domestic issues. Taking time (even just 10 minutes) to water plants and smell the roses (literally!) diffuses conflict and provides a peaceful and conducive setting to let go of troubles and stress.

We run an after-school gardening club. These sessions are educational, fun and include all aspects of gardening – from vegetable growing and harvesting to snail and wheelbarrow racing!

Garden tales

The garden was designed not just for science but for every curriculum area. One way in which we have developed our cross-curricular goals was to invite Margaret Bateson-Hill, a local author, to work with us on a writing project. Margaret worked outdoors to help the children to use their imaginations in the Secret Garden: she turned garlic upside down and made it speak to the children; they imagined themselves so small that they were engulfed by the pumpkin plants; there were kings and queens, slugs and snails. The children used what they saw to help them imagine.

Margaret worked with the children over a period of six weeks, guiding, inspiring, supporting and encouraging them to write. She gave the pupils notebooks in which they wrote down their ideas, including vocabulary, developing them into full stories by the end of the six weeks. The editing process was rigorous. However, the children were able to manage it because they were comfortable with the material they were using and they felt a sense of ownership about the garden.

Our art specialist, Andrea Konc, worked alongside Margaret and gave the children the opportunity to develop artwork to illustrate their stories. When Margaret was not in school, the artwork continued the discussions and ideas for their stories.

After editing, a book of the children's stories was designed using an online publishing tool. The published book was eagerly anticipated, and all the children involved enquired continuously about progress until the books were delivered. We now have a set of six beautifully published storybooks featuring writing and illustrations: *A Scatter of Garden Tales*; *Garden Magic*; *Above and Below*; *Buzz, Flutter, Snap*; *Seeds in Space*; and *Frogs and Snails and Fairy Tales*. Each book contains stories inspired by the garden, and they are regularly read by all the children in the school, not just the authors, and there is also a set in our local library.

Each year, the garden has inspired the pupils to write different stories – from 'The Frightening Fox Returns' in which Foxerlogz steals the fruit and vegetables, to 'The Neighbourhood Cat' in which a robin defends her nest.

Recently, the school grew the rocket seeds which had been sent to schools by the British astronaut Tim Peake. We researched the solar system, and our thoughts about seeds in space inspired the following from a Year 6 pupil:

> *Tumbling down from space, a startling white light leaves a shimmering trail of stardust behind it. But look again at that star. In the middle is a seed, and that particular seed is looking for a home – the Blue Planet. One minute it is floating aimlessly, the next it is speeding down towards Earth ...*

Breathing life into the curriculum

With the introduction of the new national curriculum in 2014, we did not want to lose what we had developed by introducing an intense programme that would restrict the outdoor learning. We invested in the Learning Challenge Curriculum, which poses questions such as, 'Where do leaves go in winter?' In Year 1, the children worked through the question and explored it using different subjects. This meant that classes could still go outside for a variety of lessons all year round.

Our maths support teacher led outdoor sessions to help staff take their maths lessons outside. With the outdoor learning team, she enabled the children to transform the back of the school from an unused space to a perfume garden full of mathematical opportunities.

Science is an obvious area to prioritise when teaching outdoors. Scientists learn by observing what happens, discovering how it happens and experimenting to see what happens if they try something else. There is also the deeper question, 'Why does it happen?' This is not always answerable, but this question may be the initial stimulus for enquiry and can sustain the scientist's determination to continue with his or her desire to discover and learn. Lessons in the garden – from planting seeds to categorising plants – involved scientific skills, teamwork and a purposeful, enquiry-led search for knowledge.

Art in the school has been inspired by nature, and our art specialist uses the outdoor spaces to inspire the children to look more carefully and really 'see' nature. As a result, the children's awareness is growing, and they produce much more closely observed artwork. She ensures that they work using a range of media, and the remarkable outcomes enhance our indoor and outdoor environment.

ICT has been used as a tool to create films, both to inform and in some cases to entertain, inspire and amuse. It also enabled us to keep photographic evidence in the form of snapshots of our outdoor learning. We are currently working on a project to map our garden electronically and create hotspots on our web page, so the pupils can link to relevant websites that will enable them to deepen their knowledge of what is growing and living in the garden.

We have reached a point where we can all agree that every class should go outside to learn at least once a week. Classes use the outdoor space that best suits the learning they want to achieve. This means that as well as trips, running our daily mile and going swimming, the children have the opportunity to go outside for another area of learning.

Growing children

We want to provide an environment that enables the pupils to thrive and grow in the middle of our inner-city concrete 'jungle'. The school gardens literally offer a breath of fresh air that relieves pressure from the closed classroom of around 30 pupils. In the garden, the children have the space and freedom to move around, to discover through nature, and engage and connect with their environment. Pupils who often struggle to stay on task in class due to poor, uncontrolled behaviour can focus more easily outside.

The garden, which changes from day to day, has a magical influence that fills our pupils with curiosity and wonder. It enables them to grow spiritually, mentally and emotionally. When compared with children from other local schools, we notice that our pupils understand how 'to be' in the garden. They are not scared of bees or spiders, they do not kill insects and they realise the importance of each creature – even the snails!

Pupils learn how to care for and respect their environment. They make friends with nature and are curious to name the insects and understand the roles they play in the ecosystem. We have a 'school for bugs' which is full of caterpillars, snails and woodlice and is run by the head teacher who is a ladybird! The 'Haribo Hotel for snug bugs' is another popular place for investigation, as well as under log piles and in our wormery.

Pupils learn and truly understand that life is sacred and that our job is to help care for and nurture our surroundings. We learn how to fix things that are broken (including ourselves) for the benefit of others. Conflict and distress experienced in class or in the playground dissolve in the garden. It is peaceful and has a positive impact on all of us. The simple act of watering and caring for plants calms even the most agitated child.

We watched our children grow in self-esteem as they took control and transformed a bare, scruffy piece of concrete previously used as a dumping ground. They built benches and flower beds (a maths project) to create a perfume garden full of roses, jasmine, lavender, gardenia, sunflowers, wisteria and all sorts of herbs. Pupils experienced directly that they have the power to shape their environment and make it beautiful by applying energy, focus and, most importantly, by working as a team.

As well as caring for the garden, they learn to care for each other. We share successes at the end of each session – reflecting on what we have done well, how we have contributed to making things better and how we are leaving our space in a better state than we found it. We have the power to turn situations and places around and to make things good.

Nurturing with nature

Just as each plant has different qualities and needs different care, so too do our children. By working with small groups of pupils in the garden, we can address and support the different challenges our young people face: bereavement, neglect, domestic violence, aggression, anxiety, depression, disturbing behaviour, speech and language delay and more. The garden fosters love and holds the space for well-being, understanding, and honest and difficult conversations. It has helped children who are hurting and don't know how to articulate their pain.

Three of our children have experienced bereavement. They chose plants to nurture to remember their loved ones: wisteria, roses and sunflowers. The children came together to water and weed their plants. As their plants grew, they opened up to each other and discussed the loss of their parents. They talked and sang together. They cared for each other. They supported each other.

The garden encourages communication. A pupil who was shy and struggled to use complete sentences got excited about seeing a bird's nest with baby birds. He bubbled with excitement and wanted to tell his teacher about what he had seen. He forgot his shyness and lack of language and found a way to share the wonder of the experience. Every child has a story. We witness daily how the garden brings joy to our young people and how they also bring love and care to the garden. The energy is palpable, and it accommodates everyone.

Autistic children find peace by having the space to be who they are and not to have to unhappily conform to the 'norm' of the classroom. Children who have witnessed and experienced domestic violence have space in the garden to talk about their fears, anxiety and pain. The garden nurtures them all and allows them to express themselves and let go. It is almost as if the garden gives them a hug and provides a continuing strength. Such is the invisible power of nature that we witness.

The daily 'Can I do gardening?' demands from pupils show that being outdoors is something our children enjoy – from the awe and wonder of seeing a small yellow flower turn into a tomato, to the delight of playing hide and seek or discovering a worm. They are developing the skills of awareness, concentration and attention to detail, which they also take back into the classroom.

Our philosophy: always leave the garden in a better state than you find it

At Christ Church, we have created a format that works for our children. Every session starts with the garden rules. The children learn them quickly because they are invited to voice them in every session. To stay safe and enjoy our time we:

- Walk in the garden.
- Use quiet voices so not to disturb the neighbours.
- Don't hurt any creatures.
- Listen to and follow instructions.

Anyone who 'breaks the rules' stands on the paving slab and counts to 100, but it is very annoying to have to miss out on the fun, so they rarely bother to break the rules again! On extremely rare occasions we may send children back to class, but their desire to remain in such a special place means that the garden rules and boundaries are clearly and quickly established.

During gardening sessions, tasks can be self-selected, especially by older children who have more experience. More specialised tasks may be directed and guided by the teachers. Easy tasks include snail inspections, litter collections, weeding and watering. More complex jobs might include team challenges, creating cloches to protect plants, constructing wigwams using canes to support plants, making a compost area, clearing stinging nettles without getting stung, and building benches or beds. The teaching staff might advise, support or offer comments on how the children tackle the challenge. However, each team is free to decide how they wish to approach and achieve their task.

The focus is not so much on gardening but on problem-solving and rising to meet challenges in a creative, collaborative way. The gardens are also wonderful spaces for writing, drawing, solving mathematical puzzles or doing science investigations.

At the end of every session we take turns (using a 'talking stick') to speak and listen to each other. We recount what we did that was good and we take time to notice and praise if we saw someone else doing something well. We leave the garden with a sense of achievement and pride in having successfully completed our tasks. Most importantly, we have had fun working together and creating enduring memories.

Sharing our tips

The following advice applies whether you are developing outdoor learning or any other project that is important for your children and families:

- Create a long-term vision. Don't worry about the money – it will come …

- Keep the vision. Know what you are doing and why you are doing it. Be passionate.

- Start small. Start with a few herbs and tomato plants on a window sill, if necessary. Create small, achievable projects.

- Delegate! Give children (and adults) daily opportunities to volunteer. We write names up on a whiteboard in the playground so it is clear who will do what and when.

- Keep it simple. Grow easy things from seed (e.g. sunflowers, rocket, radishes) or plant bulbs like tulips and daffodils – and enjoy the taste of success quickly.

- One step at a time. Little steps contribute to the long-term vision.

- Seek and accept help. Think about who might help you – research local sources of funding and groups of people who might be able to do some of the heavier jobs.

- Keep records so you can see how far you have come. Create a gardening book, take photos, draw pictures and make videos. Invite the children to create and celebrate their success.

- Protect your garden. Love all the creatures in your garden but understand which are friends or foes. Protect plants from snails, squirrels and foxes.

- Enjoy it! Remember to play hide and seek, and don't forget to dance in the rain!

Conclusion

What makes outdoor learning exciting is that it is a journey of discovery that does not end – it changes and grows just like the outdoors. Our garden is forgiving: it allows us to make mistakes and to grow through learning.

As a result, our pupils are developing into fine young people who grow in confidence and resilience through their outdoor work. They are learning to solve problems and face real-life challenges. They learn to work and care for each other, and they are learning to enjoy and take responsibility for respecting and caring for their environment.

We track the progress of each pupil on the school's pupil tracker database so that we can show the progress they are making. We also use 'outcome stars' for each pupil, so that we can tailor personal growth objectives and the children can observe how their own star is 'growing'.

The outcome stars don't measure academic achievement, but rather they measure a pupil's ability to solve problems, to listen, to use their initiative, to complete tasks, to follow instructions and to work as a team. We work to build confidence, resilience and self-worth. Our pupils are learning to concentrate and to care about their actions. By strengthening their inner core qualities, they can apply these learning skills to any aspect of the curriculum and also to life.

Importantly, we recognise the need for improved mental health and well-being, not just for pupils but also for staff. At a time when poor mental health affects so many pupils, and teachers are leaving the teaching profession due to high levels of stress, we see our outdoor learning as being an antidote to pressure and a refreshing solution to offer balance and well-being.

We continue to support the LOtC Manifesto because it clearly works for our children and we owe it to them to provide the best learning environment possible. Learning outdoors is fun, healthy and exciting – for pupils and adults alike.

Further reading and useful links

Cohen, W. (2010). *Kids' Garden: 40 Fun Indoor and Outdoor Activities and Games for Growing Kids*. Cambridge, MA: Barefoot Books.

Robertson, J. (2014). *Dirty Teaching: A Beginner's Guide to Learning Outdoors*. Carmarthen: Independent Thinking Press.

Learning Outside the Classroom Manifesto: http://www.lotc.org.uk/about/manifesto/

About the contributors

Colette Morris

Colette Morris has been a teacher for over 20 years, and has taught in several urban settings from nursery to Year 6. She has also worked as a storyteller in pre-school settings. She became interested in teaching outdoors as she discovered that, in her experience of working with children, both behaviour and learning seem to improve by taking learning outside.

After her appointment as head of Christ Church CE Primary in 2009, LOtC became an important part of the school's curriculum and since then it has been developed right through the school. Colette's research at Roehampton University into horticulture as a vehicle for learning enabled her to investigate the impact of learning outside and led to a MA in education.

Susan Perry

Susan Perry is the head of outdoor learning at Christ Church CE Primary School. Prior to this, Susan managed the education department at Chelsea Physic Garden, and also organised botanical and garden tours worldwide for the Royal Botanic Gardens, Kew. Susan has worked extensively to promote her love of nature and enjoys working with children who struggle to learn in the classroom. She imparts her joy of discovery and respect for nature to her pupils and has been instrumental in helping to develop and care for the gardens at Christ Church.

Chapter 7

Partnership Enrichment Through Shared Stories, Creativity and Gardening

Rachel Woods, co-founder, Parable Garden

In this chapter Rachel Woods describes an example of an enrichment partnership implemented by Parable Garden, an organisation which supports communities, including schools, in using gardening and shared creativity to enrich learning and develop community and spirituality. The partnership with Launton Church of England Primary enabled the school to fulfil its priorities of developing the children's creativity, involving and motivating the whole-school community and embedding the school's ethos and values in 'transformative and sustainable ways'.

The enrichment project was based around a range of learning activities centred on the stewardship of the natural world, together with related initiatives in the creative and expressive arts, all linked to the powerful impact of the parables of Jesus and their timeless relevance for the lives and learning of the pupils and the wider community.

In their inspection report (2016: 2), the Statutory Inspection of Anglican and Methodist Schools (SIAMS) observed that the pupils 'speak with pride about the work they have done in the school grounds to develop planters and beds as part of the parable garden project and speak confidently and knowledgeably about the four parables they link with'.

Background

Parable Garden, which I co-founded in 2014, offers communities, including churches and schools, fresh approaches to exploring spirituality through creative engagement with gardening, the natural world and the parables of Christ.

From our interest in gardening, we developed Into the Garden, which is our partnership methodology for primary schools, which can support schools on a creative and collaborative journey of enrichment, in alignment with the SIAMS schedule. Its areas of focus include the school ethos, community building, character education, core values and spiritual literacy.

The motivation for the development of Into the Garden arose from a desire to answer questions frequently asked by senior leaders, teachers and governors, such as:

■ How can we encourage the emotional, social and spiritual development of pupils throughout the school but also sustain academic achievement?

■ How can we balance priorities to raise academic standards across the school with ways of inspiring and motivating pupils, staff, parents and governors to explore and communicate the school's ethos and values in transformational and sustainable ways?

Growing learning, *growing character* and *growing community* are Parable Garden's terms for core educational objectives.

Aims and objectives

The aims and objectives of Parable Garden's enrichment partnerships are summarised below:

- To nurture relationships and school community cohesion through shared experiences, cross-phased teamwork between children and staff across different age groups, and partnership work between schools, local churches and gardening clubs.

- To harness and release creative gifts and energy for staff, clergy and parents to contribute ideas and activities.

- To affirm personal expression within each child through accessible, collaborative activities on a selected theme.

- To encourage attitudes of mutual respect and listening skills.

- To inspire and foster each pupil's sense of connection with the natural world, the seasons, cycles of growth and gardening activities.

- To develop pupils' spiritual and self-awareness through reflection, with accessible reflective activities for different age groups in practical sessions.

- To provide a sustainable framework of support including follow-up classroom activities, access to online resources and the establishment of regular review processes.

The approach has been piloted in several schools, and there is evidence of its positive impact on the development and achievement of the whole child, on school community growth and wider relationships.

Gardening: growing sensory and seasonal awareness

Nature quietly weaves calm, beauty and wonder into our lives. Through our focused attention, nature points us to T. S. Eliot's 'still point of the turning world' (1969 [1933]: 173) – to that centre where we find God. Playgrounds, school fields and garden areas offer endless opportunities for creative learning experiences; allowing pupils to stretch out, not merely physically, but creatively, imaginatively and spiritually.

Parable Garden is not alone in advocating for whole-school gardening where children can develop gardening skills as well as confidence in working outdoors. The Campaign for

School Gardening, run by the Royal Horticultural Society (RHS), is committed to practically supporting and resourcing the development of pupils' gardening skills across the whole school. Building relationships with local garden centres is also actively encouraged; many garden centres promote and support school gardening as well as offering sponsorship in kind, through donating materials and plants for projects and gardening workshops.

In 2016, the healthcare think-tank The King's Fund produced the report *Gardens and Health*, which was commissioned by the National Gardens Scheme. It found that qualitative studies in this area reported positive well-being effects on children from school gardening in terms of personal achievement, pride and empowerment.

The Christian Bible has many references to cultivation and gardens, and many rich metaphors relating to planting, nurturing growth, pruning and harvesting. In the Old Testament, the language of cultivation is used to describe the activities of the Jewish people and spiritual relationships. God is described metaphorically as 'the gardener'. These scriptures have inspired generations of Christians to explore and write about the connection between gardens, seasons, animals, plants and spirituality.

When working on Parable Garden initiatives, I have found that children can use the metaphors inherent in gardening as a framework and language to reflect on their own physical, social, emotional, academic and spiritual growth. The weeds choking the 'good seed' in the Parable of the Sower could represent obstacles to learning. Weeding the quiet or themed garden can be an inclusive way to think about these things, and get an important job done at the same time!

Partnership with Launton Primary School

Launton Church of England Primary is one of the schools that has successfully partnered with Parable Garden. The school is set in the heart of a rural village near Bicester, in Oxfordshire, with 146 pupils on the school roll. It has garden areas at the front of the building, which the school gardening club have been looking after, along with tubs with plants for seasonal colour around the school. To the rear of the school is a playground with a group of tall trees, and beyond is a large playing field edged with trees and hedges which is also used by the community at weekends.

Launton School wanted to respond positively and creatively to priorities identified by reports from Ofsted and SIAMS. They were also keen to develop the use of the school grounds for outdoor curriculum learning and for social, moral, spiritual and cultural enrichment.

Stage 1: Creative and collaborative planning

The Parable of the Sower, the Parable of the Good Shepherd, the Parable of the Talents and the Parable of the Mustard Seed were chosen because they embody many of the core values that underpin the development of character, learning, community development and spirituality. The Parable of the Sower was chosen as the foundation parable because it could help the children to understand the concept of growth and growing in relation to learning, character and community, as well as spirituality.

The parables were integrated into workshops which were delivered by the staff, clergy and myself, working collaboratively. A member of the clergy led an assembly prior to the first Parable Treasure Hunting Enrichment Day to establish the pupils' understanding of the Kingdom of God and explain how Jesus explained what God is like through telling stories called parables. The children learned about the Parable of the Sower and considered how a sower or gardener prepares the ground before planting seeds. They were encouraged to think about what helps a community to grow together, develop values and character and travel together on a spiritual journey. Questions for discussion included: what is our school's big story? What are the parables? How do parables help us to understand God's love?

Stage 2: Parable Treasure Hunting Enrichment Day

In the morning assembly, I welcomed the children and then explained the purpose of exploring parables and finding treasure in them through the workshops they would be taking part in during the day. The meanings and purpose of the parables were revisited in helping them to think about what it means to be a Christian school, part of God's big story, linked to Christian values.

The creative and collaborative nature of the workshops was explained, and the importance of working well together and the shared values underlying the planning of the day were highlighted. For example, the children were encouraged to consider the following: listening, inclusion, encouragement, teamwork, partnership and reflection.

The pupils were introduced to the Christian idea that God speaks to people through the natural world – for example, through reference to gardens and seasonal gardening activities, such as preparing the ground and planting seeds. Nurturing, weeding and harvesting are also useful tools for personal reflection and spiritual growth. The plant life cycle was mentioned and how it might reflect stages of the children's own spiritual journeys.

After each activity, the children would be asked, in cross-phase pairs, to reflect on what connections they had made, felt and learned and to think more deeply and personally about the parables – for example, expressing what they might mean to them and what they enjoyed about the workshops.

Stage 3: Creative and collaborative workshops

A cross-phase carousel was organised outdoors across the whole school and several workshop areas were set up in indoor and outdoor areas for the children to participate in throughout the day. The children were divided into four house groups and they rotated around the school to participate in the creative activities on offer.

The levels of concentration and engagement from all abilities were high. The children were encouraged to work as a team with their 'buddy' in exchanging ideas and supporting each other. It was clear that there was a sense of adventure and excitement about creating something together for a cooperative artwork.

The creative workshops included:

■ **Parable banners.** Each house group focused on one of the four parables. They created drawings to communicate the parable which were then translated by Parable Garden into an overall composition to retell each parable as the basis for a series of banners for the school hall. An element from each child's drawing was included in the final banner design, affirming their worth, creativity and contribution as individuals.

■ **Tree planting on the school field.** Each house group planted a tree to celebrate the tree of life and to start a school orchard. In time, as they mature, these trees can be used for creative reflection on the seasons.

■ **The Sower's Garden.** Clay props inspired by different elements of the Parable of the Sower were made by each child to contribute to the retelling of the story in the reflective garden at the front of the school. Flying and feeding birds, seed pods, corn cobs and thistle cane tops were created and then later glazed and fired in follow-up workshops. These were eventually placed in the parable-themed garden to help the children retell the Parable of the Sower.

■ **Sunflower seed planting and parable stone poetry.** The children planted a selection of sunflower varieties, partly as a scientific experiment and partly to represent seeds falling on the good soil. These were set out in planters at the front of the school, near the Sower's Garden. Each pupil wrote one word from the Parable of the Sower on a stone in permanent marker. The stones were then laid down to make a 'parable path' in the Sower's Garden.

■ **Gardening the heart.** Pupils in cross-phase pairings used reflective questions in small booklets to think about what they like to use a garden for, areas of their lives or attitudes that they want to change and how gardening activities can focus our attention on these things.

Stage 4: Conclusion to the day

As a finale to the day, we held a whole-school assembly to celebrate the creative outcomes and give pupils and staff an opportunity to reflect on the experience. Pupils from each year group shared their thoughts, feelings and discoveries from the day. As Parable Garden leader, I thanked the pupils for engaging so creatively and enthusiastically, and then explained what was going to happen next with the collaborative artwork they had produced. The completed banners were intended for display in a prominent position in the school hall to inspire ongoing reflection during collective worship.

Ongoing enrichment

Gardening together

To help embed the initiative, Parable Garden has encouraged Launton to engage in seasonal gardening activities for 40 minutes once or twice a term, to be undertaken by pupils in cross-phase groups. We see such activities as a priority for a school community in order to provide a framework for the progressive exploring of spirituality and with opportunities for pastoral care. The school's gardening club continues to maintain the Sower's Garden and further elements will be added over time.

Spirituality Safari Day

After a year of working in partnership with Parable Garden, Launton School held a Spirituality Safari Day based on the Parable of the Good Shepherd. It involved a carousel of six cross-phase workshops. We started the day with a whole-school assembly and prayer, and then the pupils were divided into cross-phase 'buddy' pairs.

The children participated in the following workshops:

■ **Planting seeds and helping them grow.** The children worked with gardening club leaders to plant out the young plants they had grown from seed in ornamental planters around the school and in the Sower's Garden. Questions triggered by the activity included: what conditions do plants need in order to grow best? What learning environment and attitudes do I need in order to learn well?

- **Talent tree of life.** A tree had been chosen to represent a 'talent tree of life' – somewhere to celebrate and show gratitude for people's talents, recognising our gifts and developing our character (this relates to the Parable of the Talents and the work of the Holy Spirit). Pairs of children created one tile as part of a composite tree of life using observational tree drawings made by Year 6 pupils. They created relief tile sections of textured bark, twigs and leaves and added relief moulded birds and insects to celebrate the way a tree supports life. Questions included: how can God support us and help us grow good personal qualities, develop our unique talents and make a difference to our school community? How can we use our talents to do what Jesus said: 'love your neighbour as yourself' and 'love one another as I have loved you'?

- **Wonder walking/prayer labyrinth.** Our prayer labyrinth is a single path, designed for ease of navigation, which leads via a circuitous route to the centre of an intricate design and back out again. The children walked the prayer labyrinth in silence to a cross in the centre and were encouraged to be still for a moment and reflect on their thoughts, experiences and feelings. Questions included: what difference does taking time to be silent and thoughtful as we walk a labyrinth make to our lives? How does it make you feel? What does it make you think of?

- **Stencil pictures.** Each child in the school contributed drawings of animals, plants and insects. An artist working with the school had hand-cut stencils from their work for the children to use on the day to add to pre-prepared backgrounds. Marine ply and outdoor paint were used to make weatherproof images of the natural world. Questions included: how can the images remind us about growing learning, character and community?

- **Making a sheep for the Sower's Garden.** This was a willow-weaving workshop with a professional sculptor and involved the children being taught how to weave a life-size sheep to be a centrepiece for the Sower's Garden. Questions included: how can our sheep remind us of how Jesus is a caring shepherd? What helps us to grow and develop as people and become aware of the spiritual part of ourselves?

- **Creating earth gardens from natural elements.** One classroom offered five mixed-age groups a large tray and a wide range of natural materials. The teacher shared examples of land art by the artist Andy Goldsworthy. She then invited each group to look at the resources available (leaves, soil, sand, shingle, flowers, twigs and glass pebbles) and then plan the basic design of their earth garden. The groups worked together collaboratively to build their garden, making a conscious effort to be open to each other's suggestions and appreciative of each other's ideas. One garden was designed as a Japanese garden and another was shaped like a dolphin. Questions included: why is it important to make beautiful things together?

Learning outcomes

Over 160 people were involved in Launton's Spirituality Safari Day. At the review stage, everyone involved agreed that the day had yielded the following outcomes:

- High levels of concentration and engagement with learning activities.

- Development of creative expression, oral skills and social literacy because the shared activities required the pupils to communicate their thoughts and ideas about the themes and activities.

- Follow-up assemblies and class discussions indicated that the pupils had gained a clearer understanding of the significance of Christian stories such as the parables, their application in everyday life and the values that underpin them.

- An increase in the pupils' sense of connection, wonder and questioning about the natural world, the seasons, cycles of growth and gardening activities.

- Reflective exercises helped the children to understand how they can use what they observe and experience to make deeper connections related to growing learning, character and community.

- Gardening activities and shared creativity brought a sense of excitement and enjoyment for every age group.

- Working in cross-phase groups and pairs strengthened relationships between the children and staff. As one Year 4 pupil said: 'We had to explain the stories to the smaller children. It helped us remember and learn too.'

Conclusion

At Launton, we found that collaborative cross-phase creativity centred around the parables and gardening enhanced learning, character and values development. The project was inclusive and motivational. By providing immersive and multisensory experiences, we observed deepening knowledge and understanding across all age groups, as well as meaningful personal expression and reflection.

The ongoing use of collaborative creativity, including gardening, provided a solid framework on which to build and sustain creativity as a life-giving, transformative ingredient within their education community. Head teacher Lisa Horton (2014–2017) concluded that the artwork and experiences the children had on the catalyst enrichment days had a very positive impact on children, staff and the wider school community.

Further reading and useful links

Buck, D. (2016). *Gardens and Health: Implications for Policy and Practice*. London: The King's Fund. Available at: https://www.kingsfund.org.uk/sites/default/files/field/field_publication_file/Gardens_and_health.pdf.

Eliot, T. S. (1969 [1935]). 'Four Quartets'. In *T. S. Eliot: The Complete Poems and Plays*. London: Faber and Faber.

Statutory Inspection of Anglican and Methodist Schools (2016). Launton Church of England Voluntary Controlled Primary School Report (9 November). Available at: http://www.launtonschool.co.uk/Files/Download/b9b75dde-3f9d-4a78-be49-5cbc9bf9824c/3cc1744f-8f03-4a92-9c45-c0c8b4e13f16/launton%20c%20of%20e%20final%20siams%202016.pdf.

Woods, R. (2016). *Into the Garden: Cultivation as a Tool for Spiritual Formation and Community Renewal* (Spirituality Series S136). Cambridge: Grove Books.

Parable Garden: http://www.parable-garden.org

RE with Soul: http://www.rewithsoul.co.uk

RHS Campaign for School Gardening: https://schoolgardening.rhs.org.uk

Understanding Christianity: http://www.understandingchristianity.org.uk

Wintershall Estate: https://www.wintershall-education.com

About the contributor

Rachel Woods

Rachel Woods developed and implemented Wintershall Education on behalf of Wintershall CIO, which is closely linked with the annual production of *The Life of Christ* in Surrey. Rachel co-founded Parable Garden in 2014. She is a lead consultant for, and co-author of, RE with Soul – an enquiry-based RE resource which is designed to complement the SIAMS schedule and new Understanding Christianity resource. She is also the author of *Visual Literacy in RE Teaching and Learning* (2008) and *Into the Garden* (2016).

Chapter 8

Languages in the Primary Curriculum

Dawn Basnett, deputy head teacher, and Roy Calcutt, Latin teacher, Ickford School, Buckinghamshire

The head teacher of Ickford School had a desire to see a modern foreign language taught to every child, including those in the Early Years Foundation Stage (EYFS), but knew he could not achieve this until he had appointed someone with specialist expertise. Despite recognising a trend for more widely spoken 'business' languages such as Spanish, German and Chinese, the head teacher chose French because he liked the language and the culture, and was learning French himself. A subject has far more chance of being a success if the person responsible for designing the curriculum has a passion or at least an interest in it.

The deputy head teacher, Dawn Basnett, a modern languages specialist, coordinates and teaches French across the school. She also runs enthusiastically attended after-school clubs in German and Spanish. The impact of specialist subject expertise, deep commitment and infectious enthusiasm is evident in the confident support of class teachers and the steadily escalating proficiency of children in languages across the school.

This is reflected in several ways:

- A rich and imaginative diversity of learning activities.

- The development of writing skills inspired by a creative stimulus.

- Constant encouragement and inviting opportunities for children to converse for a variety of purposes.

- A systematic and sympathetic but rigorous programme of assessment.

- Carefully designed and meticulously presented displays, illustrated by pupils, that describe the activities in which they engage.

- Regular weekly input from a classics scholar who teaches Latin to able and interested Year 6 pupils.

- Enthusiastic support from parents who tell of their reliance on their children as guides, mediators and interpreters on visits to France.

- The regular French café, steadily gaining in local fame, which is organised and run with the help of parents and is a source of great excitement and pleasure for parents and children alike.

Background

Ickford School, which has been an academy since 2016, is a rural village school with a maximum roll of 140, with an equal split of boys and girls. The school accords modern foreign languages a position of high status in the curriculum and regards the study of languages as a key influence on the children's education.

At Ickford we attach a huge importance, and devote significant time and resources, to ensuring that all our children acquire and master a foreign or second language, and have the opportunity to become acquainted and engage with more than one language beyond that. This is because we believe that learning a foreign language equips children with a vital skill that may well be of inestimable value to them in vocational and professional terms in later life.

But it does much more than that. A second language provides an opening to other cultures, civilisations and ways of living, and to a deeper appreciation and understanding of the world. It enables pupils to express their ideas, thoughts and feelings in another form and provides them with the glorious opportunity to engage and respond in speech and writing to those who speak that other language. In the process of such exchange, a wider world is revealed and new ways of thinking and viewing matters are developed. The opportunity to read literature beyond our own, to discover and understand other drama, film and entertainment also comes within reach.

Furthermore, learning a foreign language provides opportunities to communicate for practical purposes. The national curriculum states that 'Language teaching should provide the foundation for learning further languages, equipping pupils to study and work in other countries' (Department for Education, 2013: 1). One travels with more confidence, and has easier access to the life-enhancing richness and diversity of places beyond our national boundaries.

At Ickford, our aims are to ensure that pupils:

- Understand and respond to spoken and written language from a variety of authentic resources.

- Speak with increasing confidence, fluency and spontaneity – finding ways of communicating what they want to say, including discussion and asking questions, and continually improving the accuracy of their pronunciation and intonation.

- Can write at varying length for different purposes and audiences, using a variety of grammatical structures.

- Discover and develop an appreciation of the language studied, a passion for languages and a commitment to the subject.

- Develop a strong awareness of the culture of the countries where the language is spoken.

When a child is exposed to a new language, they begin to see patterns and learn transferable skills. For example, some children in the school as young as 6 or 7 know that nouns in French are either masculine or feminine. This is also true for German, Spanish and Italian. The children understand that describing words (adjectives) in many languages come after the words they are describing, unlike in English (e.g. 'The BFG ate a humongous breakfast').

Teaching and learning

All pupils in the school have a weekly French lesson. French for the EYFS children focuses on speaking and listening to the language. Teaching is visual and practical, using a wide range of physical resources, music and songs. On display around the school is a mix of written work, including poetry.

In Key Stage 1, we enjoy learning songs and playing games in French, as well as acting out café and shopping scenes; the emphasis is on speaking the language. Key Stage 1 children have a 30–45-minute lesson and those in Key Stage 2 have a 60-minute lesson. In Key Stage 2 we place a bigger emphasis on written French but ensure that the children speak as much as possible in the language. We act out scenarios such as *'chez le médecin'* ('at the doctor's') or fashion shows.

Differentiated tasks, open-ended challenges and support prompts enable children in all year groups to develop at their individual pace and level. As the scheme of work that follows illustrates, the teaching focuses on familiar and routine matters; the exposure to real-life scenarios (e.g. at the market stall, at the café) and the use of authentic materials (e.g. magazines, leaflets from France) ensure that the learning is experiential and meaningful.

French scheme of work

Class	Term 1	Term 2	Term 3	Term 4	Term 5	Term 6
1	Numbers 1–10 Song – *Un, deux, trois* Basic greetings *Je m'appelle* *J'ai …. ans* *Jacques a dit*	Numbers 1–20 Song – *Dix au lit, Brille petite etoile* Colours Christmas in France	Numbers 1–30 Recap basic questions (name and age) and colours *Je voudrais* Basic café vocabulary Set up French café – role play	Weekly recap of numbers, basic questions and colours *Animaux de la maison* Pets – combine with colours Introduce concept of position of adjectives Easter in France	Weekly recap of numbers, basic questions and colours Basic fruits *Je voudrais …* *S'il vous plait, merci*	Weekly recap of numbers, basic questions and colours Basic vocabulary – summer *Je voudrais une glace* + flavours Link with colours
2	Recap numbers 1–30 Basic body parts Song – *C'est moi*	Weekly numbers Questioning Sea life animals – sentences using 'il y a' and colours (emphasis on word order)	Weekly recap of numbers and basic questions Weather: *Quel temps fait-il ?* *A Paris il pleut,* etc.	Weekly recap of numbers and basic questions School subjects *J'aime* *Je n'aime pas* Easter in France	Weekly recap of numbers and basic questions *Au marché* Role play – buying fruit and vegetables	Weekly recap of numbers and basic questions Sentence structure – *il y a, aussi, et* *Les vacances* – describing a beach scene

Class	Term 1	Term 2	Term 3	Term 4	Term 5	Term 6
3	Recap numbers, greetings, basic questions Physical descriptions (hair, eyes, size and personality) Wanted poster	Recap basic numbers, greetings, questions Recap body parts – *Chez le médecin* Role play Cartoon strip Christmas in France Song – *Quelle est la date de ton anniversaire ?* Christmas in France	*En ville* Shops *Il y a …* Rooms of the house Advert for a French holiday home	*Les vêtements* Clothes (combine clothes and colours, size, materials, price) Fashion show Easter in France	*Les vacances* Buying ice creams, recap and extend *au café, au restaurant, au supermarché* Recap and extend school subjects – likes and dislikes	Recap and extend *la météo* (weather) Write weather forecast Recap all units from year – French assessment in June
4	Recap numbers, greetings, basic questions Physical descriptions (hair, eyes, size and personality) Wanted poster	Recap basic numbers, greetings, questions Recap body parts – *Chez le médecin* Role play Cartoon strip Christmas in France	*En ville* Shops *Il y a …* Rooms of the house Advert for a French holiday home	*Les vêtements* Clothes (combine clothes and colours, size, materials, price) Fashion show Easter in France	*Les vacances* Buying ice creams, recap and extend *au café, au restaurant, au supermarché* Recap and extend school subjects – likes and dislikes	Recap and extend *la météo* (weather) Write weather forecast Recap all units from year – French assessment in June

5	Introduce perfect tense – Mrs Vandertramp Sentences in past tense about summer holidays and last weekend	Song – *Quelle est la date de ton anniversaire ?* Christmas in France	Autumn poetry – link in with description (colours, sentence composition) French assembly scenes Evacuation in French – link to Second World War Christmas in France	The future tense Plans for the next weekend, next summer Horoscopes in French Planets in French	*Le sport et le weekend Qu'est ce que tu aimes faire le weekend ?* Sentence composition Easter in France	French spring and summer poems Read and write own poems	All about me (family, physical descriptions, personality, where I live, school subjects and preferences) Range of tenses and opinions

The teaching includes an appropriate balance of spoken and written language, which enables the children to understand and communicate ideas, feelings and facts about themselves and others in speech and writing.

The focus of the learning is communication: to read and understand fluently, to speak confidently, to write imaginatively and to understand the culture of French people. Across all classes, there is a focus on using the French language in everyday settings, such as asking their class teacher for *un crayon* or *une gomme* rather than using the English word. At Breakfast Club, the children are encouraged to ask for their cereal in French, using *Je voudrais …*

We have recently purchased a new CD so that each class can learn new French songs – this has been well received from reception to Year 6. Learning French through song is undeniably a sound way of learning a language.

Real-life scenarios

In Key Stage 1, we act out scenes at the café and at the market (*au marché*). This entails bringing in croissants and pains au chocolat, setting the classroom up as a French café with red, white and blue bunting and French flags, and playing French music in the background. The children politely request in French, '*Je voudrais un croissant, s'il vous plait,*' and, of course, we respond in French with '*Voilà!*'

The market scene involves setting up the tables with a mixture of plastic fruits and vegetables (as well as real ones), toy cash tills and plastic euro coins. The more able linguists in the class act as the market sellers and the other children rotate between the tables asking for fruit and vegetables in French.

The most authentic activity has to be our residential trip to Hardelot in Normandy. In alternate years, Years 5 and 6 can practise their French and experience French culture at first hand. The children go on a range of excursions, including the largest aquarium in Europe, the Normandy landing beaches and a French market, plus they get to savour French cuisine such as escargots.

Ma visite en France

La semaine dernière, je suis allée en France avec mes amis. J'ai voyagé en grand car rouge, bleu et blanc. Je suis arrivé a Pré Catelan, c'était magnifique ! La maison était blanche avec les fleurs jaunes, il y avait le badminton et les arbres verts.

Mardi j'ai visité Nausicaa. C'était énorme ! A Nausicaa j'ai vu beaucoup les poissons bleus et oranges, bruns et blancs – petits et grands ! Aussi j'ai vu le requin, les phoques et la méduse. Après j'ai visité la boutique il y avait beaucoup des animaux la mer. Après nous sommes a la plage a Hardelot. La mer était verte et bleue avec blanche. C'était trop froid ! Sur le sable il y avait les coquilles gris et blanches. Les filles aiment les coquilles.

Customs and traditions

We teach the children about French customs and traditions, especially at Easter and Christmas time. On 1 April, for example, French children put paper fish on each other's backs and cry 'poisson d'avril' before running off – a tradition the Ickford children find hilarious and copy. They also find it fascinating how the church bells are said to fly to Rome on Good Friday and not return until Easter Sunday (when the church bells ring loudly to mark the resurrection of Jesus).

On a weekly basis, we award seven language certificates (one per class for French, Latin and either German or Spanish) and we provide opportunities to present the children's work on display boards and in an annual French assembly which takes place at Christmas – all the children in the school take part and perform to the parents.

We also hold termly whole-school language competitions, with certificates and prizes awarded in assembly. In autumn the children write a French poem, at Christmas all the children design and make a card in French and at Easter they make French Easter cards. Here is the first and last verse from a Year 4 pupil's poem:

Les feuilles tombent
Tombent, tombent,
Les papillions d'automne,
Jaune, orange et rouge

Tombent, tombent,
Les pommes d'automne,
Rose, vert et rouge. ...
Tombent, tombent,
Les glands d'automne
Couvert par l'écreuil,
Tombent, tombent,
Les pommes de pins d'automne
S'ecartant partout.

[The leaves fall
Fall, fall,
The butterflies of autumn,
Yellow, orange and red
Fall, fall,
The autumn apples,
Pink, green and red. ...
Fall, fall,
The acorns of autumn
Covered by the squirrel,
Fall, fall,
The autumn pine cones
Scattered everywhere.]

The Ickford parents are incredibly supportive and actively encourage their children to practise French outside of the classroom. Many go on holiday to France and both children and parents are always eager to relay stories of speaking French. The parents also ask in French for their coffees and teas at our French café.

In order to deepen the children's awareness of other culture and languages, we introduced an after-school languages club in spring 2015. Originally a German club, the children expressed an interest in learning Spanish. This has been very successful and we now alternate between German and Spanish each half-term. We run the club after school on

Tuesdays from 3.30–4.30 p.m. and we have places for 25 children. One pupil said: 'Spanish is awesome! I can't believe how much I've learned already!'

A parent's perspective

As a parent, I am delighted that French is taught comprehensively throughout the school. I especially enjoy the French assembly where they/we can practise their/our skills. These are always well attended (very soon there will be standing room only) and require us parents to dredge up our own rusty school French and translate to each other, such is the skill level!

The children also write poetry, create artwork and sing songs in the language. I often hear my children singing about the *'bonhomme de neige'* at home. Our lively café (a fantastic idea) is also incredibly popular. Traditional French pastries are served warm from the oven alongside steaming mugs of coffee. The atmosphere – bunting flapping and jaunty French music playing in the background – gives our children a real appreciation of the culture, which I feel is important to their learning.

I asked my daughter how she felt about learning French at school. She said she loves it and always looks forward to the lessons. She added that she is very keen to get to France to show that she can politely order her own food and drink in French without any help. You can't ask for more than that!

Pupils' perspectives

French is fun – we learn new words every lesson.

French day is a special day.

The French competitions are really fun in French and German.

Thursdays are my favourite day – I have Latin and French.

Assessment

It is very interesting to track the attainment of French, particularly as we frequently discover that children who find literacy a struggle often feel more confident learning French. We believe that this may have something to do with the fact that usually the whole class are at a very similar if not exactly the same start point, that there is initially more focus on the oral language (although writing is introduced in EYFS) and because their role model is absolutely correct, which is not always the case when the children are developing their native language skills.

We assess the children's knowledge of French through observations and continuous oral questioning. Summative assessment in the form of an assessment booklet was introduced in spring 2015 for Years 2–6. A tracking file for each child has been set up in order to monitor and ensure progress. It is noteworthy that there are currently more children working at mastery level (see Dweck, 2016) in Years 3 and 4 than in any other year, which is not necessarily mirrored in their literacy and numeracy abilities.

Progression is tracked as the pupils move up through the school – for example, the older children begin to write lengthier paragraphs and use more challenging grammar, such as the *passé composé* (past tense).

Future plans

The French café continues to be very successful and both parents and children enjoy the occasion. It has become almost routine to add a French café to other activities, such as sporting events and the May Day dancing. The café takes place every other week during the summer term.

Of course, as any teacher will tell you, there is always further to go and more to do. The challenges we are currently working on at Ickford include:

■ To encourage the children to speak French outside of their French lessons (such as at Breakfast Club, at playtime, asking to go to the toilet and buying ice creams).

■ To ensure that there is a deep understanding of spoken French so the children recognise, understand and can respond to vocabulary and phrases when outside of the classroom and in non-contextualised situations.

■ To further develop the children's abilities to express themselves in other languages and to become confidently literate in more than one language. The poem in this chapter reflects the quality of writing our children can now achieve.

Language enrichment

In Year 6, as part of the enrichment programme for more able pupils, several children are given the opportunity to learn Latin. Head teacher John Ronane is convinced that specialist input from the school's Latin teacher, Roy Calcutt, is essential to the pupils' motivation and progress.

The focus of the teaching is to provide a linguistic foundation for understanding texts and appreciating classical civilisation. Mr Calcutt uses the Minimus language course as well as stories from Greek mythology to support his teaching; the children act out scenarios and role play in Latin. In 2017, he taught Latin to seven children who were already competent in French, while the remaining children concentrated on improving their French. This arrangement enabled those children to work in a smaller class group which supported their progress and helped them to achieve the expected level of attainment in French.

Teaching Latin at Ickford

Having studied for a Classics degree before pursuing a career in law, I have retained a keen interest in the ancient world. I recall clearly how much I enjoyed Latin when I first had lessons as a child, and the excitement of the classical world that gripped me when I first encountered it has stayed with me to this day. The prospect of volunteering in a school to teach Classics for an hour per week, offering me the ability to immerse myself in the subject again and to pass on my interest to some of today's young minds, was a very attractive one. I was therefore very enthusiastic when the head teacher and the languages lead at Ickford School gave me the opportunity to teach Latin and broader aspects of the classical world to their Year 6 pupils.

The class began by pursuing the Minimus course developed by Barbara Bell, which follows the lives of the eponymous mouse and the family living at Vindolanda on Hadrian's Wall in AD 100. However, as the confidence of the students developed we diversified into work beyond the Minimus course – for example, pupils have translated simple sentences from Latin to English and English to Latin. The stronger students have moved on to translate stories from Latin on mythological subjects such as the building of Troy and the Judgement of Paris.

Pupils appear to enjoy exploring the roots of English words and rendering Latin into English and vice versa. We have concentrated on understanding the grammar, including the role of nouns, adjectives, verbs, adverbs and prepositions in Latin. In a mixed ability class, some students clearly find the grammar more challenging than others. For this reason, the rigour of the approach needs to be tailored to the abilities of individual students. While some choose to attempt a passage for translation, others might undertake an exercise from Minimus.

Study of the language itself needs to be leavened with other aspects of the classical world which all of the pupils can enjoy together. Greek myths and Greek and Roman gods and goddesses have proved very popular; we have explored these subjects both by reading stories together (e.g. from the Minimus books) and also by looking at paintings with classical subjects, such as Titian's *Diana and Actaeon* and *Bacchus and Ariadne*. We have also talked about the founding of Rome and looked at pictures of the famous sights of the city. We have discussed classical Athens, the origins of democracy and the phenomenon of ostracism.

Whether the students continue with Latin beyond primary school or not, I believe that the lessons have helped them to understand the development of the English language, expanded their vocabularies, reinforced their existing knowledge of grammar and, in conjunction with their pre-existing knowledge of French, provided them with a good basis for foreign language learning in the future. I hope that it will also have imbued at least some of the children with a lifelong interest in the richness of the classical world; a world which is such a big part of the foundation of our own culture.

Est melius in Latina – It is better in Latin!

Roy Calcutt

Conclusion

Head teacher John Ronane credits the success of languages at Ickford mainly to the personality and expertise of his specialist teachers. He believes strongly that children should all learn at least one other language from the earliest possible age – not simply as an add-on or gimmick to appear 'different', but because having a second language is empowering throughout life. It is a skill of which one can be very proud, and it opens doors to other places, peoples and cultures.

Despite the dominance of English as the language of the digital age, our children will grow up in a world where the capacity to engage in the language of others – for practical, business and commercial purposes – will remain as important and rewarding as ever. Resistance to this, whether due to complacency or indifference, makes us less receptive to advanced modes of thinking and inventive and progressive ways of doing things – to our detriment and loss.

Further reading and useful links

Barton, A. and McLachlan, A. (2016). *Teaching Primary French: Everything a Non-Specialist Needs to Know to Teach Primary French*. London: Bloomsbury.

Bourdais, D. and Finnie, S. (2015). *Games for Teaching Primary French*. Carmarthen: Crown House Publishing.

Department for Education (2013). Languages Programmes of Study: Key Stage 2 National Curriculum in England. Available at: https://www.gov.uk/government/uploads/system/uploads/attachment_data/file/239042/PRIMARY_national_curriculum_-_Languages.pdf.

Dweck, C. (2016). *Mindset: The New Psychology of Success*. New York: Ballantine Books.

BBC Schools – Primary Languages (French): http://www.bbc.co.uk/schools/primarylanguages/french/

British Council – Partner with a School: https://schoolsonline.britishcouncil.org/partner-school

Institut français du Royaume-Uni: https://www.institut-francais.org.uk/.../primary.../for-teachers/mobility-programmes/

Minimus: http://www.minimus-etc.co.uk

About the contributors

Dawn Basnett

After completing her PGCE at Oxford University, Dawn Basnett worked at Cannock Chase High School before then moving to Windsor Girls' School, where she was head of modern foreign languages. Having started a family, Dawn later set up a French club at her daughters' primary school and taught literacy and numeracy at a local secondary school. In 2011, she was offered a part-time job teaching French at Ickford School. By 2012, she had become so impressed and inspired by the attitudes towards learning she found there that she accepted the offer of a role as the Year 6 teacher, French teacher and, eventually, deputy head.

Roy Calcutt

Having obtained a Classics degree at Pembroke College, Oxford, Roy Calcutt qualified as a solicitor in 1993 through a legal conversion course. Initially he specialised in property law in private practice before joining the Government Legal Service in 2001, where he worked in the transport sphere – with railways and aviation in particular. Roy was the legal adviser to the Airports Commission, which reported in 2015 on the airport capacity needs in the south-east of England.

Chapter 9

Role Play and Stories

Isy Mead, head of learning and participation, the Story Museum, Oxford

This chapter begins with a persuasive claim for the place of story at the core of human existence. Isy Mead of the Story Museum in Oxford argues that stories are everywhere, they are 'at the heart of our culture' and in all the art forms. Stories have the capacity to contribute richly and profoundly to the whole curriculum.

She conveys something of the extraordinary atmosphere of the Story Museum, and the almost Gothic nature of some of the exhibition spaces, with their haunting sense of fairy tales, legends and folklore, and their capacity for enchantment, enthralment and fearfulness. As we read, we can imagine the visiting child's animated searching and movement along twilight byways and round corners, encountering one wonder after another, pushing their way through the wardrobe into Narnia itself or opening a gate into a secret garden.

Isy Mead also suggests some valuable principles to bear in mind when using stories with children, whether in a dedicated space such as the museum or in a school library or classroom, as well as ideas and inspiration for creating magical spaces within a primary school.

Background

The Story Museum in Oxford was established in 2003, motivated by a vision to enable children to grow up rich in stories, inspired by their power to transform their lives, and to develop the linguistic, intellectual and emotional skills they need to understand themselves and the world, and connect with each other.

The museum aims to achieve its vision by collecting 'great stories' and sharing 'great ways' of engaging with them. It does so in a variety of ways, including an extraordinary range of displays, exhibitions and events, together with regular input from renowned authors, educators, literary authorities and storytellers who enrapture schoolchildren and family visitors with their craft and performances.

What role can story and stories play in today's schools?

Alice was beginning to get very tired of sitting by her sister on the bank, and of having nothing to do: once or twice she had peeped into the book her sister was reading, but it had no pictures or conversations in it, 'and what is the use of a book,' thought Alice, 'without pictures or conversations?' (Carroll, 1865: 1)

So begins Lewis Carroll's *Alice's Adventures in Wonderland*, just before Alice throws herself unceremoniously into a colourful world of extraordinary sights and bizarre conversations. It is likely that Alice's rhetorical question, with its insinuation that books from the outset can be unappealing and boring, has very strong echoes in what might be heard from so-called 'reluctant readers' in the classroom today. Alice doesn't say outright that she doesn't like reading. If anything, she wishes to access it; after all, she 'peeped into the book' of her own volition. However, Alice does imply that she sees multisensory approaches as fundamental elements of a book: the visual through 'pictures' and the auditory through 'conversations'. These approaches are far more than simply accessory; they are *integral* to the reading experience. Indeed, a book has 'no use' without it. Alice wants books to be participatory and interactive engagements with story.

What Alice wants is to access story through tangible, dynamic and multisensory experiences. How do we bridge the gap between the experience Alice craves for and the more intellectual experience Alice's sister is enjoying? These questions form the heart of pedagogy: enlightening the student through inspired teaching methods to make material accessible, understandable and increasingly but suitably challenging. In recent years, a niche has started to emerge in the non-formal learning sector that promotes enthusiasm for, and creative responses to, story.

Making spaces for story

Distinct from the academic environment that is inextricably linked with the demands and anxieties of measurable achievement, there are a range of cultural venues across England which develop the concept of reading for pleasure by realising engagement with story and creative writing in tangible ways. These places include, among others: Discover Children's Story Centre in Stratford, east London (opened in 2004); Seven Stories, the National Centre for Children's Books in Newcastle (opened in 2005); the Roald Dahl Museum and Story Centre in Great Missenden, Buckinghamshire (opened in 2005); the Ministry of Stories in Hackney (opened in 2010); and the Institute of Imagination in London (founded in 2011, due to open in 2020).

Bridging libraries, museums, arts organisations and theatres, these story-focused venues respond to an increasing need to make central the universal and timeless powers of the imagination, critical thinking and human interaction. The timing of this phenomenon seems more than simply correlation with the cultural climate, characterised by features often seen as acting to the detriment of the imagination: controversial curriculum changes, the rise of the digital experience and, most recently, the sprawl of fake news across social media. The Story Museum in Oxford hopes to play a vital role within this new sector.

For the first five years, the Story Museum ran creative learning projects in schools and communities in the most disadvantaged areas of Oxford, using storytelling to raise literacy levels and achieve other learning and social impacts, captured by extensive evaluation. Having established a need for the services we offer and having proved the effectiveness of our approach, in 2009 the team acquired the lease on a dilapidated set of buildings in central Oxford and began planning for their transformation into a world-class museum of story.

In 2014, the Story Museum opened a semi-redeveloped home and began a rolling public programme of exhibitions and activities, focused on creating fantastic encounters with stories in all forms. Since then, we have welcomed over 100,000 people – mostly families, children and young people – to enjoy the museum and to create and share stories of their own. We also continue to run targeted projects in local schools and communities around Oxfordshire which are challenged by economic and educational disadvantage.

The power of story

Stories have the power to transform lives because children who grow up surrounded by stories develop the vital intellectual and emotional skills we need to understand the world and connect with each other. Albert Einstein himself is popularly credited with saying, 'First, give him fairy tales; second, give him fairy tales; and third, give him fairy tales!' People use stories to transmit knowledge and ideas, belief and identity, making stories as important a legacy as the places, objects or facts that each generation passes on to the next. Bruno Bettelheim, in his groundbreaking book *The Uses of Enchantment*, postulates how fairy tales are important for children to grow and learn about the world because they provide a safe space in which they can enact their emotions, dreams and anxieties. Fairy tales are rehearsals for life; they 'represent in imaginative form what the process of healthy human development consists of' (Bettelheim, 1991: 12).

Contemporary children's authors passionately echoed this argument in interviews carried out by the Story Museum in 2014. It is indisputable that children need stories:

> Stories are a way that we understand not just the world but ourselves. It is important for children to be exposed to stories from this country and around the world … It's also about teaching empathy, being able to see the world through other people's eyes. You open a book, and it's like opening a door to new thoughts, new ideas, new feelings, new peoples, new worlds. That's what makes them so special. So I think it's really important we have somewhere we can reflect on that. (Malorie Blackman quoted in Rochester, 2014: 124)

A space full of stories

The Story Museum is distinctive in that it commits to collecting and sharing 'great ways of engaging with great stories'. Stories existed prior to the printing press through oral traditions and continue through to the digital formats we see today. The 'great ways' celebrate stories in all their myriad forms, exploding beyond the page into the multisensory approaches that would appeal to Alice. Such an egalitarian approach means that everyone, with their varying needs, preferences and cultural perspectives, can access story in some way.

Meanwhile, the 'great stories' are part of a continuing project, begun with Michael Rosen in 2012, to identify the 1001 tales that represent the most important stories to our heritage. These will obviously shift and change and be revised year on year as our world changes. Stories are everywhere. Music, dance, drama, poetry, mime, song, puppetry, sculpture – all art forms contain stories. Science holds stories. Cookery holds stories. Sport holds stories. Stories lie at the heart of our culture.

Architecture, too, holds stories. Since 2009, the Story Museum has gradually been transforming a large, dilapidated building as its permanent home, located in Oxford's old medieval Jewish quarter. In this area, scribes first began to transfer traditional oral stories into written form. Indeed, Berechiah, the 'Jewish Aesop' who wrote the Fox Fables, is believed to have worked in the area and two copies of his manuscripts are held at the Bodleian Library. Merton College acquired the site at the end of the 13th century after Edward I ordered the expulsion of Jews from England. In 1921, Merton College sold the site to Her Majesty's Postmaster General to build a sorting office, storage, offices and canteen.

So, even prior to the museum, the building has been playing host to a network of stories of all kinds and forms, spanning times of war and times of peace, and latterly enabling the exchange of stories by post and telephone, from birthday messages to breaking news.

Meanwhile, classic authors were writing near the site: close by are the college rooms of Christ Church and Pembroke Colleges where Lewis Carroll wrote his Alice stories and Tolkien created a hobbit with furry feet. When the Post Office moved out in the late 1990s, the building lay in a derelict state for some years before being bought for the charity by a generous benefactor.

This rich history infuses the building with a haunting, intriguing quality. The labyrinthine, rough-about-the-edges corridors and rooms contain an atmosphere evocative of classic stories in which so much more can lie behind seemingly tired furnishings and trivial objects. An old wardrobe can lead to the enchanted snow-covered land of Narnia; a neglected, ivy-covered wall can shield a secret garden; a 'tiny ring of cold metal' can hold an intricate quest through the swirling histories of Middle Earth. It is such narrative worlds as these that become places one desires to visit. A story museum, or even a library or a story room in a school, can be a place to explore these worlds and encounter the characters that inhabit them.

Story characters

An early exhibition in 2014, '26 Characters', showcased this concept. It contained a series of immersive narrative environments in which visitors could enter the world of a story and become part of it for a few moments. For the exhibition, the Story Museum invited 26 of Britain's most exciting contemporary children's authors to name their favourite story characters from their childhoods. The authors were then transformed into these characters and photographed. With the help of theatre, film, interior, graphic and sound designers and artists, each photograph was displayed in a three-dimensional realisation of a scene featuring a powerful encounter with the character.

Holly Smale, author of the Geek Girl series, chose to dress as the White Witch from *The Lion, the Witch and the Wardrobe*, so the museum recreated the unforgettable moment in which Edmund enters the wardrobe and meets the enchantress. Visitors opened a mysterious creaky wardrobe, burrowed through fur coats and entered a darkened, snowy forest where a dimly lit lamp post heralded a sleigh draped with elegant white furs, where somewhere was hidden a little jewelled box containing the lingering smell of Turkish Delight. In another secret area of the museum, Kevin Crossley-Holland as Merlin gazed down a corridor of tangled ivy, dust, golden afternoon light and birdsong; a thick, yellowed book lay chained at his feet. Elsewhere, Benjamin Zephaniah, as Anansi, jumped from a hut of spreading palm leaves, amid dappled sunlight and the sounds of tropical creatures. A cheetah and a snake lounged in a basket nearby ready to take their roles in Anansi's tales of trickery.

Story worlds

Of course, such narrative worlds can be replicated elsewhere. However, there is a distinct difference between the Story Museum's approach and that of Disneyland or a film set. This is the quality of being 'unfinished'. This trait manifests itself in two ways. The first is physical. The Story Museum is characterised by a lack of gloss and superficial veneer. The galleries are not so much complete realisations of story as a set of clues to decode and interpret using all the senses. You may smell incense, feel a distinct change in temperature or perceive a mysterious form among the shadows, but no more than that. The rooms are there as stimuli to imaginative play, to a range of interpretations, to endless skeins of discussion and investigation. The museum spaces try to replicate the experience we have when we hear an oral story or read a book. This is when each one of us becomes part of making the story. The experience then becomes an active process rather than a passive entertainment, enabling us to internalise the story even more strongly. As a visitor once wrote on TripAdvisor: 'Be prepared to do something …!'

This leads to the second manifestation of being unfinished: the need for people. The Story Museum spaces cry out for an enlivening human presence. This is apparent in the uncanny sense that a fictional character has just left the room. It is also there in the need for people to embody roles; whose unique and boundless imaginations can interpret and transform the spaces.

Storytellers

The spaces we create can be seen as a series of stage sets for characters, where visitors interact, experiment and discover and, above all, communicate. Visitors to the story spaces are subconsciously using critical thinking skills, building connections and strengthening enquiry. They become story characters and storytellers.

The learning follows naturally from these encounters, without the fanfare of specific learning objectives. This active engagement then fosters a sense of ownership over the space and the story, which reflects the organic process of story itself, as stories are exchanged from storyteller to storyteller. Indeed, the overwhelming response to the exhibitions from students is the sense of ownership they gain; by enacting and living a story, they feel it somehow belongs to them. This sense of ownership then works reciprocally in terms of a deeper engagement with story: adults moving through Narnia often felt nostalgic and were inspired to reread the fantasy; children became curious and, on reading the story, reported feeling an odd sense of occupancy of the story world, of déjà vu.

The Story Museum's story guides also aid this experience by telling themed 'pop-up stories' to the visitors in different areas of the museum that echo the atmosphere of a particular space. Picture books are incorporated regardless of the age range, as all ages benefit from the multimodal evocations provided by this delightful and subtly complex medium. We also use spontaneous storytelling – collaborative stories with visitors – which involves using objects and details from the environment alongside gentle questioning and prompts such as, 'But then it didn't go as planned! Because ...'

Story time

A sense of ownership and a unifying need to 'complete' spaces with a visitor presence was realised in another exhibit which opened in January 2015, 'Time for Bed'. The room held a giant bed, complete with a patchwork quilt, large enough to seat a class of 30 students (or 60 extra-small ones). Visitors were encouraged to put on dressing gowns, clean their teeth with outsized brushes (shower brushes), take off their shoes and sit on the bed for a story. The room celebrated and heightened the process of choosing a book: picture books were hidden in lockers along with multisensory objects featured in the story, so the story could be enacted. Thus, the room itself was unfinished; it had not fulfilled its function until the visitor was there to complete it. Not only this, there was an intellectual layer to this unfinished quality which called for the visitor to participate. The outsized bed recalled the familiarity yet peculiarity of a dream state, and was therefore immediately both welcoming and disorienting, and ultimately intriguing.

A cabinet within the room also held a world evocative of Mary Norton's *The Borrowers* – tiny Sylvanian Families characters read miniature books in beds made out of matchboxes under postage stamp pictures on the walls. These contrasts, challenging our perceptions of scale, were identified by children's playwright, director and Story Museum trustee David Wood OBE as not only fun but stealthily deploying the role of the imagination: 'There is something immediately appealing to the imagination about giant-scale or small-scale objects or people' (Wood, 1997: 49). This intellectual unfinished quality calls for visitors to enter the world of the story imaginatively and readjust their perceptions to accept the story world as it is.

All in all, the room was incomplete without the presence of people to continue the story tradition, just as stories will become extinct if there is no new generation to hear or tell them.

> Because it seems to me that without stories, and without an understanding of stories, we don't understand ourselves, we don't understand the world about us. And we don't understand the relations between ourselves and those people around us. Because what stories gives us is an insight into ourselves, a huge insight into other people, other cultures, other places. So, it's a gathering of all the knowledge and understanding that we need. For me that's probably the most important kind of museum that you can have, providing that you can also hear the stories and see the pictures, that it is presented in a way which is lively and imaginative. (Michael Morpurgo quoted in Rochester, 2014: 126)

Starting with the story

Of course, all museums, by definition, have an unfinished quality, encouraging a human presence to explore, discover and continue to investigate. But the Story Museum reverses the concept of the traditional museum which starts with objects and explores the stories around them: these stories may evolve and change as further historical or scientific research and discoveries are uncovered – although, arguably, only to a finite extent. The Story Museum starts with the story and then searches for the objects that evoke it, and this opens itself to boundless possibilities, dialogues and conversations, and in so doing centralises the need for a continuing visitor presence.

For the Story Museum, the objects will always change, as differing interpretations, versions and retellings will produce ever-shifting items of paraphernalia. Are Dorothy's slippers red or silver? Should we commission an artist to render the dagger Macbeth sees before him, or would that be a hopeless exercise seeing as it was just imaginary (or was it)? Was Cinderella's shoe made of glass or fur? Was Mowgli discovered in a baby's basket or swaddled in saris? Does Tinkerbell have a wand? When Robin Hood wins his archery contest, what does his silver arrow look like? How decorative was Arthur's sword in the stone? And what impact would any of these answers have? The Story Museum is currently engaged in exploring these questions, consulting with audiences on the most important story objects to collect and the most exciting story worlds to create for children to visit.

In a school, a class could create its own version of a story museum within their own classroom or the school library. With their teacher's or librarian's help, the children would need to consider various questions to jointly decide which stories to focus on – for example:

- Selected works from one favourite author.
- A particular type of story (such as those featuring fantasy or animal characters) from a range of authors.
- A story theme, such a pirates or magic.
- A type of story vehicle, such as comic books or fairy tales.

But the children would also need to decide the key principles of engagement for visitors to their 'museum'.

Principles of engagement

The Story Museum's principles, which were developed in 2013 by the museum's co-founder Kim Pickin, could also serve as a manifesto for story engagement in the classroom:

- **Start from the story:** *The elements that make 'great stories' also make great experiences: strong images, suspense, surprises, the power of 'what happens next?' Start with the story and let it tell you how to touch hearts* *as well as minds. Make sure audiences can experience all of the story, or enough to care what happens next.*

■ **Go universal:** *Focus on stories that touch us all, that work across times, cultures, ages and levels of prior knowledge, that are part of our shared heritage.*

■ **Hand-pick treasures:** *Hand-pick the stars among stories and the treasures among objects then build out from those. Less is more. Too much is bewildering and tiring, especially for the young.*

■ **Create wonder:** *Offer immersive experiences that help visitors to step into stories. Use contrasts to stimulate the senses: large and small, light and dark, fast and slow, loud and soft, opportunities to move or sit or lie down. Help people focus with enclosed spaces or story landscapes, atmospheric light and sound, interesting textures and real objects to touch, and sometimes smells. Stimulate imaginations with amazing and unusual objects. Use live storytellers and costumed story guides to aid the depth of engagement.*

■ **Add layers and connections:** *Offer different layers (and heights) of interpretation to suit different abilities and types of learning – and offer visitors diverse ways into and through the exhibitions. Leave space so visitors can add their own layer to the exhibition. Make connections between different stories and explore their influences and impact. Connect stories with what people already know and what they could know next about story heritage.*

■ **Be playful and participative:** *Encourage visitors to engage and play. Use visual and verbal wit. Visitors have more fun and are more likely to learn. Encourage and enable participation – and show that we are listening. But don't force visitors to respond if they don't want to, or to analyse their own experiences. This is a conversation not a transaction.*

■ **Open doors:** *Ask questions. Offer challenges. Evoke curiosity. This is a place of beginnings and 'what happens next' will be an important driver. Signpost further experiences – places to visit, objects to see, stories to enjoy or create, things to do. Set examples of habits and rituals that might be nice to continue at home. (Pickin, 2013)*

The Story Museum's outreach projects

Personally, I worry that our stories will die out, be forgotten. Fortunately, at the moment, there's a boom in children's literature and storytelling generally, but you just never know what the future is, so now is the time to do it. (Benjamin Zephaniah quoted in Rochester, 2014: 127)

The Story Museum has a wide-ranging engagement and outreach learning programme which delivers activities in various communities to spread the museum's approach, and stems from the seven principles outlined on pages 149–150. In general, the Story Museum aims to develop miniature 'museums of story' across schools and institutions.

Storydays

An early project, 'Learning through Stories', characterised much of the learning department's initial exploratory work and showed incredible impact within a range of schools. The project worked with over 100 Oxfordshire schools, all of whom received 'storydays', which built on a concept developed with professional storyteller and educator Dr Chris Smith.

Storydays started with a whole-school storytelling performance by a professional storyteller, followed by an interactive exhibition in which exhibits were sequenced to follow the story narrative. Therefore, having heard the story, the students experienced and interacted with the story a second time using sight, smell, hearing and touch, experiencing a range of stimuli including music, natural sounds, perfumes and oils, photos, paintings and various kinds of objects. The stories included Theseus and the Minotaur, The Tree of Life, *Alice's Adventures in Wonderland*, five traditional tales and a newly written environmental story.

For example, for the Theseus and the Minotaur interactive exhibition, visitors could try on a Queen Pasiphaë's cow disguise, smell the incense King Minos burns when he prays to the Oracle, dress up as Bacchus, work out a way through a maze, make Icarus' wings from feathers and wax, change ship sails from white to black, and listen and respond to 'Jupiter' from the orchestral suite *The Planets* by Holst. Teachers shared that their students remembered the stories for much longer than they would normally and that their writing was improved by the experience, using unusual new insights and authentic sensory description.

Story spaces inside schools

Further projects have included creating museum spaces within schools, a concept developed by Kate Sayer. In 2016, the museum created installations within a disused library space for Windale Primary School on the Blackbird Leys estate in Oxford. A campfire, a dark starlit sky and furs and logs were used as a backdrop for oral storytelling. Launching from Britain, the students 'travelled' to the Americas, Australia, India and Africa, using traditional oral stories to guide them.

This was followed by an immersive 'story ship' installation, featuring cabin benches, sails, prow, stern and portholes. Books on the theme of journeys, the sea and pirates were supplied and placed in 'treasure chests' to be discovered. The students came on board 'ship' and one student was elected as the captain to choose stories from the treasure chests for the session leader to share with the class. As the project progressed, the stories became stories on any subject, and the ship became a metaphor for students to sail away on a sea of stories. The entrance, through curtained 'portholes', physically emphasised the idea that the students were stepping into an unfamiliar environment – a world of story.

Extreme reading adventures

Another example of our interactive and multimodal approach is 'Extreme Reading Adventures', a project designed in 2015 to help children make emotional connections with books to stimulate their desire to read. Funded by the Maggie Evans Trust, this project is aimed at 8–12-year-olds who had been identified by teachers as 'reluctant readers' for a range of reasons, and provides six 'adventures' linked to identified reading material.

Each week, the students received the book for the following week wrapped as a present. The associated immersive adventures were designed to prompt imaginative and engaging responses to the worlds the students had been exploring through independent reading. The reading material included newspaper articles, a how-to comic book, a recipe book and a biographical book on Sir Ernest Shackleton's journey to the Antarctic. The accompanying session for the latter involved learning bushcraft, campfire making and survival skills, just as Shackleton and his crew would have done when stranded on the ice floes or at sea.

Other books and related activities included meeting a magician, learning tricks and playing Quidditch alongside listening to audio versions of *Harry Potter and the Philosopher's Stone*, and a treasure hunt through Oxford to trace the journey of characters in locations cited in Philip Pullman's *I Was a Rat!*

The participants and their families gave enthusiastic feedback on the programme. The pupils involved had a more positive attitude to reading for pleasure through these 'live' encounters with story. Non-readers started to become committed readers. They also came away with an understanding that stories do not have to be fiction or appear in black and white type in paragraphs. Grateful parents wrote in to express thanks for the way the programme had transformed their child's relationship with reading, emphasising how they now looked upon books in a unique way – as full of possibilities and brimming with pictures and conversations.

Conclusion

Our pilot projects have already built up a wealth of data to show the positive impact on attainment and well-being and proving the increasing need for story in today's world. Yet we merely aim to showcase what already exists everywhere.

Most schools, to a greater or lesser extent, already contain creative elements that belong in a tangible museum of story – whether that is a narrative space (such as a display area or reading corner) for the current class text, a wall celebrating individuals' favourite stories, or a cabinet containing objects from a school play. Every school has children, and every child can have a museum of story in their head.

It is of fundamental importance that we create and preserve spaces devoted to understanding, exchanging and exploring every one of these inner museums, where a story remains embedded: a visceral moment of drama, an indelible quote, a haunting land, an unforgettable character. These multiple museums that we carry within us, whether through tangible rendering or a conversation exchange, cement these worlds for us and confirm that, wherever we are, our dreams are valid.

Further reading and useful links

Bettelheim, B. (1991). *The Uses of Enchantment: The Meaning and Importance of Fairy Tales*. London: Penguin.

Carroll, L. (1865). *Alice's Adventures in Wonderland*. London: Macmillan.

Lewis. C. S. (1950). *The Lion, the Witch and the Wardrobe*. London: Geoffrey Bles.

Norton, M. (1952). *The Borrowers*. London: J. M. Dent.

Pickin, K. (2013). *Seven Interpretation Principles*. Oxford: The Story Museum.

Pullman, P. (1999). *I Was a Rat! … or The Scarlet Slippers*. London: Doubleday.

Rochester, A. (ed.) (2014). *26 Characters: Celebrating Childhood Story Heroes*. Oxford: The Story Museum.

Rowling, J. K. (1997). *Harry Potter and the Philosopher's Stone*. London: Bloomsbury.

Smale, H. (2013–2017). *Geek Girl* [Books 1–6]. London: HarperCollins.

Tolkien, J. R. R. (1937). *The Hobbit*. London: George Allen & Unwin.

Wood, D. with Grant, J. (1997). *Theatre for Children: A Guide to Writing, Adapting, Directing and Acting*. London: Faber & Faber.

Story Museum's 1001 audio stories: http://www.storymuseum.org.uk/stories/audio-stories

About the contributor

Isy Mead

Isy Mead has 12 years' experience in both formal and non-formal learning contexts. She is currently head of learning and participation at the Story Museum, and was previously learning manager at the Roald Dahl Museum and Story Centre. Formerly a secondary English teacher in east London, she worked as a Voluntary Service Overseas (VSO) teacher trainer in a Rwandan village for two years before moving into the museum sector. She holds a bachelor's degree in English literature and history of art, and a master's in history of art – both from the University of York.

Chapter 10
Creating a Community of Learners

Geerthi Ahilan, senior leader, St Ebbe's CE Primary School, Oxford

This chapter is an account of a far-reaching development in pedagogy and learning, conceived and implemented by staff at St Ebbe's CE Primary School. This was initially motivated by concerns about the educational underachievement of a significant cohort of children from ethnic minority groups. The staff involved instigated a rigorous investigation of the apparent barriers to the pupils' progress and achievement.

Two measures were adopted by the school to respond to the dilemmas highlighted by the study. Firstly, they adopted a co-coaching model to redress any shortcomings in aspects of existing pedagogical practice, and secondly, they promoted a storytelling approach to the curriculum, which improved language skills, progress and outcomes for all the children, not just those with English as an additional language (EAL).

Geerthi Ahilan describes the decisive role of story in the teaching and acquisition of language. More importantly, she reminds us that narrative is central to the education process. She offers a valuable insight into the effective teaching of English and EAL; in particular, the gains achieved by meticulously planned and organised co-coaching, and by the powerful impact of narrative across the curriculum, not only in critical areas of language but at the heart of learning itself.

Background

St Ebbe's is a two-form entry Church of England school in the heart of Oxford serving a socially, economically and culturally diverse community of 400 children. The school has a long-standing reputation in the local community for its commitment to enabling staff and children to take a collaborative and creative approach to teaching and learning.

However, increasingly, school data and teacher observations raised concerns about the underachievement of some of the children from minority ethnic groups, those who are from EAL backgrounds and those in receipt of the government's pupil premium funding. This underachievement was particularly highlighted in literacy, both in terms of reading comprehension and writing.

Teacher-led research

Over a four-year period, colleagues decided to objectively analyse key barriers to learning for specific groups. Initially, we started with EAL pupils, but later this was extended to examine children in receipt of pupil premium funding. Using the EAL data as a starting point, teachers set up a project to shed further light on the apparent underachievement of our predominantly second-generation Pakistani and Bangladeshi children.

The school-based research established two key aims: (1) to examine teachers' pedagogical practices for minority ethnic EAL pupils and how these affected the children's learning experiences, and (2) to facilitate collaborative learning for the teachers involved, so the team could reflect on and learn from the experience to inform classroom practice.

To enable participants to reflect on their pedagogical practices, a co-coaching model with an emphasis on lesson observations and follow-up discussions was adopted. The lessons were videoed to provide further reference points to the post-lesson observations.

The model adopted is promoted by the Centre for the Use of Research and Evidence in Education (CUREE).

Barriers to learning and achievement

The teacher-led study highlighted three key barriers to learning for EAL children:

1. Poor participation of some EAL children during whole-class teaching, discussions and even in child-initiated activities, such as role play. For instance, the Early Years Foundation Stage (EYFS) classroom observations and video evidence highlighted that while many children took advantage of the child-initiated activities (e.g. role playing in the home corner and then moving on to the construction site), others seemed less confident or even aware of what to do. We observed that those who did participate in these practical activities tended to instigate dialogue with both adults and peers. The adults, in turn, probed and interacted effectively with these children, therefore moving their learning on.

    This highlighted the work of two major educational theorists: Jean Piaget (2002 [1923]) and Lev Vygotsky (1986 [1962]). A central component of Piaget's thinking was that children's learning and development was crucially facilitated by their interaction with the environment. Teachers can be seen as facilitators of learning by providing resources and materials that are matched to the child's particular stage of cognitive development. At St Ebbe's, we noticed that if we carefully planned the organisation of the learning environment to enable EAL children to construct knowledge through exploration and enquiry, then they were able to enjoy more meaningful interaction with adults and their peers, which crucially developed their language and clarified their thinking.

2. Overdependence on adult support. For instance, after supported group work, some children were observed to be reluctant to feed back during whole-class discussions, and in certain cases, well-meaning support staff were speaking on behalf of the children. This was hindering the school's commitment to developing independent and resourceful learners.

3. Prevalence of 'expert' and 'non-expert' status of children within the classroom. This status was largely determined by the degree to which specific children were selected by teachers for questioning or sharing knowledge.

Curriculum review

As a school committed to ensuring that our practice is rooted in research, we set up a review of the literacy curriculum, underpinned by the following key principles about teaching and learning:

■ Learning as a social phenomenon where collaboration is encouraged and nurtured through shared experiences. This idea stems from the work of Vygotsky (1978), whose idea of the zone of proximal development argues that in order for learning to occur, learners need to be prompted or 'scaffolded' by a more expert teacher or peers. Equally, we wanted to provide rich experiences for children to learn through exploration.

■ The importance of creating language-rich environments. Colleagues worked together to build capacity for learning through their classrooms and through providing opportunities for context-embedded and meaningful speaking, reading and writing. In our classrooms, language, books and stories permeate every aspect of the school day (e.g. in literacy, maths, science, history, assemblies).

■ The importance of vocabulary. Vocabulary development is promoted by adults consciously teaching appropriate vocabulary at the point of need. Our teachers encourage the children's natural curiosity about language by using challenging words. For instance, one teacher said, 'Please take copious amounts of notes,' prompting a child to say: 'What does copious mean?' Teachers also appreciate the importance of modelling language to enrich children's word knowledge, so adults introduce the children to new words and model their use. For example, when a child says: 'He's not right,' the teacher rephrases, 'Oh, so you disagree with him.'

Our teachers realise the importance of moving children beyond social language (basic interpersonal communication skills) and towards academic language (cognitive and academic language proficiency (see Cummins and Swain, 1986). This is echoed by Victoria Murphy and Maria Evangelou (2016), who emphasise the importance of vocabulary knowledge for learning to read, particularly for pupils in Key Stage 2. Hence, you could have two children with specific language difficulties, but the child with a broader knowledge of words will make greater progress with reading because he or she is more able to anticipate words using context cues than the child with limited vocabulary knowledge.

■ The significance of positive self-esteem. We observed that low self-belief, where children lack confidence ('I can't do it, so what is the point?'; 'Others are better at this'; 'Everyone will laugh if I get this wrong'), led to passivity in the classroom and pupils feeling as if they didn't belong or didn't have the right to ask questions and contribute to discussions.

Further investigations into barriers to learning and achievement revealed some themes that were common to both EAL and pupil premium-funded children. These were:

- Low aspirations: 'It's not for me.'

- Barriers to communication, language and literacy (e.g. limited vocabulary).

- Reluctance to tackle the abstract nature of certain concepts/learning.

- Unfamiliarity with cultural references such as book, film or television characters, historical associations or language traditions such as fairy tales or nursery rhymes.

- Issues with personal, social and emotional development.

- Reduced attendance and poor punctuality.

- Infrequent or reluctant parental engagement.

To start to address some of these barriers, the school set about leading a review into our literacy curriculum.

A creative language and literacy curriculum

The Year 3/4 team took a lead in exploring different approaches to language and literacy development. They concentrated on the power of narrative and focused on increasing opportunities for children, through storytelling, to engage in writing and raising achievement.

In 2015, inspired by the '26 Characters' exhibition at the Story Museum in Oxford (see Chapter 9), we embarked on our own replication of the project in which every student dressed as their own favourite story character and posed for a professional photo. Here a collaborative investigation of a book's major themes and narratives opened up into fascinating conversations. This involved the children's own intellectual discussion of the stories: which story to choose? Which character? Which moment? Should it be the most emotional moment for the character or the most mundane? The character in their finest hour or at their most flawed? Scrooge at his most belligerent or Scrooge at the moment of redemption? Which is more important? Or more memorable?

This experience was a turning point in the way we incorporated visits into our planning. Previously, we learned things in school, prior to a museum visit, and perhaps wrote an account afterwards in the form of a diary or thank you letter. However, the '26 Characters' exhibition visit, at the start of a term, led to a whole term's follow-up work around the theme 'Tell me a story'. The exhibition and theme gave the children an opportunity to think about their favourite books and characters. At the museum, the children were intrigued to see what familiar authors, such as Michael Morpurgo and Jamila Gavin, looked like in their photographs, and were interested to see which books and characters they had chosen to represent. Benjamin Zephaniah had chosen traditional tales about Anansi the Spider, while Julia Donaldson had chosen *The Owl and the Pussy Cat* by Edward Lear.

We decided to work in partnership with a parent who volunteered her time to take professional photographs of each child, in costume, representing their chosen story. All staff and children in Years 3 and 4 took part in what we renamed '86 Characters'. This project created another powerful and shared experience, and reinforced our goal to create a community of learners through story. We invited the Story Museum to visit our exhibition, which further increased the children's sense of pride, and our exhibition was featured in the Story Museum's evaluation of their own '26 Characters' event.

Based on this partnership, the school was invited to co-curate the Story Museum's 'Animals' exhibition. Each class in Key Stage 2 was allocated an area of the world (Africa, China and Japan, Oceania, India, Britain, Europe or the Americas). Having listened to an animal story from their region, the children worked in groups to learn the story and retell them orally. These were then recorded for the audio part of the exhibition at the Story Museum for visitors to listen to – a wonderful example of using language for a real purpose. The project also gave the children a chance to work with an artist to generate ideas for the fabric collage illustrations which accompanied the stories.

Resources for story

There are several valuable storytelling courses on offer, but we were overwhelmingly convinced by the simplicity of the Storytelling School's programme, materials and handbook (Smith and Guillain, 2014). The core aim of this approach is to equip children with a bank of stories to draw from, while simultaneously supporting the development of language and vocabulary. Oral storytelling as a prerequisite for writing is highly emphasised throughout the programme. Therefore, the teacher has the key role of storyteller – the person who guides the children through the language, structure and rhythm of narratives.

For teachers and pupils, the programme provides a clear structure for the process of learning to tell stories through collaboration and creating shared experiences:

- The teacher learns and tells a story from memory (they could choose any story or they could take one from the handbook or website).

- The children listen carefully and then discuss the story as a class.

- The children map the story's plot using story frames, sketches, diagrams or arrows.

- The children 'step' the story, highlighting and sequencing key events or episodes, thereby already actively engaging in the reproduction of the story.

- The children retell the story orally to their partner.

Here is an example of one Year 3 child's innovative response to a traditional Kenyan story:

> *In a deep, dark forest was a shining bright light. That shining bright light was in fact a light of a cabin. In the cabin lived an ordinary poor hunter. The day we are going to talk about is the day the hunter wanted to catch a deer ...*

The process of learning to tell stories while creating shared experiences also offers valuable opportunities to match the learning to the children's developmental stage. This is achieved by the three 'I's principles:

1. Imitate – the process of learning to tell stories from memory through hearing and retelling means that the language of the story becomes part of the children's language repertoire (e.g. hearing and reproducing the language and conventions of storytelling).

2. Innovate – adapting known texts in a variety of ways to create new versions (e.g. changing the setting/problem or character). Initially, this is modelled by the teacher through shared writing and focused feedback and is followed by opportunities for independent innovations, where learning is used and applied (e.g. the children adapt their story maps to create their own version of the story).

3. Invent – drawing on a growing repertoire of text structures, rich language and a range of experiences and ideas to write independently and creatively.

Teachers were also attracted to the programme because it takes a whole-class, inclusive approach which enables high levels of modelling and scaffolding for those children who have been highlighted as 'at risk' of underachievement in teacher-led study, while allowing teachers to provide opportunities for those who needed to be challenged.

Co-coaching

From the outset, there was agreement among the Year 3/4 teachers that if we were to effectively implement the language and literacy curriculum and excel in the storytelling process, there would have to be opportunities for teachers to work collaboratively. We would need to create occasions for less experienced members of the team to observe and learn from those who were more experienced.

The co-coaching model was adopted as the teachers found it to be an empowering approach to teacher development: a second community of learners had been created.

Storytelling Fridays

We introduced Storytelling Fridays to Years 3 and 4. The more experienced member of the team would tell the story (selected by the team of teachers during the planning meeting) to the children, while the three other members of the team observed. Following each session, there was an opportunity for the team of teachers to engage in discussion about what they had observed, to pose questions and to consider how to take the learning forward in the next session, including any additional resources that might support the children's understanding and retention of the story. Initially, the storytelling, mapping and stepping were led by the lead practitioner in the school hall or the playground.

However, within a few weeks of being immersed in the process, classes began to work on the story mapping in their own classrooms led by their class teacher. During the course of a term, we had moved from the lead practitioner leading every aspect of the story learning process, to a teacher mapping the story while the story was being told, and finally to class teachers increasingly taking the lead with their classes.

These inclusive Storytelling Fridays became the highlight of the week for many. We saw 100% participation rates, and children developed greater independence as they were exposed to story language and conventions. These became part of the children's own language repertoires. The sessions created an atmosphere of collegiality as all the children had experienced the stories together, and because the stories reflected the many parts of the world that the school community served, there was a fluidity between the 'experts' and 'non-experts'.

For instance, the story of 'The Three Dolls' from South Asia hooked children in because they were invited to pose a riddle that the wise old teacher could not solve. Immediately, the children were keen to share their puzzles. All the children had the opportunity to innovate simply by formulating their own riddles. The story also sent out a strong message about the nature of learning: cleverness is not just about learning facts and answering questions correctly. The storyteller's daughter, the story's protagonist, had managed to outwit her wise old teacher because she loved stories and was able to use them creatively.

To maximise the impact of these sessions, the children were set the task of orally retelling these stories to a member of their family. During the year, the children learned three or four stories from their teachers, as well as many more from their peers as they were set the task of collecting traditional stories to retell to their class. From the oral retellings, the children were empowered to write several stories over the course of the year. At each stage of the writing process, there was an emphasis on sharing and critiquing ideas, language and structural choices. This reflective approach to learning further supported progress.

Those children who had the furthest to go with developing their language and literacy, the EAL children and those in receipt of the pupil premium, were also encouraged to follow the programme at home with their families by listening to stories from the Story Museum website, which they could access for free. While this was good practice in principle, its success varied depending on family involvement. Where parents and carers could listen to and discuss the stories, the children's progress with storytelling and literacy skills was further enhanced.

Storytelling and literacy

Over time, with the introduction of the new curriculum in 2014, the storytelling approach was incorporated into the school's English curriculum, partly because it supported EAL children so effectively. It is a model that has further evolved. Storytelling is now embedded in our cross-curricular thematic approach, which has been rolled out across the school so that storytelling no longer sits separately from the rest of the curriculum.

A further appeal of this approach is that it is sustainable: the school does not necessarily have to invest huge funds in training and resources, and because teams have adopted a co-coaching model, when a member of staff leaves we have not lost our investment. Indeed, colleagues who have moved to other schools and counties have taken the approach with them and adapted them to their new settings.

Storytelling beyond the school

The storytelling approach was embedded into the school curriculum and underpinned our approach to improving outcomes for our EAL pupils, children in receipt of pupil premium funding, and other vulnerable groups.

Using funding from the National Lottery's Awards for All, we worked with a professional storyteller, Richard Neville, to provide opportunities for parents/carers and children to listen to and share stories. The funding allowed us to host story events on the housing estate where some of our families live, as well as broaden the children's experiences of stories by organising visits to museums and galleries and overnight stays at an outdoor education centre for children and mothers.

We also extended the project by giving some of our children and their families the opportunity to visit our partner school in Bucharest, Romania, with the support of funding from Erasmus through the European Union.

Using stories to engage families has been very successful because we all have stories to share, regardless of our backgrounds, circumstances and levels of formal education. Stories provided a wonderful vehicle for increased parental engagement with the school, and we saw parents being increasingly aspirational for themselves and their children as their confidence grew. Furthermore, it allowed mothers, including those still learning English themselves, to learn alongside their children, which was very powerful in motivating and engaging the children in oracy and language development for both adults and children.

Story and maths

It was soon easy to see how the story-based approach could be applied to other areas of the curriculum. For example, in maths, a list of abstract questions about a graph may be rephrased as, 'What is the story behind this graph?', which emphasises the idea that everything has a story, whether it is a graph, a painting or an object. When children realise that mathematicians, scientists and historians are all telling a story, it can create a buzz of excitement in the classroom. The open-ended nature of this way of learning seems to encourage a diverse group of children to share things of interest, question assumptions and refine their own thinking.

Having become convinced about the benefits of using stories to engage children and develop content and skills, the school has since piloted the concrete, pictorial, abstract (CPA) approach to teaching maths (Singapore Maths). This promotes and develops the mastery approach to maths. The children are encouraged to work collaboratively to unpick mathematical problems in the context of a story, using models, maps and images (similar to story mapping) to make maths meaningful to all. As with the storytelling model, the emphasis is on the learning process, with the teacher modelling and scaffolding the children's learning.

Story-based partnerships

We have found other partners to further support this approach, including a local theatre company, Creation Theatre, and our local cathedral (Christ Church), where we were involved in a film about its history, the story of its patron saint, St Frideswide, and the stories contained in its very stones.

We also joined and collaborated with our local branch of the Federation of Children's Book Groups (FCBG). There are local branches of the FCBG in many regions, which run events for families and schools designed to inspire and actively engage children in reading, the enjoyment of books and a love of storytelling. We have found our Oxford Children's Book Group membership very fruitful, especially in relation to the Oxford Storyfest, with which we were involved in the autumn term of 2016.

Storyfest

In 2017, three schools in Oxford were invited to join in a national initiative, the Jean Russell Storytelling Project, organised by the FCBG through selected local branches. The other Oxford schools were St Aloysius Catholic Primary School and New Hinksey CE Primary School. A professional storyteller, Anna Conomos (see photograph on page 155), had been selected to be the national FCBG storyteller who would work with us. She is an award-winning, international storyteller but had, in fact, grown up near Oxford.

The Storyfest was a two-day event (Thursday and Friday). Anna spent half a day with each of the three schools, working with two classes of Year 4 or 5 children in each school. She rehearsed one third of the story of Jason and the Golden Fleece with each school. She came to us for the morning of the first day, and returned on the Friday afternoon because we had offered to host the finale in our school hall.

Six classes, with 180 children in total from the three schools, came together on the second afternoon, each having rehearsed their school's part of the story of Jason and the Golden

Fleece. Every single child was an Argonaut but also had a second part to play, even if it was only in the action-packed choral speaking pieces.

Anna's storytelling style and techniques offered the children a chance to make suggestions and shape the story which guaranteed their ownership of it all. She used song, chant, repetition, actions, props and visual cues, all of which gave meaningful support to all the children, especially those with EAL. This was true not only for the children from St Ebbe's but also for those from the other schools.

Anna skilfully narrated the story and held the three schools together, so that the performance, after only one brief run-through, was an acknowledged success. The children thoroughly enjoyed acting out and retelling the story to an audience of adults and other St Ebbe's pupils. A professional film-maker captured the event so the children could watch the performance later.

Storytelling with a global partner school

Our partner school of three years, Scoala Gimnazialǎ Numarul 195 (Scoala Hamburg) in Bucharest, Romania, has adopted many of the principles of the storytelling approach to developing children's language and literacy skills and mathematical understanding. Just as St Ebbe's has taken on and made the storytelling approach their own, so our partner school has done the same. Through funding from the European Union (Erasmus), colleagues and children have been able to extend this idea of a community of learners and develop further co-coaching-based projects to enhance story-led literacy and maths in the two schools.

When applied across the two schools, the co-coaching model has enabled colleagues to learn from each other. It was very powerful to see English and Romanian colleagues reflecting on their practices and the barriers to learning and achievement which were the basis of our original curriculum review. Susie Bagnall, head teacher of St Ebbe's observed: 'This opportunity has enriched our school tremendously. We have had the chance to learn from our Romanian colleagues using storytelling as our common language.'

Conclusion

Through working closely with each other and with all our partners, we are convinced more than ever that the collaborative, storytelling-based curriculum has helped us to answer the following questions: why develop a community of learners in schools? How can it be done? How can it benefit our vulnerable pupils and our EAL pupils? Why is it successful?

Colleagues from St Ebbe's agree, in answer to the last question, that creating a collaborative, story-based curriculum results in teachers and children engaging in the learning process, reflecting and acting as critical friends to ensure enduring learning outcomes. It promotes capacity building and long-lasting change and empowers children and teachers.

In answer to the question of why schools should adopt a story-telling approach to learning, my experience at St Ebbe's has convinced me of the following: stories are at the heart of the human condition and are therefore accessible to all. It results in inspiring and stimulating thematic programmes of study, supporting a broad and balanced curriculum, and it enriches children's language and thought and offers them a chance to encounter new language and imaginative possibilities.

The irresistible essence of story is how it gives an insight into the human situation and condition, and all its predicaments, challenges, joys, tribulations and marvels. Stories are meaningful and engaging for children from an early age; at St Ebbe's, we are convinced by the power of stories to transcend the constraints of time and place, to thrill the imagination and to enable all children, including EAL pupils, to respond to and shape their own language and identity.

Further reading and useful links

Baker, C. and Hornberger, N. (eds) (2001). *An Introductory Reader to the Writings of Jim Cummins*. Clevedon: Multilingual Matters.

Conteh, J. (2015). *The EAL Teaching Book: Promoting Success for Multilingual Learners in Primary and Secondary Schools*, 2nd edn. Los Angeles, CA: Learning Matters.

Cummins, J. (1986). Empowering Minority Students: A Framework for Intervention, *Harvard Educational Review*, 56(1): 18–37.

Cummins, J. and Swain, M. (1986). *Bilingualism in Education: Aspects of Theory, Research and Practice* (Applied Linguistics and Language Study). London: Taylor and Francis.

Murphy, V. A. and Evangelou, M. (2016). *Early Childhood Education in English for Speakers of Other Languages*. London: British Council.

Piaget, J. (2002 [1923]). *The Language and Thought of the Child*, rev. edn. New York: Psychology Press.

Smith, C. and Guillain, A. (2014). *The Storytelling School: Handbook for Teachers*. Stroud: Hawthorn Press.

Vygotsky, L. S. (1978). Interaction Between Learning and Development. In *Mind and Society: The Development of Higher Psychological Processes*. Cambridge, MA: Harvard University Press, pp. 79—91.

Vygotsky, L. S. (1986 [1962]). *Thought and Language*, 2nd rev. edn. Cambridge, MA: MIT Press.

Bell Foundation: https://ealresources.bell-foundation.org.uk/teachers/eal-nexus-resources

British Council: http://learnenglishkids.britishcouncil.org/en

Centre for the Use of Research and Evidence in Education (CUREE): http://www.curee.co.uk

Federation of Children's Book Groups (FCBG): http://www.fcbg.org.uk

Mantra Lingua: http://uk.mantralingua.com

National Association for Language Development in the Curriculum (NALDIC) – the national subject association for EAL: https://www.naldic.org.uk/eal-advocacy/mission-and-details/

Story Museum: http://www.storymuseum.org.uk/schools/

About the contributor

Geerthi Ahilan

Geerthi Ahilan trained as a primary teacher at the UCL Institute of Education, in London. She was a class teacher and senior leader at St Ebbe's for 13 years, having initially taught in the London Borough of Tower Hamlets. She is currently working as an assistant head at a school in Surrey. Geerthi believes passionately in the power of collaborative learning for children and staff alike to bring about sustainable improvement in educational outcomes for all.

Chapter 11

Writing Reclaimed

Emily Rowe, classroom teacher, Jenifer Smith and Simon Wrigley, co-founders of National Writing Project (UK)

The issue of children's writing is assuming growing importance in the formal evaluation of the effectiveness of primary education and of schools, and it is doing so for two main reasons.

Firstly, the quality of children's writing is taken to be a major signifier of teaching competence and acceptable pupil attainment in evaluations based largely on the outcomes of SATs in English.

Secondly, because writing offers easily visible evidence to inspectors, it figures prominently in inspection judgements of schools. Judging the quality of writing might be quite proper and beyond question as a means of seeking assurance about standards, were it not for the fact that many educationalists regard such tests as representing a restricted and ill-informed view of the essential nature of writing and the vital experiences, influences, prerequisites and expertise that shape and nurture it.

It seems irrefutable that the teaching of writing and the time, resources and concern devoted to it have become dominant features of everyday life in many schools, a key focus of attention and effort, but teachers seem to be increasingly unsure as to how to teach it. Indeed, some teachers seem to believe that teaching writing may be a specialism beyond them. No matter how expert they are in other areas of their practice, or how personally confident of their professional capacity, teachers have become diffident to the point of uncertainty about their understanding of the writing process and the degree to which they can teach it well.

All of this has inclined some colleagues to seek assurance in an ever-growing range of published guidelines; some of which are valuable in many respects, while others are formulaic, focus on limited strategies and are designed simply to meet the requirements of SATs.

In this chapter the contributors raise our awareness to the possibility, inherent in the current pressure for the attainment of specific outcomes, that the critical requirements of authentic writing competence and confidence are in danger of being neglected in schools.

Writers know that the prerequisites for success include:

- Compelling, varied, affective and illuminating experiences that stimulate the need and the compulsion for expression.

- Involvement in a language-rich environment that nurtures the acquisition of the skills of communication, explication, enquiry, argument, debate, persuasion and presentation.

- The development and application of high-level reading skills in a context where all forms of literature are highly valued, constantly available, cherished, shared and discussed.

- Continuing opportunities for pupils to participate in writing for a variety of purposes and, thereafter, to read it to others, apply their feedback and aim to 'publish' it.

■ The presence of skilled and practised writing mentors to guide the developing writer.

■ A recognition that the skill of writing is gradually acquired and flowers best in a climate of recognition, encouragement and informed and sympathetic guidance.

Through their work with the National Writing Project (NWP), Jenifer Smith and Simon Wrigley offer teachers the opportunity to engage meaningfully with the writing process for their own personal satisfaction. By joining a NWP Writing Teachers group, colleagues can share their expertise of the writing process and develop helpful strategies and approaches to teaching their pupils the craft and joy of writing. Emily Rowe teaches in a small school in Suffolk and belongs to a Writing Teachers group. She provides a powerful account of the impact that a teacher who develops as a writer can have on the quality of the writing of the children in their own classroom.

This chapter suggests that, by gaining valuable insights into the writing process, teachers can become more effective in their teaching of writing.

Background

In 2008, Professor Richard Andrews, who was based at the UCL Institute of Education in London, suggested that a National Writing Project should be established in the UK, along the lines of what had proved so effective in the United States. He did so because he thought that formulaic approaches to the teaching of writing were limiting thought and expression – and hampering the creativity of teachers and pupils alike. He realised that, under the national strategies, with their emphasis on structures and outcomes, teachers had lost confidence in their own knowledge about writing and their instinct that writing needs to be experienced 'from the inside out' (Andrews and Smith, 2011).

Writers need to think for themselves and negotiate with others; learning cannot happen effectively when pupils are not free to experiment and teachers are not free to exercise their own judgements. It could be argued that these are moral issues. Necessary conversations about education are in danger of being silenced by political and economic imperatives, and policies are introduced and passed without question. It is time for a cultural shift.

To learn more about what writing could do for us, and how it might best be cultivated in schools, we decided to go back to first principles. In 2009, we established NWP (UK) as a grass-roots teachers' collective and research project, having piloted a teachers' group in

Buckinghamshire. With support from the University of East Anglia (UEA) and the National Association for the Teaching of English (NATE), we have now set up 30 writing groups around the UK, supported by a website: www.nwp.org.uk.

Over the last decade, NWP teachers have discovered more about writing; realising that, in its free, provisional and experimental modes – with the reading and discussion which underpin it – writing has much more to offer learners (for thinking, organising, remembering, creating, collaborating) than merely preparing for tests or passing exams.

Teachers writing together

By writing together, teachers start to deepen their personal and professional understanding of writing. They become their own experts, rather than frustrated operatives in a system that threatens to be 'dysfunctional', where writing is valued only as a tool to answer questions limited in scope and value and imposed by others. Over the years, the NWP team has collected evidence to show what is possible when teachers' personal experience as writers informs, and begins to determine, the writing policy and practice in their schools.

Writing Teachers, a group that has been meeting in the School of Education at UEA for over 10 years, provides one model of an NWP teachers' writing group. It meets once a month for two after-school hours. Many of the primary and secondary teachers who attend studied for their PGCE at UEA. The atmosphere is relaxed. There are drinks and biscuits. There is plenty of talk and laughter. And there is the nourishment of belonging to a community of writing teachers.

Freewriting and word association

We usually begin a Writing Teachers session by writing something short. It is often simply a list of words, and we hear those spoken around the circle. We listen out for words that sound good and for patterns and surprises: *pipistrelle, button, sideboard, kidney.*

We enjoy the very sounds of words: *pamper* followed by *samba. Armitage Shanks* makes us laugh. Sometimes there is a theme to the list of words: *pear drops, peppermints, liquorice laces, humbugs ...*

Freewriting – writing without stopping or allowing the editor in the head to interfere – often follows. Maybe the list of sweets jogs our memories. Sometimes a prompt from something like Natalie Goldberg's book about writing memoir, *Old Friend from Far Away* (2007), might start us off. Freewriting might be shared, but it often leads us into places we had not expected. It is writing as a process of discovery which becomes important. Often this is about increased attention to and awareness of ourselves. The act of writing can restore us.

Crafting a piece of writing

We next move on to a more crafted piece of writing of some kind, often related to the teachers' current themes and preoccupations. The writing we do is for ourselves and not designed for the children, but teachers often recognise how they might adapt the ideas to suit their classes. What is gained is not so much 'top tips' for tomorrow's lesson, but a web of experiences, feelings and knowledge that informs the way we plan for and respond to young writers.

Often, writing is inspired by a reading of poetry or prose or by exploring unexpected texts; wordless picture books, 1950s textbooks, comics, museum catalogues. Writers find their own way through the writing and have time to share what they have written with others. The experience of writing and reading together offers the chance for us to review and reorientate. We find new, deeper understandings of what writing means to us, and we take that with us to our teaching.

Discussion – talking about our writing

Conversations move easily between what we have written, our experience of writing and what is happening in our classrooms. We understand that time to share ideas and problems is a crucial part of the meeting, each taking from it what suits us and integrating that into our teaching. Later, we bring that experience back to the group and ideas extend and evolve so that the community becomes a centre for ideas and development. The writing is often playful.

We use lists and words cut from packaging, small toys and postcards, as well as boxes containing mysterious items and natural objects collected on a walk. We ask: how did I experience that? How might the children? Once, when exploring quest stories, we drew and named characters that could be moved across a jointly created landscape. Questions attached to landmarks challenged the traveller – and the writer: 'A dragon guards this bridge, how will you cross?'

One teacher reshaped the idea to create Gothic tales with her Year 8 class. A reception teacher discovered that children played endlessly with the landscape maps they had created, adding to them and introducing small-world characters and props to realise their narratives. This, in turn, prompted teachers to further explore young children's creation of narratives as they begin to write themselves.

The writing community

However individual teachers approach their writing, all who attend a Writing Teachers session agree that the community is a significant part of the attraction. They know there will be people there who want their practice to be interesting and better. There is a range of experience in both teaching and writing, but everyone brings their own perspectives: 'I know that the teachers who go to the meeting consider writing in a thoughtful way.' One teacher says that, for her, the group has 'changed literally everything'. She thinks she 'can judge now when to intervene and when to leave it. It is not the same with every child.'

Although teachers do come away with ideas, the deeper learning comes from the combination of writing, reading and talk within a community of professionals. There is not a single way of teaching writing, but an inner core of knowledge that orientates the teacher. That inner knowledge informs planning and resourcing and, crucially, the moment-to-moment progress of the writing classroom.

A writing school

Could the small village primary school in Suffolk, where Emily Rowe teaches, be described as a 'writing school'? What might that mean, and how to achieve it? Every teacher in the school, including the head teacher, has experience of Writing Teachers groups. Each colleague approaches writing differently, drawing on their own experience and preferences. There is no single system, but there is a strong culture of writing being regarded as integral to a child's life at school. Writing is simply something that everyone does. Pupils and teachers simultaneously regard writing as ordinary and expected and as something very special. There is an openness and sense of adventure; a discourse of possibility.

In the first week of November, a reception child (G) in a mixed R1/2 class wrote on a whiteboard: 'the wolf blo the has don'.

He had asked his teacher how to write 'the' and she directed him to the display on the wall. He found and wrote the word for himself. Then he had asked for 'wolf', and when his teacher suggested he sound it out, he did. Off he went to write the rest of this important sentence that arose from hearing the story of the Three Little Pigs, retelling it with and without puppets. Ten weeks earlier, this child did not really know what writing could be. He could shape, very tentatively, only the first letter of his name.

What the children value most is the way they are relatively free to find their own way through the many activities on offer. Older children value writing and share their pleasure. Phonics lessons are fast and fun, and the content of these lessons is tailored, as far as possible, to the children's interests. This class is already full of writers and, in the course of eight weeks, G has become part of this writing community.

Writing for the school library

In the library there is a beautiful display of books, written and illustrated by children in the Year 3/4 class. The teacher here constantly seeks a strong purpose for writing of which they can be proud. The stories on display take their inspiration from the picture book by Neil Gaiman and Charles Vess, *Instructions* (2011).

From the outset, the children knew that they would illustrate their stories in the style of Charles Vess' paintings. Their texts draw on Gaiman's text: its open-endedness, its use of the second person, its patterns and repeating rhythms. Their inspiration to write comes from reading, enjoying and noticing the language, and it is there in the music of their writing:

> *When you have reached Melo's Mild there's goblins who bite and dragons who spurt out poison. Next cross the wobbly bridge. But don't look down. Speak to the old lady in slinky clothes. She will point the way … Touch the handle that's old and wet. Twist the wheel. A drawbridge will open and will make a creaky noise. Step quietly, make no noise, you shall see an old staircase with red carpet. Go up the stairs. Go to the door on the right. You will have to make a wise decision …*

> *Then you will see two old men sitting on a log. Sit next to the oldest one, don't trust the little one. He will bite your fingers off, but the oldest one will give you magic powers like super-strength night-vision goggles …*

Year 3 and 4 pupils

A teacher's perspective

As the Year 5/6 teacher and language coordinator, Emily Rowe, our third author, plays a key role in developing the writing culture of the school and is a regular at the UEA Writing Teachers group. In the section that follows she shares her experiences.

Being part of a Writing Teachers group empowers teachers by giving them confidence through shared experience. It has helped me to establish a supportive environment where each child's writing is valued; a classroom in which children can explore their own and others' writing in a safe and supportive environment. I have learned that a writing teacher can feel comfortable in writing alongside children and giving personalised feedback drawn from their own reflective experience. Teaching writing is difficult if you cannot understand its complexity, its difficulty and its joy. Writing Teachers has helped me to understand all three of these.

In my Year 5 and 6 classroom, my experience of being part of a Writing Teachers group impacts my daily practice both consciously and subconsciously. It echoes through the lessons, and the writing and culture of the children. It is visually evident through the giant 'wordscape' on display, the collection of favourite words that the children have gathered on the wall, and the piles of handmade journals on the shelves.

Freewriting

Freewriting is crucial in the writing development of the children in my classroom. The value of freewriting should not be underestimated. Just as a runner runs each day to stay fit and develop their technique, so a writer needs to write to become better at writing. Freewriting does not necessarily mean that tasks are entirely without structure; I often give a phrase, word, picture or idea to start the writing. I usually use freewriting at the beginning of each lesson to enable words to start hitting the page – many children (and adults) find this the hardest thing about writing.

Short, warm-up exercises can last for three to ten minutes, although there is no single correct formula. I consciously began to weave freewriting into my lessons as I found it so enjoyable at Writing Teachers meetings. The fear of being wrong, writing poorly or not knowing what to write is swept away by freewriting. The exercises are playful and non-intimidating, and this is exactly what makes it ideal for children.

The results of freewriting can often be pleasantly surprising as well. Without the constraints of learning objectives or success criteria, the children explore vocabulary, grammar, authorial voice, form and structure at their own pace. I find that I gain a better understanding of the children from their writing. For some, it is a place to confront events and emotions which are troubling them.

Sometimes the children have so enjoyed their short pieces of freewriting that they have revised and extended them on another occasion. For example, the opener of a five-minute freewriting task, 'The cardboard box took up half of the room …', led to the rest of the lesson being scrapped in favour of some very exciting stories being written. Freewriting helps children to write with better stamina and with fewer inhibitions. A boy who had previously never written more than a handful of sentences during a literacy lesson now writes up to an A4 page during 10 minutes of freewriting. This is one example:

> *The cardboard box took up half the room. A way in but no way out. A death machine or what? Inside the box was the way out. But how? Cannot touch it else evaporation. Cannot hide from it else death. So what? Plain sight, of course. But then … GONE!*

Incidentally, this challenge enabled him to produce some of his best writing thus far. Freewriting is not magic or mysterious. It merely allows children the space to write and develop as a writer through playful, unpressured tasks.

Journal- and book-making

Journal- and book-making greatly contributes to the children's writing development. I have found that making books has been instrumental in raising the quality of the children's work. Making your own book and writing for an audience can elevate the quality of the writing. The children have ownership of this in a way that is not present in a class exercise book.

One book-making project was based around the children revisiting a tree on the village green each week. This term-long project produced beautiful results. The children made sewn mini-notebooks which they used for observations of the tree. To present their work, they made large, folded books and incorporated research findings and non-fictional writing with descriptions of their interactions with the tree.

Writing club

The writing club at the school, run by Emily and Jenifer, meets once a week. It is a popular choice, especially among the youngest children, even though it is timetabled against the sports club. Originally, there was some understandable scepticism about our decision to make the club open to all children. Children of all ages are now firmly, and enthusiastically, established in a school-wide culture of writing. Their presence has made us think carefully about what we offer and has affirmed the power of drawing and making as integral to being and becoming a writer. In this school, anyone may join the writing club.

If you were to pop your head round the door of our writing club you would find a busy, settled atmosphere. Older children help younger ones. Children sit side-by-side, following their own paths or working together. Everyone likes to share their work and listen to each other. Sometimes a child will go and show an adult what he or she has done. When the head teacher drops in, he sees the club as a powerhouse for writing culture in the school. Watching the youngest children creating books, he can see them laying down the foundations of their writing lives.

We begin with a word game. Immediately, we have words 'on the air'. Sometimes we ask for certain kinds of word – wintry words, words that contain an 's' sound, quiet words. The words set the scene. Then we introduce an idea. We very often start with a book made from a folded sheet of paper – an idea suggested by Paul Johnson in one of his many books. We have an initial thought for how writers might write, although everyone knows they can follow their own ideas. We prepare the books in advance, mainly for speed. As Johnson points out, the form of the book sometimes does the work by offering a framework for the writer's ideas. It presents the writer with the constraints and possibilities of its structure. Even the number of pages can dictate how a story might unfold. We make available a range of pens and pencils, and sometimes stencils, stamps, stickers and tape. We read short picture books, poems or other texts to fuel the fire.

The shapes of simple folded and cut books invite a playfulness that prompts complex texts. We love the simple concertina books with cut roofs and opening doors. Add the question, 'Who lives here?', and children immediately create polysemic texts which have more than one meaning. They may write on the doors, inside and out, and add sound effects and speech bubbles. The story can continue around the doors and on to the plain reverse of the book. On the door of one house, the writer stamped the house number and 'Knock, knock …' On the inside of the door, 'I am a goldfish and my name is Bob.' Through the door, we can see Bob, bubbles rising, saying, 'Keep on swimming. Keep on swimming.'

When we introduced a graduated book in the style of Eric Carle's *The Very Hungry Caterpillar* (1969), Year 2 children had been making a list of stories that repeat. One child decided on a cumulative story (see photographs on page 169):

When Emily introduced bear stories, we thought of bear-like words and phrases – *fuzzy, grizzly, honey, in the woods, brown, fluffy, fierce*. And then everyone was given a beautiful folded book, its centre pages cut to make a bear's face. The youngest children drew and wrote with great concentration. Older children took the opportunity to write bear adventures of all kinds.

> *One day a little bear called Bobo went to get some honey and on the way to get some honey he saw some people having a picnic. He didn't like the people. They were scary to him and he was lost but he felt like he lost his smile.*
>
> *He did lose his smile. He was sad. He was lonely. He saw some bees going to their hive to make honey. He was still sad because he had lost his smile. He got some honey from the beehive, but he got stung from the bees.*
>
> *He was sadder than he was. But when he went to look at the pond and he saw his reflection showing and he saw his smile. He was excited and happy.*

Year 2 pupil

We could see this pupil had been influenced by *Augustus and His Smile* by Catherine Rayner (2006), but this story is absolutely her own and establishes the sadness of scary people and of loneliness. We love the rhythms of this story and its original phrasing: 'They were scary to him'.

Children feel free to interpret the suggested prompts however they wish. There are those who prefer to draw first and those who move between writing and drawing. We see how integral drawing is to writing throughout the primary years. We also note how vital it is to have the freedom to choose. To have agency over one's writing strengthens and challenges writers in positive ways. There is no competition, age differences are balanced out, and each child helps and appreciates the others. The youngest children often write for their families, while older children may prefer each other as audience.

Writing club represents an orientation towards writing that is both structured and free. In our writing club, we recognise its particularity and its versatility, its public and private qualities.

Conclusion

Writing, in its freer forms, contributes to enquiry and discovery. If writing is controlled, narrowed in scope and tested from the centre, and if children and teachers only own part of the process, its full potential and benefits will be limited.

The solution to such reductive approaches is the same as it was 10 years ago: effective, responsive and engaging teaching which requires teachers to be informed, experienced, reflective and creative practitioners. For the success of the reforms to the curriculum that HMI and Ofsted now acknowledge we need, teachers must be empowered to be the agents of change so they can reclaim the writing curriculum.

When teachers develop the confidence to write alongside children, to share their surprises, false starts and discoveries, and, crucially, to give children ownership of the process, then the climate for writing and learning in the classroom changes for the better. When teachers reorientate themselves as fellow practitioners, rather than assessors, they cultivate a trustful climate for writing. In such classrooms, a few minutes of freewriting together can support learning and engage pupils with unexpected delights. The children understand and will experiment with writing structures and conventions, if they can explore them in non-judgemental contexts.

The more school leaders understand – and experience – the nature of writing creatively, expressively and purposefully, the more likely writing is to thrive in our schools. And the time to reclaim this vital part of the curriculum is now.

Further reading and useful links

Andrews, R. and Smith, A. (2011). *Developing Writers: Teaching and Learning in the Digital Age.* Maidenhead: Open University Press.

Carle, E. (1969). *The Very Hungry Caterpillar.* New York and Cleveland, OH: World Publishing Company.

Gaiman, N. (2011). *Instructions*, illus. C. Vess. London: Bloomsbury.

Goldberg, N. (2007). *Old Friend from Far Away: The Practice of Writing Memoir.* New York: Free Press.

Harwayne, S. (2001). *Writing Through Childhood: Rethinking Process and Product.* Portsmouth, NH: Heinemann.

Johnson, P. (2005). *Get Writing! Creative Book-Making Projects for Children, Ages 4–7.* London: A&C Black.

Johnson, P. (2008). *Get Writing! Creative Book-Making Projects for Children, Ages 7–12*. London: A&C Black.

Loane, G. with Muir, S. (2017). *Developing Young Writers in the Classroom: I've Got Something to Say*. Abingdon: Routledge.

Rayner, C. (2007). *Augustus and His Smile*. London: Little Tiger Press.

Smith, J., Rowe, E. and Georgia (2017). Our Right to Write: The Power of Writing [video], TEDxNorwichED (3 April). Available at: https://www.youtube.com/watch?v=QaNKKRQrJzE.

Smith, J. and Wrigley, S. (2016). *Introducing Teachers' Writing Groups: Exploring the Theory and Practice*. Abingdon: Routledge.

Federation of Children's Book Groups (FCBG): http://www.fcbg.org.uk

National Association for the Teaching of English (NATE): https://www.nate.org.uk

National Writing Project (NWP) (UK): http://www.nwp.org.uk

About the contributors

Emily Rowe

Emily Rowe is a teacher of Year 5 and 6 pupils in Occold School, a rural primary school near Eye in Suffolk, where there are around 65 children on roll. Emily is responsible for leading English across the school, whose head is Dr Paul Parslow-Williams. She is passionate about children's writing and recently presented a TEDx talk, alongside one of her pupils and Jenifer Smith. In 2017, her pupils were awarded the 'best overall' prize for their entries in the Suffolk Young Poets competition. She is currently studying for her master's in educational practice at UEA.

Jenifer Smith

For over 20 years, Dr Jenifer Smith has been a teacher-educator and sometime course director for the primary PGCE at UEA. An English and drama specialist, she is especially interested in the teaching of writing. With Simon Wrigley, she is a co-director of NWP (UK), and is currently making a longitudinal study of writing in a primary school. Her publications include *Introducing Teachers' Writing Groups* with Simon Wrigley; a poetry pamphlet, *Reading Through the Night*; and an artist's book, *Pivotal*, created with her daughter, Alice Finbow.

Simon Wrigley

Simon Wrigley began teaching English in India in 1973. After graduating from Oxford University, he taught in comprehensive schools for 17 years before becoming a local authority adviser in Bedfordshire, then in Buckinghamshire. He served on NATE's primary and secondary committees before assuming the position of chair between 2004 and 2006. Working with Jenifer Smith, he established a teachers' writing group in Buckinghamshire, and this led to the co-founding of NWP (UK), which he co-directs. Now he is building the NWP (UK) website and learning more about writing. In 2017, he launched the thirtieth NWP group in Glasgow.

Chapter 12
Dance and Music in the Classroom

Lynn Knapp, head teacher, Windmill Primary School, Headington, Oxford

This chapter describes a remarkable and diverse range of dance, music, singing and performance throughout a large primary school on the outskirts of Oxford.

Characterised by the widest involvement of children (including in out-of-school time) in the expressive and creative arts – which have been integrated into wider curriculum areas (e.g. visual arts, technology, literature, writing, local history, geography and health education) – and developed by accomplished and specialist teaching, including from professional composers and performers drawn from outside the school, it has led to high levels of attainment and skill in writing, composition and choreography. There is also notable engagement in high profile adult and professional performance, and parents and the wider community are frequently involved in arts activities at the school.

A wide and generous education is on offer at Windmill School, centred on a broadly presented curriculum and enriching the experience of the pupils and their lives long into the future.

Background

Windmill Primary is a large three-form entry primary school in Oxford, with over 500 pupils on roll. The vision statement which we hold at the heart of our school culture is: 'Achievement through creativity, community and challenge'.

Despite the increasing pressure on schools to meet the expectations of the revised 2014 national curriculum, Windmill School has ensured that a broad curriculum, the teaching of the creative arts, and the mastery of skills and knowledge have not been compromised. We feel very strongly that art, drama, dance and music support children in attaining well in English and mathematics, and actively use the arts as a way of bringing the so-called 'academic' subjects to life. We recognise that a multisensory approach to teaching enhances learning for many of the children in our classes (see Madan and Singhal, 2012).

Dance plays a large part in Windmill School's curriculum. It is used as a strategy for learning as well as being part of the extracurricular opportunities that we offer. Although a busy head teacher, I run a regular dance club on a Monday lunchtime which attracts boys and girls from reception through to Year 6, and children across the school take part in a range of dance activities throughout the year. Each week in dance club, we come together to dance our favourite dances and work together to choreograph new ones.

Thanks to visits from professional dancers and watching a wide range of dance via the Internet and DVDs, the children discover new steps and moves which inspire their choreography for new dances. For example, children in Year 5 choreographed dances to bring a battle in the English Civil War to life using music and marches from the time period, while Year 4 children learned traditional Indian dance steps as part of their year group topic on India.

Dance in the curriculum

Dance is incorporated into curriculum plans to link with the topics that the children are studying. The dance component may be delivered as part of the PE curriculum or as a stand-alone lesson to help the children to develop their understanding. For example, the

Year 3 children, working in groups, choreographed a dance incorporating a sequence of movements to represent a volcano erupting. They were expected to be able to use the technical vocabulary that they had been learning in the classroom when they explained their reasons for specific steps or sequences of moves. This enabled the class teachers to evaluate the level of understanding that the children had developed in relation to their knowledge of volcanoes, as well as being an opportunity to assess the children's coordination and group-working skills.

Junior Strictly Oxford

We regularly take part in many dance-based projects. For the last four years, Windmill School had as many as 100 children taking part in the Junior Strictly Oxford competition, which involves me and other teaching staff attending an after-school ballroom dancing lesson to learn the dances that we will then teach the children.

The whole event is organised and coordinated by a local dance school, which ensures that the teachers are well trained to deliver the dance steps to the children taking part. The children then spend lunchtimes, and closer to the event, class time, learning and perfecting the dances which they perform in a competition with children from other schools at a local theatre. Over the years we have learned to cha-cha-cha, waltz, jive, tango and perform an 'American Smooth'. We believe that it is essential that every child gets to take part in the performance, regardless of whether they are better dancers or not, as the confidence they gain from participating is worth the time it takes to train so many children. Learning dance steps really helps them to develop their coordination skills and movement memory.

For most of the children, ballroom dancing is a completely new skill. The same applies to the teachers who volunteer to attend the dance classes to learn the steps. It is good for the children to see that their teachers are learning something new, and on many occasions finding it challenging too. This annual event has become a high point of the year and the children genuinely look forward to taking part and learning new dances.

Oxford Dance Festival

Each year, we work with children from Year 2 to choreograph a dance as part of a dance festival which is performed at the New Theatre in Oxford. Dances that we have performed range from the chimney sweep dance in *Mary Poppins* to 'Everybody Needs Somebody to Love' from *The Blues Brothers*. The children are selected because they love to dance, regardless of how much dance experience they have. They learn and perfect the routine over a period of six weeks, spending curriculum time rehearsing. On the day of the performance, they travel to Oxford to have a rehearsal on the stage and that evening they perform along with other schools from across the county.

Watching the other schools perform is a very valuable experience for them as it adds an aspirational element to the experience. To see our 6- and 7-year-olds dancing on a real stage is very special. Overcoming their nerves and going out in front of a theatre full of families and friends to perform their dance is a skill that they will take with them through life.

Summer dancing

In the autumn, children from across the school have a chance to perform a dance at the school's Autumn Fayre, with as many as 130 children choosing to take part. But the most important date in our annual calendar is our whole-school morning of summer dancing, when every child in the school performs a dance with their class or year group.

The range of dance styles is broad and ranges from traditional maypole and Morris dancing to street dance with breakdance moves and dances from other cultures. It is important that a progression of dance skills is seen across the school, and the older children take a significant role in choreographing their own routines.

The children learn their dances in class time, but in the week leading up to summer dancing you will find classes and year groups in many areas around the school rehearsing their dance steps. The fact that all children in the school have such a positive response to dance confirms how embedded the dance culture is in school. The event regularly coincides with our Health Week, so the link to dance as a route to fitness is emphasised.

And it is not just the children who dance. Three years ago, we decided that the teachers should perform their own routine to the school community. For many of the staff this really tests their own growth mindset and places them well outside of their comfort zone. The dance is purely voluntary but almost all members of staff choose to take part. This is always a highlight for the children and families who come along to our summer dancing event. The morning is rounded off with everyone getting up to dance together, which amounts to approximately a thousand people all dancing in the open air and having fun!

Morris and folk dancing

Dance has become a regular feature of our community life. Interestingly, our locality has a historical association with folk dancing. William Kimber (1872–1961) was a famous Headington Quarry Morris dancer and musician, and a key figure in the English Morris dance and folk music revival of the early 20th century. A few years ago, we joined with the Headington Quarry Morris Dancers and two members of the folk-rock band Bellowhead to stage a dance and music project in his memory with the children in Years 4, 5 and 6. William Kimber created the 'Bean Planting' dance which the Year 4 children were taught by the local Morris dancers. We all then went to the Story Museum in Oxford to perform our dance as part of the opening ceremony of the Oxford Folk Festival.

This project was initiated by the organisers of the Oxford Folk Festival who approached the school to see if we would like to take part. This was a very exciting opportunity for the children as they trained and performed alongside professional musicians and dancers. The musical pieces that the children learned were challenging and required them to work closely as a group to perfect their timing and accuracy. For the children who learned the dance, it was the first time they had tried a traditional Morris dance and the direct link to our local community made it even more special.

Dance and literature: Winter Lights

In 2013, as part of the Winter Lights celebration of the arts in Oxford, we worked with 30 children from across Key Stage 2 to choreograph an atmospheric dance to tell part of Philip Pullman's *Northern Lights* story. We were invited to take part by Fusion Arts in Oxford and the dance element was part of a wider range of arts activities taking place over the Winter Lights weekend, with the theme of dark to light.

A professional contemporary dancer came to work with the children to help and inspire our choreography. The workshops took place in curriculum time and involved children from Years 3 to 6. We watched sections of the film *The Golden Compass* and together read some chapters of *Northern Lights* linked to the parts in the story that our dance would tell to help the children explore their ideas.

The children performed their memorable 15-minute dance in a church hall in Oxford to a large audience. The element of dark to light was developed using fairy lights pinned to the children's outfits so that, as the dance began in pitch darkness, they were able to gradually turn on their lights, giving the feeling of a starry sky slowly coming to life. Parents who were in the audience commented on the sophistication of the children's routines and the atmospheric feeling of the performance. Not only was this a wonderful opportunity for the children to demonstrate their dance talent, but it also gave them access to a high quality text to explore and represent in dance. This was a one-off event but one that could inspire future projects which combine music and literature.

The translation of a narrative into dance moves and gestures is a complex task, but you can start with short extracts or scenes from well-known stories. For example, the scenes where the bad fairy places a spell on the princess in 'Sleeping Beauty' could incorporate the music of Tchaikovsky or something more modern. A repetitive story, such as *The Gruffalo*, could inspire repeated or sequential dance moves. The possibilities are endless.

The Artsmark award

The school has trained up three members of staff who are able to support Artsmark award projects. Where a dance or music event lends itself to becoming an Artsmark award project, one of these adults will take a lead in ensuring that the children do the appropriate background work which will support them in qualifying for an award. For example, for the Winter Lights dance, the children researched the events in *Northern Lights* which led to their choreographed routines.

Music and singing in the curriculum

Music is an important part of the curriculum at Windmill School. Originally, we used the music scheme, Music Express, to support non-specialist teachers in teaching music in their classes. But, for the last two years, music has been taught in classes by a specialist music teacher, Penny Dwyer, who teaches music to every class in the school. She also runs our school orchestra, which all our musicians are invited to join. Music is adapted to make it accessible to all levels and to ensure that the orchestra is fully inclusive.

Classes are timetabled to 30–40 minutes of music per week depending on the age of the children. Additional activities such as the choir and orchestra are run after school. Oxfordshire County Council's Music Service also has a team of peripatetic instrumental teachers who come into school each week to teach specific instruments. Continuing professional development opportunities are also run by the Music Service and this supports non-specialists in delivering music in the school.

Singing in the curriculum

At Windmill, we consider singing to be a very therapeutic activity and we place a lot of emphasis on the children singing regularly. We have signed up to Sing Up, which places a strong emphasis on children singing every day, as well as providing an extensive bank of songs upon which to draw.

All the children take part in a singing assembly every week in which they learn and sing a wide range of songs. Every year, every child in the school will also take part in a year group production, based around songs that tell or link to the story of the performance. Songs are also regularly used in classes as a learning strategy and to engage their attention with, for example, times tables and counting.

The school choir

Penny Dwyer runs two choirs as the demand to be in the school choir is so great. There are now choirs for Years 3/4 and Years 5/6. They meet weekly, one at lunchtime and one after school. The choirs are fully inclusive and every child who would like to attend is very welcome. The choirs sign up to a variety of choral opportunities throughout the county, which gives them a focus for performance. At Windmill, we believe a shared goal is very important because it gives the children a genuine purpose for their practice and development.

The choir always takes part in the Festival of Voices, organised by the National Association for Primary Education, during which the choir joins with other schools from around the county to celebrate singing in Dorchester Abbey. Some other examples of our singing experiences are summarised below. While they may be specific to our context, there will be similar opportunities in other areas, wherever one can find musicians and choirs.

Oxford Lieder Festival

Each year, Oxford hosts a Lieder Festival (lieder is the German word for song). In 2015, selected children from Years 5 and 6 took part in five half-day workshops at school in curriculum time. The project culminated in a rehearsal and short concert in the Sheldonian Theatre, which opened the festival that year. The children chosen were those we thought would benefit most from the experience of working with professional musicians and who had demonstrated an interest in and a talent for singing. The work they did enabled them to achieve the 'Discover' part of the Artsmark award.

The children worked with John Webb, a composer and workshop leader, and a professional singer, to create their own lyrics and songs in response to Shakespeare's *The Tempest*. Throughout the workshops, the children did an extensive amount of work on the story to prepare them for their own composition, as well as for the drama they were performing. The singer sang them several different settings of Shakespeare texts to expose them to a range of music styles.

Liz Stock, the then head of Oxfordshire Music Service, wrote:

> *Well done to all the staff and children for their performance in the Sheldonian Theatre on Friday for the launch of the Lieder Festival. Their performance was one of the best I have seen at the end of the project. … Thank you for giving the children the opportunity to have flexibility with their usual timetable to be involved. We just never know how life-changing these sorts of experiences can be for the young people.*

Cathedral singing project

Another valuable project with Christ Church Cathedral was jointly organised by the Christ Church Cathedral School and Oxfordshire Music Service. It involved all the children in Year 4 and was timetabled into the curriculum. The children took part in workshops in school, when some Christ Church choristers and their music teacher came to work with them on learning the songs. They worked on several pieces, one specially written by a local composer, Debbie Rose, with follow-up work to do in school between the sessions. The project culminated in an early evening concert in the cathedral, jointly with other schools and the choristers.

The performance was very special, and the whole project gave the children an opportunity to work with specialist teachers and students from a very unique environment. Opportunities like this can be aspirational for children who have never been inside a cathedral or performed alongside such talented musical students.

Singing with a local choir

For another project, the Year 5 and 6 choir had an opportunity to work in partnership with the Oxford Bach Choir. The children were required to learn a very difficult piece of music that had to be performed to a high standard. The performance took place in the Sheldonian Theatre on a Saturday evening, and the choir were accompanied by a professional orchestra. As an audience member it was inspiring to hear the choir singing alongside the adult choir in such a magnificent venue, making it an unforgettable evening for everyone concerned.

Singing with twinned city schools

The Oxford International Links committee organised a performance of Benjamin Britten's one-act opera *Noye's Fludde*, including schools from our twinned partners across Europe. This event brought together professional soloists, the Ernst-Moritz-Arndt-Gymnasium school choir from Bonn, the Leiden Youth Symphony Orchestra, young adult dancers from Perm in Russia, children from the East Oxford Community Choir and choirs from local schools. In all, 280 children and adults, plus a host of volunteers engaged backstage, collaborated on the performance, under the musical direction and leadership of John Lubbock, conductor of the Orchestra of St John's.

The schoolchildren involved came from Oxford schools St Ebbe's, Windmill, Our Lady's and the Blackbird Academy Trust. They joined the large school choir from Bonn to play and sing the roles of the animals in Noah's Ark. The children learned the songs in their own schools and then came together for two joint rehearsals before the evening performance. Chris Milton, learning projects manager at the Britten–Pears Foundation in Suffolk, came to talk to the cast and give a pre-concert address to the audience.

For the children it proved to be a unique and transforming experience:

■ They were a vital part of a production that in terms of extent, ambition, cultural range, importance, social diversity and experience, they had never encountered and, indeed, under normal circumstances were never likely to.

■ They had to become familiar with and master complex and challenging musical forms, hitherto alien to them.

■ They were helped to an insight into the brilliance of a great composer who adapted a story – known, in part at least, to most of them since childhood – into a powerful and sophisticated narrative of human behaviour, illuminated by sublime and engagingly inventive music.

■ They became an important and integral part of a complex production that called, on their part, for new learning, rigorous work, perseverance and discipline in ensuring their crucial part in the opera matched the expectations and standards of the other participants, some of them professional.

■ They worked with local artist Diana Bell in designing and making the sumptuous animal costumes and bird masks required for the opera personae.

191

- They learned to respond to other specialist music teachers who were drafted in to support their own teachers in teaching them to master the thrilling but demanding music.

- They had the rare experience of meeting, relating to and working with pupils and adults from other countries and cultures.

Opera was as new an art form to many of the parents as it was to the children themselves. They had never experienced a venture of this nature, or the performance of such a rare and, in its way, exotic, work, which eventually proved wholly captivating and spellbinding for all of them.

Something of the impact and value of the event is conveyed in the comments of those who taught, learned, participated or simply observed:

> It was such an incredible sight to see groups from different countries working together for a common goal, each one bringing a beautiful piece to make a fantastic whole.
>
> **Parent**

> [What] came across was the enjoyment of the performers (as well as the audience) and the feeling that a group of people had worked hard together and achieved something of which they could be proud. It illustrated perfectly the importance and significance of twinning.
>
> **Member of the audience**

Looking ahead

At Windmill, we place a great emphasis on maintaining a commitment to the arts. While we are fortunate to have a music specialist, we believe schools do not necessarily need subject specialists to develop the creative and expressive arts to a high standard. It just needs some enthusiastic staff who are prepared to have a go. The Sing Up website has a huge bank of resources for the non-specialist music teacher and these can be used to get a choir up and running. There are many other websites that can be used to support choreography for dance sessions and usually there will be children in each class who can support with leading and supporting less confident dancers.

Opportunities to take performances beyond school can come through making links with community events. Many cities now have an annual carnival, local churches and community groups have celebratory events, and local music groups (opera, orchestra, folk) organise a range of events that schools can sign up to. Making links with our local theatre and university has supported one-off opportunities for music, drama and dance which can then be exploited further. The projects that I have described in this chapter are just examples of the many dance and musical opportunities that are available to children if their schools reach out to local dance and music organisations and groups. In our experience, the more you say 'yes', the more opportunities come your way!

Conclusion

I firmly believe that dance and music are both activities that can contribute to children's mindfulness and well-being. This, in turn, gives them skills that they can take with them through life. The endorphins produced through singing and dancing actively support children being 'happy'. Links to the academic curriculum have also been made, but claims which have been made to show a link between music and mathematical achievement are still unsubstantiated (see Gaab and Zuk, 2017). However, it is generally accepted that learning to play music can support children to develop their gross and fine motor control. Movement memory is deemed to be even more powerful than auditory memory, so adding dance moves when learning key facts (e.g. times tables) can improve recall.

As a singing leader with the British Council's World Voice programme, Lin Marsh claims that the impact of learning to sing, play an instrument and dance is much wider than just having fun. Cognitive and social benefits follow, and these benefits and skills should be part of each child's educational entitlement: 'By communicating freely with the voice, face, and body, children learn to express ideas with confidence, empathise with others from diverse cultures and backgrounds, and feel at home in their own skin. Song, music and dance can help children become more imaginative, self-aware and collaborative global citizens' (Marsh, 2015).

As with all the creative and expressive arts, music and dance can be fully inclusive and give children a chance to demonstrate and develop their creativity and, in many cases, experience working with specialists and professionals. This provides a wealth of learning for the children involved, and gives them access to the world of music and dance, as well as creating and strengthening links with the local community, which has so much to offer.

Further reading and useful links

Burnard, P. and Murphy, R. (2017) *Teaching Music Creatively* (Learning to Teach in the Primary School Series), 2nd edn. Abingdon and New York: Routledge.

Gaab, N. and Zuk, J. (2017). Is There a Link between Music and Math? *Scientific American Mind* (1 May). Available at: https://www.scientificamerican.com/article/is-there-a-link-between-music-and-math/.

Madan, C. and Singhal, A. (2012). Using Actions to Enhance Memory: Effects of Enactment, Gestures, and Exercise on Human Memory, *Frontier Psychology*, 3: 507. DOI: 10.3389/fpsyg.2012.00507.

Marsh, L. (2015). Why song and dance are essential for children's development, *British Council* (25 June). Available at: https://www.britishcouncil.org/voices-magazine/why-song-and-dance-are-essential-childrens-development.

Pullman, P. (2011). *Northern Lights* (His Dark Materials: vol. 1). London: Scholastic.

Artsmark: http://www.artsmark.org.uk

BBC Learning School Radio – primary dance teaching resources: www.bbc.co.uk/schoolradio/subjects/dance

Music Express: https://collins.co.uk/page/Music+Express

National Association for Primary Education (NAPE): http://nape.org.uk

People Dancing – the Foundation for Community Dance: https://www.communitydance.org.uk

Sing Up: https://www.singup.org

Siobhan Davies Dance: http://www.siobhandavies.com/work/primary-school-programme

About the contributor

Lynn Knapp

Having been brought up in south-east London, Lynn Knapp moved to Oxford as a student to study biology. She qualified as a teacher in 1982 and has been teaching in Oxfordshire ever since, working in four schools. She became the head teacher of Woodcote Primary School in 1997 and moved to Windmill Primary School in 2007. Lynn has recently been recognised as a national leader of education (NLE) and the school has been given teaching school status.

Chapter 13
Drama Across the Primary Curriculum

Helen Heaton, drama teacher, Ansford Academy, Castle Cary, Somerset

While many primary schools continue to preserve the tradition of a drama production, especially at Christmas or at the end of the school year when the pressure of tests has eased, there is worrying evidence that drama is being curtailed as an established and practised part of the curriculum. This is due to an out-of-date perception of drama as an unproductive indulgence when the demands of the core curriculum are much more urgent.

It is probably true to say that apart from a brief period in the 1970s and 1980s, when creative drama was in vogue in primary schools, it has been much more common for the subject to be a focus of performance and show rather than a means to cultivate and animate core elements of the curriculum. Exceptions to this are usually still to be found in the primary sector, particularly in schools where a drama specialist (or an informed and competent enthusiast) fosters and celebrates drama for its inherent worth and potential as an instrument of wider learning.

This chapter represents a notable example of such a situation. Helen Heaton, an experienced specialist who has worked in both primary and secondary schools, makes a compelling argument for the value of drama in cultural, social and general developmental terms, and as a potent agent in the whole learning process. She highlights the potential of the subject as a stimulus to learning in other curriculum areas, particularly in the domain of language. This is combined with practical advice and encouragement about the implementation of drama in the classroom.

Background

Ansford Academy is a secondary comprehensive school with nearly 600 pupils aged 11 to 16. It is located in the town of Ansford, which lies on the northern edge of Castle Cary in Somerset. The school has a small but active creative arts department, featuring music, drama and art. Ansford recognises the importance of the arts and makes it compulsory for all students at Key Stage 3. There is a transition programme in place featuring drama, sport and team-building activities for primary children moving up into Year 7.

The value of drama

Having worked with drama and theatre for nearly 20 years, I am constantly reminded and amazed by how this subject is so wide reaching and multifaceted. From an early age we start acting out scenarios, mimicking our parents as soon as we can walk and talk, and then role playing visits to the supermarket, doctor and post office. We develop characters from the people we meet, see and interact with, and play out our favourite days and moments to help our ongoing need to please ourselves.

In primary school, we carry on role playing but now it is time to play out scenarios that we may not have personally encountered, and this can help us to problem-solve and build relationships with those with whom we share the scenario. Much research has taken place on the benefits of drama which encourages children to use their imagination (see Cockett, 1999).

Interestingly, the Education Endowment Foundation, in partnership with the RSA, is working with 400 schools across five new research studies, where primary school pupils will take part in daily singing or weekly drama and TV news reporting lessons as part of a £1.1 million research programme – the UK's largest ever study of cultural learning. 'Learning About Culture' is a two-and-a-half year investigation (2017–2020) into the role that cultural learning plays in improving educational outcomes for children (see Londesborough et al., 2017). Its intention is to develop more evidence of what works and to support schools and cultural organisations to use the evidence collected to continuously improve their practice.

Drama can help children to become more confident and more willing to stand up and talk in front of peers in a classroom setting. A report published by the New Schools Network (Fellows, 2017) shows that those who study drama at GCSE level are higher achievers than those who do not. We are likely to have memories of taking part in our first school play, whether it is playing Mary in the school nativity or being the angel at the back of the choir. We are born to act and play, and therefore drama should maintain a central position within the primary curriculum rather than being squeezed out of the timetable.

Confidence building

From an early age, most children have a fearlessness which lessens as they get older. They can be confident beings, rarely fazed by playacting or performance. However, the fear starts when they are told they cannot do something or when they are laughed at for making mistakes, whether that is at home or at school. As a result, we are likely to become more careful of what we say and wary of what people might say about us.

This can present a massive problem when teaching or using drama. However, it is easily overcome if we make it clear to the children that everyone is working together, on the same equal basis, towards a piece of work for which no one is going to judge them as individuals.

At times, drama can be a chance for children to play, with permission. It provides opportunities to release inhibitions and forget about the usual 'rules' of how you should be in a classroom setting. When children play they become more relaxed, and therefore are more willing to give their all to a situation or problem.

Getting started

When working with primary school groups, I usually begin with them in a circle, with me standing in the middle. I lead a very gentle warm-up which generally ends with them having to shake various limbs and pull funny faces. This is the icebreaker. They have all performed something extremely silly (in their eyes, at least) and already feel slightly less tense. I also play a quick game of 'pass the clap' which instantly engages the children and helps them to focus on the task in hand. There are many variants of this game (such as 'zip, zap, boing' and 'splat') which are age-old favourites when it comes to warm-up games.

For younger children, get them to hold hands in a circle and 'pass the squeeze' instead of the clap. At various points ask a member of the class to guess where the squeeze has ended up. With a class who you may not know very well (such as when looking after someone else's group or coming in as a supply teacher) a name game works well. Ask each child to come up with a movement which they will do instead of saying their name. Someone stands in the middle and must copy the movements from each person in the circle.

Building drama into the curriculum

The next step is to look for ways to link drama to some work being covered in class. In the past, I have introduced an exploration of the rainforest (in geography), devised a Roman invasion (history), created soundscape journeys (music and geography), acted out various incidents in *The Jungle Book* (English) and created space adventures (science).

For instance, taking the idea of the rainforest, we first make a soundscape, where we create sound effects using our voices and bodies. The initial step is to show the children how they can use their bodies and voices to create a world of sound. As a warm-up to this they can create a rainstorm. It goes something like this: the children rub their fingers together to create a quiet swooshing sound and gradually building in a patter using the tables (or floor). Then move to them clapping, patting their thighs and stamping their feet. Then gradually go back to the thighs, clapping, pattering on the tables and then the fingers. This is an amazingly effective exercise, and the children feel a real sense of achievement as they hear how easy it is to build up a wall of sounds.

I then play the class an audio clip of a rainforest and get them to write down the sounds they hear. This is a good opportunity to split the class into two and ask them, in their group, to come up with their own mini soundscape, making sure they build it up in lay-ers like the storm they created earlier. After creating a soundscape (and sharing it with the class), groups of children can then build in some freeze-frames or frozen tableaux of animals or people they might find in a rainforest. They can then create perhaps five epi-sodes to reflect the stages of their soundscape and put them together. This can be further developed by showing them a rainforest growing from primary to secondary growth set to music (I find Saint-Saëns' *Aquarium* from *The Carnival of the Animals* lends itself well to any kind of 'growth' work).

Hot seating is the quickest and easiest technique to incorporate into the classroom. Hot seating is putting a character on a chair in front of the class and asking them questions about themselves. This is an effective way for the class to become more creative and think more deeply about the inner workings of the main protagonists of the current class book or the roles of people involved in a class topic. I have found that this technique works best in an English lesson where the children have got to know the characters extremely well. I usually try to do it a couple of times during the course of the novel so the children can add to previous answers, but also to identify progression in the characters and notice which answers change.

I have found the book *The Way to Sattin Shore* (2008) by Philippa Pearce to be a perfect example for hot seating, especially as the book holds so many mysteries for the reader. The class can use their imagination to come up with answers for the characters – particularly for Kate, the main protagonist. After reading the first chapter of the book, I ask a member of the class to become Kate for the moment and sit on a chair in front of the class. I encourage the children to ask her several questions about her age, who she lives with, whether she has any pets and so on.

Then, a couple of chapters later, I help them to explore the character's feelings, with a different child taking the part of Kate ('Right now, Kate, how do you feel about your dad? What secret do you think your family are keeping from you?'). This kind of hot seating exercise can be done at any point during the book or at the end ('How do you feel? How do you feel towards your mum?'). Of course, this can be expanded to explore other characters in the story or to exercises such as 'role on the wall' and 'thought tracking'.

Role on the wall is ideal for in-depth character exploration. First, ask a child to lie down on the floor on a big piece of paper and draw around them. The children then add information about external features of the character around the outline (age, name, family) and then add internal features inside the outline (feelings, hopes, dreams). These can be acted out to ensure everyone understands the meanings of each word. The outlines can then be displayed and added to during the collective reading of a class book. This is particularly helpful for English as an additional language (EAL) pupils and those who like to learn in a more visual way.

Thought tracking involves taking a roll of wallpaper and drawing a timeline of the book along its length to which the children can add events and plot episodes as the narrative unfolds. At the same time, they can create an 'emotions timeline' to keep track of the thoughts and feelings of the characters as they react to the story's events and to each other.

There is also place for the quick, one-off drama lesson, such as on a special occasion or celebration days. My favourite is Chinese New Year. I usually tell the children the story of the origins of the Chinese New Year and then encourage them to have a go at being some of the animals moving around the space. Next, I split them into 12 groups and assign them each an animal from the Chinese zodiac. They then rehearse the story of the animals' grand race to reach the Buddha, with each animal team working as a group to represent their assigned animal.

Teamwork

One of the most valuable lessons learned in drama is effective teamwork. In the past, I have given children a scenario to work through (this is perfect for discussions on characters in books for English, or moral issues in RE), split them into groups and then asked them to work together to agree an outcome. Sometimes, this can be rather chaotic to start with, so I leave it to them for a couple of minutes before bringing them back as a whole group. We then discuss what the problems are within the groups – the children usually suggest things like 'listening skills', 'communication' and 'everyone getting a turn'. With these in mind, I send them back to their groups to come up with a solution and then act it out.

I always reinforce these rules with older children, too, because the rules don't change. At this point it is good to experiment with different sized groups and see what works and what doesn't. Once a class has got into the routine of respectfully working with one another, most children work well together and don't complain. For groups that perhaps don't gel as well, I sometimes use a sports analogy, telling them that they are part of a team – much like in football. This normally helps them to get into the right mindset. These social and teamwork skills are even more valuable as children work through the school system, so it is of fundamental importance to establish them at the beginning of children's school careers.

Drama games can also help with focus and discipline – for example, by inviting the children to play a quiet game such as 'wink murder', where one pupil secretly winks at others in the circle to 'murder' them and another pupil takes on the role of the detective. Another way of engaging disengaged children is by assigning them a leadership role such as 'personal assistant' ('Can you assist me in this game, please?') or getting them to direct something. Praising these children when they have done well works wonders, in my experience. Giving them a purpose during a lesson means they are likely to want to do the job again and thus will engage in the lesson next time.

Imagination

A great exercise to stimulate the imagination involves choosing a painting and asking the children to create a piece around it. My favourites are *Tiger in a Tropical Storm* by Henri Rousseau or some of Dali's surrealist dream paintings. Children read so much into them and let their imaginations soar. Indeed, they often read much more into the pictures than adult groups with whom I have done the same exercise.

Before launching into the exercise, a word association game can help to start the creativity flowing, initiating word chains such as *admiral, boat, catamaran, dinghy, funnel* ... Or *ant, bat, cat, dog, elephant, guinea pig, horse* ... This can obviously be tailored to any primary group according to the interests and abilities of the class. Start throwing in some more obscure words to start the chains off, such as *airport, dream, journey* or *choice*.

Then ask the children to look at the chosen painting and try to find, or make up, the story. Ask them to create some characters and move about inside the picture using the space in the classroom or hall. Encourage them to create the story with actions and with a beginning, middle and end. Give them the chance to rehearse their mini pieces within a given time limit; a visible stopwatch or big egg timer is very useful.

Drama projects

Children enjoy working towards a project – something that will grow and take them beyond a single lesson, something that will run for half a term or turn into a school production. In so doing, their sense of achievement is so much greater.

I have found the Vikings have proved to be a subject with limitless possibilities. I once turned a school hall into a Viking longboat using chairs and boxes which had been donated by parents. The children played out Viking myths and customs, devised their own scripts and put on a mini-performance for the rest of the school. What was particularly good about the project was that the children not only had the opportunity to act and perform, but also to learn about scriptwriting, directing, scenic art and preparing props.

Writing for others

Drama can support many other subjects, but it is especially helpful in providing a genuine purpose for writing as children can create their own scenarios. Scriptwriting can appeal to and benefit those children who find writing more of a challenge because the lines can be short and consist of dialogue alone. For those who find writing easy, they can write and then pass it on for someone else to read – much as it works in the theatre industry for a new show. The children may be fascinated to discover that they are using techniques employed on Broadway or in the West End!

Scriptwriters need to learn some important skills. They need to describe the scenario to their cast, express what they want the outcome to be and ask the actors to try saying the lines in unusual ways – to 'give it a go'. Their efforts can be recorded or filmed and then the 'writer' can pick and choose what they want to keep. This exercise can be easily done using tablets. These tools and processes help children to work at their own pace, teach skills in editing and drafting, and give them a chance to improve on their work with reworking and refinement.

The process can be enriched by filming the final performance and then, if the school ICT requirements can handle it, downloading some editing software (I have found VideoPad to be one of the best for schools because it is free, has an easy-to-follow format and can be easily uploaded to school networks) and then children can have a go at editing their own films. Children engage with this activity well, particularly when they find out how to add music and sound effects.

For children who find generating ideas quite difficult, there is a useful set of dice called Rory's Story Cubes which come in all sorts of genres including Prehistoria, Mythic and Fright, to name but a few. No pupil who has used these has ever suffered from 'writer's block'!

Another strategy is to have a bag of random objects such as plastic animals, mini furniture, objects or cards which children pick out without looking. They then have to say out loud five words which first come to mind, then use their ideas to write. Quirky *objets d'art* or jewellery can also be useful to spark the imagination. A former teacher of mine used to wear a small perfume bottle on a chain which always had a coloured liquid in it. As a class, we had to guess who had owned it, where it came from and how it had come to belong to our teacher. Collections of footwear and other accessories can be a useful talking point in the classroom and offer potential starting points for young writers.

Problem-solving

Drama can be used as an effective way for children to find solutions to problems. For instance, you might set up a scenario where a pupil overhears two teachers talking about a test paper and then you ask the class what that pupil should do next. Having set up the dilemma, the class can be divided into small groups to discuss and then act out some alternative outcomes. These are then performed and the class can vote on which is the 'better' ending for the scenario. This leads into all kinds of work, develops good debating skills and sometimes brings out children who are usually very quiet. This model can also be used for characters in a book or poem, moments of history, ethical issues and personal, social, health and economic (PSHE) education.

Another way to use this is for the children to come up with some problems which may have arisen in other topics (such as the conflict between King John and the nobles over Magna Carta). They can dramatise the conversation and situation and come up with a conclusion. Items from problem pages from magazines can also work well (although you should be familiar with the children you do this with and be sensitive to any problems at home that you may be aware of).

The school production

As I have always been a drama teacher, I have always looked forward to the school production. However, I know many in the profession who are daunted by it.

There are many advocates for getting children to perform (the charity Action for Children's Arts to name but one). On a more academic front, much research has been done on the benefits of physical activity levels, which can include drama and performance, particularly for those children who are disadvantaged and do not have access to after-school clubs and activities (see e.g. Clipson-Boyles, 1999; Bolton, 2009; Brooks, 2014). Therefore, being part of a school production can help close the attainment gap for those children who most need it. This has also been highlighted by prominent drama practitioners such as Dorothy Heathcote and Jonothan Neelands.

Summer is my preferred time of year for a large production. The tests and exams are usually over by then, and teachers seem to be more relaxed with their classes and more willing to support each other.

The question that needs to be answered first is whether to use a ready-made, traditional script with specific parts or to opt for an ensemble piece in which the parts are more equal and differentiated. Scripts that have been adapted from classics can work well with an ensemble cast – for example, *Alice's Adventures in in Wonderland* (many versions available), *Arabian Nights* by Dominic Cooke (2009), *Treasure Island* by Stuart Paterson (2007) and *Wind in the Willows* (many versions available). David Wood has written some excellent plays for use in primary schools, both original works and adaptations (my favourite is Roald Dahl's *The Witches* (1993)).

As someone who has undertaken many productions, I have established the following principles:

1. Always have a 'deputy' on hand. A teaching assistant or parent who enjoys drama can be worth their weight in gold.

2. Have a rehearsal plan and allow more time than seems necessary. Although the audience of parents will not mind whether the final production is polished to perfection, a rough outline of what you wish to achieve by the production date can certainly help when considering what may be viable in the time available.

3. Always add a song. It doesn't have to be a showstopper but children tend to learn the lines of songs better than those in a play. Consider using a song that the audience know as well so they can join in. Remember to consider copyright and apply for it if necessary.

4. Don't overly complicate the set/props/extras. In the primary setting, the children care little about what they are wearing, as long as it is different from their everyday uniform. A basic set, simple props, costumes and make-up are all you need to enable them to suspend disbelief and 'become' a character.

5. Enjoy yourself and relax, so the children can also enjoy taking part. It is easy to get overly stressed about a production, but parents and colleagues are rarely as judgemental as we fear. Onlookers will just be proud that their son/daughter/ grandchild is on the stage, developing valuable skills and giving it their all.

Drama as part of the everyday classroom

To embed drama within the everyday curriculum, it is always sensible to have a few props to hand in a box that you can readily reach out and use. So, if the children are solving a maths problem and you feel it needs some drama, ask a student to pick out a hat and then solve the sum on the board in the character of whichever hat they have picked. I have used this many times in the classroom myself, mainly to make sure that a certain mathematical method will be remembered: 'Do you remember when Sophia solved that long division while dressed in a princess hat? She used such a funny voice that I will always know how to do long division now.'

Children enjoy it when their teacher dresses up and goes into role. They can be introduced to a new topic by interviewing a 'stranger', and they will accept that the adult has adopted a different persona through the use of a different voice, prop or costume.

Children's views on drama

I currently work as a secondary teacher, so all my students have made the transition from primary to secondary school. My first question is always, 'How many of you have done drama before?' Worryingly, many say they have never done it before or say they did not do it enough.

However, those with experience of drama in primary school tend to demonstrate a passion for it which continues into the secondary phase, and into drama as a specialist subject. In the primary setting there are very few children who don't enjoy drama, and those who find it more challenging usually gain in confidence and develop a quiet respect for the subject over time.

Parents' views on drama

When drama in the classroom is mentioned to parents it is likely to get one of two responses: 'Fantastic!' or 'What's the point of drama?' It is encouraging to hear stories from parents who say that their child has talked for days about a drama project they did at school. It shows that there is a profound need for drama in the school curriculum, especially if it comes with a multitude of skills and outcomes.

Unfortunately, the place of drama in school curriculums will always be in question, but I have never known a person to turn down a ticket for the theatre or a screening at the cinema. And we all know where exceptional dramatic performances are rooted: in drama classes, in school productions and in the encouragement of teachers who have used drama in their everyday lessons.

Conclusion

Current government thinking would lead us to believe that drama can be simply side-lined, especially with the creative arts being relegated to the backseat in the secondary national curriculum because it is not part of the English Baccalaureate. It has long been considered a 'soft' subject or a practical subject with no strong pedagogical foundation.

However, our worldwide counterparts think differently. In countries such as New Zealand and Australia, a drama curriculum is standard in most schools. Other countries, such as Finland and Iceland, are following suit. In the UK, according to a report from the National Theatre, more people attend theatre shows than Premier League football matches (see Perry, 2014). Doesn't it make sense that we should nurture this subject as a key staple in the primary curriculum, rather than as a subject only brought out on special occasions?

Drama is in danger of being removed from the curriculum because it is perceived as being the exclusive domain of those who want to act in later life. However, I hope that this chapter has shown that drama can be integrated into any subject and can be valuable when used within everyday teaching time. Using drama at the primary stage builds children's confidence, character, resilience, imagination, personality and team-working skills, which are essential attributes whatever path they may follow in later life.

Further reading and useful links

Bolton, G. (1992). *New Perspectives on Classroom Drama*. Cheltenham: Nelson Thornes.

Bolton, G. (2009). Changes in Thinking About Drama in Education, *Theory Into Practice*, 24(3): 151–157.

Brooks, F. (2014). *The Link Between Pupil Health and Wellbeing and Attainment: A Briefing for Head Teachers, Governors and Staff in Education Settings*. London: Public Health England. Available at: https://www.gov.uk/government/publications/the-link-between-pupil-health-and-wellbeing-and-attainment.

Casado, D. (2014). *Teaching Drama: The Essential Handbook: 16 Ready-to-Go Lesson Plans to Build a Better Actor*. N.p.: CreateSpace.

Clipson-Boyles, S. (1999). The Role of Drama in the Literate Classroom. In P. Goodwin (ed.), *The Literate Classroom*. London: David Fulton Books, pp. 134–141.

Clipson-Boyles, S. (2011). *Teaching Primary English Through Drama: A Practical and Creative Approach*. Abingdon: Routledge.

Cockett, S. (1999). Evaluating Children's Learning in Drama in the Primary School, *Westminster Studies in Education*, 22(1): 63–73.

Cooke, D. (2009). *Arabian Nights*. London: Nick Hern Books.

Dahl, R. (1993). *The Witches*. Adapted for the stage by D. Wood. London: Samuel French.

Farmer, D. (2012). *Learning Through Drama in the Primary Years*. N.p.: CreateSpace.

Fellows, E. (2017). *The Two Cultures: Do Schools Have to Choose Between the EBacc and the Arts?* London: New Schools Network. Available at: https://www.newschoolsnetwork.org/file/nsn-arts-report-the-two-culturespdf-0.

Heathcote, D. and Bolton, G. (1995). *Drama for Learning: Dorothy Heathcote's Mantle of the Expert Approach to Education* (Dimensions of Drama). London: Heinemann.

Londesborough, M., Partridge, L., Bath, N. and Grinsted, S. (2017). *Learning About Culture: Programme Prospectus*. London: RSA Action and Research Centre. Available at: https://www.thersa.org/globalassets/pdfs/reports/rsa-learning-about-culture-report.pdf.

O'Connor, P. (ed.) (2010). *Creating Democratic Citizenship Through Drama Education: The Writings of Jonothan Neelands*. Stoke-on-Trent: Trentham Books.

Paterson, S. (2007). *Treasure Island*. London: Nick Hern Books.

Pearce, P. (2008). *The Way to Sattin Shore*. Oxford: Oxford University Press.

Perry, K. (2014). Almost twice as many people visit the theatre than attend Premier League games, *The Telegraph* (30 July). Available at: https://www.telegraph.co.uk/culture/theatre/11001177/Almost-twice-as-many-people-visit-the-theatre-than-attend-Premier-League-games.html.

Theodorou, M. (2013). *Games, Ideas and Activities for Primary Drama* (Classroom Gems). London: Pearson.

Winston, J. and Tandy, M. (2008). *Beginning Drama 4–11*. Abingdon and New York: David Fulton Books.

Zachest, K. (2016). *Drama Games for Young Children*. London: Nick Hern Books.

Action for Children's Arts: http://childrensarts.org.uk

Arts on the Move: http://www.artsonthemove.co.uk/education/primary/primary.php

BBC Learning School Radio – primary drama teaching resources for Key Stage 2: http://www.bbc.co.uk/schoolradio/subjects/drama

David Wood: http://www.davidwood.org.uk/my_plays.htm

Music Theatre International – holds the rights to many popular show tunes: http://www.mtishows.co.uk

PPL – helpful information about music licences: http://www.ppluk.com/I-Play-Music/Businesses

Rory's Story Cubes: https://www.storycubes.com

VideoPad: http://www.nchsoftware.com/videopad/index.html

About the contributor

Helen Heaton

Helen Heaton holds a degree in drama from the University of Aberystwyth. She started her career as a Royal Academy of Dramatic Art (RADA) trained stage manager but gradually became more interested in the educational side of the theatre. Having started off as a drama technician at Ellesmere College, Shropshire, she did her PGCE training and then moved to St Peter's School, York, where she taught LAMDA (London Academy of Music and Dramatic Art) speech and drama and the Trinity Arts Award. When she first moved to Somerset, she gained experience and knowledge in both the primary and secondary sectors. She currently teaches drama at Ansford Academy in Castle Cary and writes drama resources for ZigZag Education, as well as working freelance with Arts Award and LAMDA.

Chapter 14
Chess in the Curriculum

Ed Read, head teacher, Cumnor CE Primary School, Oxfordshire and Dr Andrew Varney, chess coach

Chess, more than most games or sports, seems possessed of a rare and particular mystique, perhaps because it is rooted deep in the history of humankind. It is rich in mythology, anecdote and folklore around epic contests, legendary players, intellectual inventiveness, audacious daring and risk. Tellingly, it has come to be seen as a decisive test of computing power to challenge and match human intelligence.

According to the charity Chess in Schools and Communities (CSC), the game has many benefits: 'Chess is a universal game, knowing no boundaries of age, gender, faith, ethnicity or disability, that promotes key intellectual skills such as problem solving, logical thinking, pattern recognition and concentration. Playing chess also fosters intellectual character.'

If one tiptoes into a classroom at Cumnor Primary School when a chess lesson is taking place, with 20 or more pupils in one-to-one opposition, it is hardly an exaggeration to say that one perceives a concentration and attention on the part of even the youngest players which would match that of any experienced adult. The spectator need have no knowledge of the intricacies of the game, or recourse to the assurance of assessment data, to understand that something precious and extraordinary in terms of learning – and something memorable in terms of experience – is happening here.

At Cumnor School, as in many others, there is specialist teaching provision by a professional coach for the more able and capable players, but all pupils have the opportunity to acquire an understanding of this complex game, and their enjoyment – or mastery – will enrich their lives for years to come.

This chapter, by head teacher Ed Read and chess coach Dr Andrew Varney, conveys their confidence in the contribution that chess can make to the education and wider development of children. Their enthusiasm for chess in schools is derived from their extensive experience of enabling pupils to play the game regularly as part of the school curriculum, and from their observations of the excellent progress made by the wide range of pupils they teach.

Background

Cumnor CE Primary School is a voluntary controlled school which has just over 200 pupils, aged from 4 to 11. It is located in a village just four miles from the centre of Oxford. It has fewer than average numbers of pupils in receipt of the pupil premium, with English as an additional language (EAL) status or with special educational needs (SEN).

Cumnor School promotes a full and broad curriculum for its staff and pupils, encouraging them to explore all facets of education both within the framework of the national curriculum and through the vast opportunities outside it. We see our role at Cumnor Primary School as creating the building blocks for our pupils to become successful, both academically and socially. By giving children a truly broad curriculum, they can discover what they are passionate about and where their talents lie. These talents may lie within the standard school curriculum or well beyond what has become an overly narrow focus.

Technology is transforming our lives so rapidly that many of the jobs that will be available to the children who are born today have not yet been created. We therefore need to prepare them for a new world in which they will need to think strategically rather than just repeat information they have been told.

It is through initiatives such as our chess programme that we are truly able to teach the children the skills they need for the future beyond their Key Stage 2 SATs and GCSEs – preparing them for the tests of life, not a life of tests. Chess can sit alongside other curriculum-enhancing programmes such as values-based education, character education and growth mindset to prepare children for their future.

Chess, thinking and learning

Educators know that children bring a range of skills, capacities and learning styles to bear upon their learning. Chess, however, crosses these boundaries and gets to the core of how children think and learn. It doesn't rely on a teacher presenting a subject in such a way as to aid learning, but supports the child in developing the skills and attitudes they need to support their learning. The skills they learn are transferable: thinking ahead, juggling different ideas simultaneously and choosing the best option, focus, concentration, visualisation and perseverance.

Chessmaster Jerry Meyers (2016) has summarised the thinking processes which chess demands of its players and the cognitive outcomes which support children's learning. Some of the academic benefits from playing chess include:

- Focusing – Children learn how to observe and concentrate on what they are doing.

- Visualising – Children are taught to think before they act, imagining a sequence of actions before they happen.

- Analysing concretely – Children learn to assess the consequences of their actions based on logic rather than emotion.

- Thinking abstractly – Children are supported to consider the 'bigger picture' rather than getting caught up in details.

- Planning – Children learn how to develop longer-term goals and take action to bring them about.

- Juggling multiple considerations simultaneously – Children are encouraged not to become overly absorbed in one thing but to evaluate lots of different factors all at once.

Chess challenges children to think about the position in which they find themselves. They cannot just repeat information or learn a rule, as is expected in so much of today's education (times tables, punctuation rules, dates and places, mathematical formulae and so on). Players have to understand that careful and logical analysis of the situation is the core to a successful next move.

There are more possible games in chess than there are atoms in the universe, so each game is unique. In 1950, mathematician Claude Shannon wrote a paper about how a computer could be programmed to play chess. In it, he calculated how many different games of chess were possible and came up with the number 10^{120}. This is an extremely large number; by comparison, the number of atoms in the observable universe is 'only' estimated to be around 10^{80}.

Lifelong learning

We want children to be lifelong learners. This means that we teach them to reflect carefully on the resolution of problems and challenges encountered, and the management of particular situations and events. It is essential that we teach them how to adapt, change their strategy or approach and develop flexible thinking.

For me, the most significant gain of playing chess is being able to assess a situation and see what tactics and resources you have at your disposal to overcome a problem. This involves analysing your opponent's game to see how it can be used to your advantage and exploring and developing strategies that will lead you to your ultimate goal. By learning these skills, the adults of the future will be able to apply these skills in the workplace: learning how they can use the skills they have acquired to the greatest effect, developing strategies to help them become successful and using the world around them to the greatest benefit. It is only the children who can adapt to the ever-changing world around them who will be successful. Chess teaches them the skills they need to adapt.

Transferable skills

Chess can teach children many transferable skills:

- Manners – playing quietly and respectfully, shaking hands at the start and end, congratulating your opponent at the end.

- Concentration – games can last hours so good concentration levels are needed to remain focused and to play the best move, which is useful preparation for exam success.

- Perseverance – the ability to persevere with sustained writing or long and complex science or maths problems.

- Memory – learning set openings, learning from previous mistakes and miscalculations.

- Resolving problems peacefully – you may be up against it, but hard work and clever thinking get you out of trouble: you use your head not your fists.

- Resilience – never give up. Even if the odds are against you, a chess game could always end in a draw or even a win if your opponent blunders.

- Accepting the consequences of your actions – if you make a poorly thought-through move you may lose your queen. If you make a poor choice in the playground you may get into trouble.

Introducing chess across the school

When my son started to play chess, I noticed how his thinking began to change as he got better at the game. But it was only when two boys from Armenia joined us and told me of their enjoyment of the game at school (chess is a statutory part of the Armenian curriculum) that I started to explore the research that had been published on the benefits of playing chess in school.

My research led me to contact CSC, who were able to talk me through how other schools had set up chess programmes and obtained funding. The most daunting parts of the project were quickly resolved by CSC as they were able to supply the chess sets, partly fund a chess coach and provide a curriculum for us to follow, broken down into weekly plans.

With my research complete, contact with a chess coach made and the potential support of CSC agreed, it was now just a case of convincing the governors, staff, parents and children that this was a good idea! Some of the key questions which were asked, and resolved, were:

- **Why have chess lessons as part of the curriculum, not an after-school club?**
  I had run after-school chess clubs before but these only attracted a relatively small number of children. The emphasis in clubs is more on the game itself and tournaments, rather than the transferable skills that can be developed. By including chess in the curriculum, all the children would benefit and the scope of the teaching could be broader. I also felt strongly that the children who would potentially benefit most from chess were those children who had difficulty with memory, concentration, resilience and problem-solving, and they were often the children who would be reluctant to come to an after-school chess club.

- **Which age groups would be taught?** A cautious approach here may have been prudent – perhaps trialling chess in one year group for 12 months and then expanding the project. However, I had become totally convinced that this was going to be a good thing for our children and wanted to involve as many of them as possible right from the start. We were fortunate to be able to secure the chess coach for one afternoon a week and he could teach two classes for 45 minutes each in this time. With his help, and the CSC curriculum, I took two other classes later on in the week. In this way, all the Key Stage 2 children in our one-form entry school could be taught.

- **How often would the lessons be?** Initially we went for a 45-minute lesson every week. This worked well and had a significant impact almost immediately. However, after the first year, we decided to make some significant changes and arrived at a model which works well for us. All the children now have a 45-minute lesson once a fortnight. As the head teacher I take half the class, and our specialist chess coach, Andrew Varney, takes the other half, with the class being split largely on ability.

- **Would chess be taught at the expense of other curriculum subjects?** We introduced chess at a time when the curriculum was being rewritten, again. There was to be less emphasis on the amount of time given to each subject, and the new curriculum was less content-driven than before. This allowed us to be more flexible and creative with our teaching, and chess was to be part of this more child-centred approach. Timetables needed to be adapted, but, in the end, no other subject lost out. Chess just slotted in alongside the other subjects being taught.

- **How much would it cost?** The CSC provided us with a curriculum and all our chess sets, and funded the majority of Andrew Varney's time. The additional expense was simply in my time and a £750 contribution to the CSC. Interestingly, as a result of our being a 'chess school', additional revenue now comes in as a result of the school hall being let out in the evenings and weekends for external chess coaching and tournaments (the Oxfordshire Junior Squad meet at Cumnor).

■ **How would chess affect attainment and progress results?** As with all research, it is difficult to attribute just one factor to any perceived improvement, and I could find little substantive evidence to prove a link between chess teaching and improved attainment levels. However, it is possible to say that the teaching of chess seems to contribute significantly to higher academic standards. For example, before we started the chess programme, the percentage of children attaining the national standard (4B+ in those days) was 86%, 79% and 68% for reading, writing and maths respectively; after four years of chess teaching, our most recent results show 91% of children achieving the 'expected level' in all subjects.

■ **How would the school community respond?** The school governors asked some interesting questions but they were happy to give the project a try. Teachers had a good appreciation of the pedagogy behind the project and were keen to develop their children's approaches to learning through chess. I explained fully to the parents why we were embarking on the project, and the feedback from them was initially – and has remained – very positive. And as for the children, they saw it, and still see it, as a chance to play games instead of having lessons!

And so we began.

How chess is organised at Cumnor

Chess now forms part of the school curriculum and involves all the pupils. Importantly, chess is offered at all levels of ability but special provisions have been made for very able players.

All children in Key Stage 2 are introduced to chess. They have a 45-minute chess lesson once every two weeks. In Years 3 and 4, I take the chess lesson and am supported by the class teacher or teaching assistant.

In Years 3 and 4, the children are taught how each piece moves, what 'good' moves look like and why. Sessions also cover basic principles including how to check, achieve check-mate or stalemate. We also look at more of the fundamental and obvious transferable skills, and focus mainly on tactics. We actively teach them, and show them, how what they learn on the chess board can also be applied to real-life situations.

In Years 5 and 6, some of the more in-depth critical thinking skills are taught: strategy, consequences and seeing the bigger picture. For example: what is a significant threat and what is a perceived threat? They learn that a small sacrifice now should lead to greater gains later on. They appreciate that when a plan goes wrong a decision is essential: should you persevere, adapt your strategy or start again?

Whichever year group is playing chess, the concentration and motivation of the children is almost palpable. In the classrooms, there is a hush appropriate to a more sacred place, broken only by the sigh and click of moved pieces and the muted exchange of necessary dialogue.

Our chess lessons are shared between two teachers. Andrew takes half the children – those who have shown a real aptitude for the game and need some advanced skills training. I take the other half of the class, continuing with teaching simpler strategies and tactics, and constantly referring to the transferable skills being developed.

Competitive chess

Although not the primary aim, some children have gone on to excel at chess. In everything we do at Cumnor, we hope to ignite a spark in every child, enhancing their lives and encouraging them to find out what they are good at and what they are passionate about. This may be art, playing an instrument, maths calculations or chess. All our children have become good chess players and learned to apply the skills acquired along the way. A few have shown exceptional abilities which may otherwise have been left undiscovered. They have gone on to play successfully in local and national tournaments, represent the county and become members of the local chess club, where they give the adult members a serious challenge!

We also run a separate after-school club for those children inspired by the game, where the focus is more on developing chess skills and strategy at a higher level and preparing them for tournaments and matches in the Oxfordshire Schools Chess League.

The professional perspective: specialist support and input

My strong belief in the educational value of the game led to the engagement of Andrew Varney to tutor pupils of above-average ability. If a school arranges for differentiated provision in all subjects, to accommodate the varied needs of learners, then chess should not be an exception.

In a brief account of his perception of the place of chess, not merely in terms of educational worth but as a life-enhancing pursuit, and his approach to teaching the game to children of all ages, levels of ability, attitudes and responses, Andrew conveys something of the richness and sheer fun that his intervention adds to the enthusiastic participation of the Cumnor Primary School chess players.

Around the time I started coaching chess professionally, I was asked how I viewed the teaching of the game. I summarised my answer as: the teaching should be enthusiastic, entertaining and encouraging, and the content should be relevant, realistic and rewarding. Perhaps the following examples may illustrate what I mean:

■ When teaching how chess pieces move, one of my Year 2 pupils spotted the word 'shop' when I wrote 'bishop' on the board. This led me to the Harry Potter joke which I now use regularly with primary schoolchildren:
Q: Where do bishops do their shopping?
A: Diagonal All(e)y – they are not allowed to go anywhere else!

■ How do I explain a threat rather than just an attack? I ask the pupils to imagine they are being attacked by a teddy bear, which always evokes laughter. 'Exactly!' I reply. 'You would laugh, and you don't have to do anything about it. But now imagine you are being attacked by a grizzly bear who could kill you with one swipe of a paw ...' This calls for different thinking and response about the level of threat in a game of chess.

Cross-curricular teaching strategies

Some teaching strategies draw upon areas of the curriculum; history frequently provides thought-provoking examples.

For example, when teaching about 'double threats' I sometimes do this by writing '1066' on the board and asking the pupils what it means to them. Sometimes they know about the Battle of Hastings, sometimes not. Very rarely do they know about the Battle of Stamford Bridge where King Harold, having defeated the invading Norsemen, was obliged to rush his army all the length of England to face, exhausted, William the Conqueror's waiting force; a classic example of the double threat! I find it of direct relevance to the difficulty of dealing with the double threat in chess and I believe the children come to appreciate it too.

I analyse, with the players, the opening stage of the chess game as preparation for the main battle:

- Central control – when preparing for any battle, you first want to control the battleground. Historically it might mean getting onto higher ground; in defending a city it might mean placing snipers in key places; in modern warfare it usually means taking out radar and communications. In chess it means controlling the centre, especially the four squares d4, e4, d5 and e5.

- Development – get your army out of bed and onto the battlefield (i.e. get your pieces out into active positions)!

- King safety – this is important because checkmate (effectively taking the king ransom) is the goal of the battle. When war is threatened, the leaders of a country are taken to safety – for example: the president of the United States is taken to Air Force One.

Eyes-head-hand

Unlike in an exam or test, because of the touch-move rule in chess, you cannot cross out your answer and write another one. Therefore, we must play chess with eyes-head-hand. This is probably my most common catchphrase, and I use it at all levels, from beginner to the most advanced students.

I believe eyes-head-hand is also of relevance to taking exams: *read the question carefully, plan the answer and write.*

Creative approaches to chess

Chess needs to be fun, creative and challenging. I use chess puzzles for different situations and at different levels. Here are a few examples from a recent autumn term, based upon 'story time'. This involves a series of sessions based on puzzles set out as stories which the children try to solve (mostly in groups). These include:

- 'Bullet Chess', based on a famous puzzle by Sam Loyd.

- 'A 36-Year Analysis', using one of my favourite real-life end-game studies.

■ 'A Matter of Direction' and 'Mystery of the Missing Piece', which are both retrograde analysis puzzles taken from the book *The Chess Mysteries of Sherlock Holmes* by Raymond M. Smullyan (2012).

As a special focus during the week leading up to Halloween, I have used: 'Tales of the Unexpected', which features dressing up in wizard's hat and cloak and dimming the lights; an analysis of a game in the 'Halloween Gambit' (a crazy variation on the Four Knights opening) referencing the pawns advancing unstoppably like zombies; handing out plenty of Halloween-themed sweets for correct or interesting answers and general participation; and a mini-tournament playing the chess variant game 'Ghost Chess' (an interesting idea from *My First Chess Book* by Jessica E. Prescott (2014)).

Chess as a learning continuum

Identifying potentially gifted chess players is not as important as some might think. We believe it is about encouraging and providing opportunities for the young chess players at their own level. For some, that means moving on with their game consistently and determinedly, step by step, even up to playing at junior international level. For others, it is a less competitive game played for pleasure, and developing, in the process, qualities of character and values: confidence, critical thinking, learning how to win and lose with grace.

Teaching chess, as with any area of learning, involves teaching along a continuum. This is one of the factors that make coaching so rewarding. Sharing in the joy of the first checkmate by a child who is never going to be the top chess player in the school is just as poignant as seeing two of the original players from a chess club you formed long ago playing in the main British Chess Championship. There is great satisfaction in seeing a team you have managed and coached winning prizes in national tournaments, but hearing from a grateful parent that playing chess has given their child the confidence they needed to take up other competitive activities is just as rewarding.

Research

Research is being carried out into the possible rewards of chess for children with SEN and claims that chess may lead to positive educational outcomes for children with attention deficit hyperactivity disorder (ADHD), although no definitive evidence has emerged yet.[1] Children with ADHD (and those on the autistic spectrum) appear to benefit because the game calls for silence, focus, concentration and the need to be calm and sit still.

Like most advocates of the game and its educational value, we are not disconcerted by a recent piece of research (Education Endowment Foundation and Institute of Education, 2016) which found no perceptible long-term gains in the assessment scores of children accustomed to playing chess. Our experience has given us ample first-hand evidence of the benefits offered to children by learning chess.

The children's perspective

When 120 of the children at Cumnor were asked about chess in the curriculum, 93% said they enjoyed chess, 89% believed that chess helped them with their thinking skills and 81% said that it helped with their concentration.

Individual responses included the following views. The children believed that chess helped them with:

- 'Thinking about things before I react.'
- 'My patience – because sometimes it takes a long time before people move their piece.'
- 'Being a lot quieter. I get time to be peaceful and still.'
- 'Keeping calm and focusing on what I need to do.'
- 'Thinking about the right thing to do next.'

Conclusion

By the time our children leave Cumnor, having had chess lessons for four years, their ways of thinking and their approaches to problems have become highly developed. The

---

1 A useful summary of recent research studies can be found at: http://www.chessinschools.co.uk/ research.htm.

children can see through problems, deal with their opponent's plans and tactics and develop quite complex strategies.

It has been noted by teachers at the local secondary school that, by Year 7, our children are able to function at higher levels than many other children, thinking through what they are being asked to do and applying critical thinking skills to their work. Parents, too, have noticed that their children are now better equipped for secondary school education: 'Parents recognise how effectively their children are prepared for the challenges of secondary school, when they leave Cumnor at the end of Year 6' (Ofsted, 2017: 1).

Chess has now become an established part of what is special about Cumnor Primary School; it embodies an approach that goes beyond the straightforward teaching of curriculum subjects. We believe strongly that chess enhances the way the children live their lives, giving them additional skills and strategies which they can apply to their work and play, and approaches that will stay with them as they grow and develop.

Further reading and useful links

Barden, L. (1980). *Play Better Chess*. London: Octopus Books.

Coakley, J. (2004). *Winning Chess Exercises for Kids*. Montréal, QC: Chess'n Math Association.

Education Endowment Foundation and Institute of Education (2016). *Chess in Schools: Evaluation Report and Executive Summary*. Available at: https://educationendowmentfoundation.org.uk/public/files/Projects/Evaluation_Reports/EEF_Project_Report_Chess_in_Schools.pdf.

Kongsted, C. (2005). *Beat the Grandmasters: Can You Rise to the Occasion?* London: Gambit Publications.

Meyers, J. (2016). Why Offer Chess in Schools? In Kasparov Chess Foundation Europe, *The Benefits of Chess in Education: Examples of Research and Papers on Chess and Education*. Available at: http://www.academiadesah.ro/wp-content/uploads/2016/08/research_kcfe.pdf, pp. 3–5.

Ofsted (2017). Short Inspection of Cumnor Church of England Primary School (Voluntary Controlled) (25 September). Available at: http://www.cumnorprimaryschool.co.uk/wp-content/uploads/2015/04/Cumnor-CofE-Primary-School-OFSTED-Report-September-2017.pdf.

Prescott, J. E. (2014). *My First Chess Book: 35 Easy and Fun Chess-Based Activities for Children Aged 7 Years+*. London: CICO Books.

Shannon, C. (1950). Programming a Computer for Playing Chess, *Philosophical Magazine*, Ser. 7, Vol. 41, No. 314.

Smullyan, R. M. (2012). *The Chess Mysteries of Sherlock Holmes*. New York: Dover Publications.

Chess in Schools and Communities (CSC): http://www.chessinschools.co.uk

Kasparov Chess Foundation: http://kasparovchessfoundation.org

About the contributors

Ed Read

Ed Read trained as a teacher at Westminster College, Oxford and then followed this up with an MA in educational research. Cumnor is his third substantive headship. During his first two headships he developed an interest in the broader curriculum – first at Stonesfield Primary, which had a values-based curriculum, and then at Kingham, where a form of growth mindset was used to enhance the quality of the children's learning.

Dr Andrew Varney

Dr Andrew Varney returned to chess when his children discovered one of his old score books from his school days. This led to him starting a chess club at his children's primary school. After taking on more and more junior chess organisation and coaching on a voluntary basis, he left his job in research and development to teach chess to children professionally. He currently teaches chess in nine different schools each week, runs an evening chess club for county-level junior players, and coaches many children on a one-to-one basis, from beginner up to junior international level. He also manages to work part-time as a superconducting-magnet design engineer.

Chapter 15

Building Goblin Cars

Liz Tansley, head teacher, James Veness and Christopher Savage, The Hendreds CE Primary School, Oxfordshire

From a wide choice of learning activities, all deserving of documentation, The Hendreds CE Primary School elected to describe their work building a Goblin car. They did so because of some noteworthy and fascinating features of the project:

■ The challenge of involving primary-age pupils in the construction of something as ambitious, daring and complex as a kit car, hopefully conveying to them that extraordinary things were within their capacity.

- The expertise required of the teachers in guiding the project to a successful conclusion; and the adoption of a project involving not merely technology, but also the acquisition of genuine engineering skills on the part of the pupils.

- The enabling of pupils to gain vital understanding into the links between mathematics, engineering and design.

- The development of an early insight into the intricacy and wonder of engineering and an awareness of its value as a domain of knowledge and expertise.

- The degree of teamwork, between both girls and boys, in the construction of the car; and the discipline, skills and self-awareness (apart from the thrill and the fun) developed in the experience of driving the car they had constructed.

- The never-to-be-forgotten participation of pupils, teachers and parents in the great 'Gathering of Goblins' at Goodwood.

Background

The Hendreds is a small primary school in the village of East Hendred in Oxfordshire. It has around 140 pupils aged from 4 to 11. The number of pupils who speak English as an additional language (EAL), who are disadvantaged or who have special educational needs (SEN) is below the national average. The school was voluntary aided by the Church of England until it became an academy in 2013, when it joined the family of schools in the Oxford Diocesan Schools Trust.

The Hendreds has a history of developing innovative practice, establishing Latin, judo and latterly engineering as part of the broader curriculum. We serve a rural catchment that is socially and economically diverse, making us an important agent in forming a community that has respect for all and the development of everyone's potential at its heart. Academic achievement is important, but it is only one aspect of developing rounded individuals who can lead a good life and be true to themselves.

Our mission statement, 'Value who we are, and who we can become', summarises our dual commitment to welcoming and valuing the children and families who come to us, and transforming their life chances. Our pupils are drawn from diverse socio-economic backgrounds, but, in a rural community, it is very easy for the diverse cultures of the various sub-groups to be hidden. Within the children's homes, the challenges facing those who are economically disadvantaged can be huge; but, interestingly, we have challenges with the more advantaged children too, who can also underperform.

A broad and balanced curriculum

At The Hendreds we are dedicated to the transforming power of education through a broad and challenging curriculum, designed to enrich our pupils intellectually and spiritually, and nurture their social, moral and emotional development. The creative and expressive arts, environmental study based on the Forest School ethos, the learning of French, Latin and PE all constitute crucial and consistent aspects of the pupils' education.

We like to think that small schools can make big people. We try to develop positive attitudes across the curriculum, including in PE. In our culture of sport for all, they become fitter, more mentally resilient and join in with a real sense of thrill and passion when we hold our sports tournaments (six times a year).

Leadership

The school drives a team-based approach to improvement. Working in a small school of five classes makes this possible, keeping in mind the adage 'observation followed by conversation'. Senior leaders engender a work ethic for younger colleagues and pupils that says: 'Every aspect of the school day is of worth.' Senior staff help to lead breakfast club, lunchtimes (we do not employ canteen staff), playtime supervision and after-school clubs. We discuss what is happening in the classrooms at least three times during the day: at the breakfast meeting, during lunchtime (when we are circulating in the hall) and at the end of the day.

'Swap-arounds' are one of the strategies that are used every year. Not only does this help to build relationships, but it also develops less experienced teachers' understanding of leading a subject across a key stage and gives them experience of seeing a subject or topic across a range of year groups. They develop an overview of standards and progression, behaviour management and meaningful relationships with all children. The children enjoy the variety of lessons and the different teachers who work with them. We are here to make the ordinary extraordinary.

Child's view/voice

The structure of the curriculum and the life of the school are consistently examined from the viewpoint of the child. This is a core function for the leadership team and is a non-negotiable of the school.

As the children progress through the school they become more independent and take on additional responsibilities: taking on a 'watchdog duty' at playtimes, being a 'lunch buddy' to a younger child and contributing towards whole-school assemblies are all examples of this.

We do not have traditional sports clubs (e.g. boys' football team); any opportunity that is worthwhile is available to all children. We wish to ensure that any individual may sing, act, give an opinion, learn a language or play in a team: primary school is all about opening doors and not closing them.

Design and technology

We have chosen to describe in this chapter a particular aspect of our work in design and technology for the following reasons: firstly, because we are convinced of the critical and growing importance of the subject in the education of children now and, increasingly, in the future; and secondly, simply because we believe that the project we describe here is emblematic of the creative, inventive and hugely productive nature of teaching and learning in the school.

The primary national curriculum guidance on design and technology states that the subject makes an essential contribution to the creativity, culture, wealth and well-being of the nation. It highlights the profoundly important knowledge and skills that pupils derive from engagement in the subject: 'They acquire a broad range of subject knowledge and draw on disciplines such as mathematics, science, engineering, computing and art. Pupils learn how to take risks, becoming resourceful, innovative, enterprising and capable citizens' (Department for Education, 2013: 1).

The critical dependence of design and technology on mathematics, science and computing for its realisation and implementation is made abundantly clear. But among the formidable range of skills set out in the national curriculum subject content – which combine to achieve mastery of the subject – is a reference in the evaluation section, easy to miss, that invites consideration of, and possible engagement with, a wider range of curriculum.

It simply urges that children should 'understand how key events and individuals in design and technology have helped shape the world' (Department for Education, 2013: 3).

It takes us back to the need for pupils to come to an understanding, at an early age, of the centrality and importance of design and technology in our lives, and to the form and nature of the world in which they will grow up. The importance of helping them to an understanding and appreciation of this can hardly be exaggerated. But education systems, down the ages, might be said to have been less than successful in conveying the inestimable worth of the discipline and profession of engineering. The country and the economy continue to suffer from a failure to recruit capable young people into the profession. This is possibly due, in part, to its association with the hard mechanical/industrial practice of another age and the undeniably challenging skills involved, with little account too often taken of its extraordinary, and sometimes seemingly miraculous, achievements.

This chapter, which is concerned with an account of the construction and use by pupils of a Goblin car, might be said to represent these disparate parts of the engineering experience: on the one hand, the challenging part (the grind, if you like) of mastering and applying the range of complex skills demanded by the construction of the car, and thereafter the realisation of a structure to delight in, the opportunity to learn and apply the adult skill of driving, and the glamour and excitement of participating in a festival of engineers.

This is a highly ingenious way of introducing pupils to the engineering process, of enabling them to master elemental but important skills, of developing confidence in their capacity for learning and, above all, providing them with an inspiring insight into the wonders that design, technology and engineering make possible. It has achieved the extraordinary aim of teaching them to build and drive a car. But to develop an understanding of something of even greater significance ('how key events and individuals have helped to shape the world'), teachers find it necessary to refer to curricular areas beyond science, technology, engineering and mathematics (STEM); for example, enquiry, debate, reading, research and investigation, language in its various forms and, most frequently, history. Of course, much of this knowledge is acquired over time and in its proper place, but it is important that children come to understand the immense importance of design and technology – not merely in terms of how it has shaped our world for the better, in all kinds of ways, but for the role it will play in influencing the circumstances and times in which the children will mature and what their part in it might be.

Building and driving a Goblin car

We were first introduced to the concept of Goblin cars in 2011 by a scientist, who was a parent of one of our children. The Greenpower Education Trust is a charitable organisation committed to inspiring more young people to become interested in, and thoroughly involved and engaged in, the so-called STEM school subjects. Their project was set up in 1999 to encourage pupils to design, build and race their own electric cars, within professionally drafted specifications, and with mentoring and some practical assistance from experienced adults.

The construction and racing of the Goblin kit car is an exciting and attractive way into practical engagement in the sometimes daunting STEM subjects and areas of learning for primary pupils, both girls and boys, aged from 9 to 11. The kit includes all the parts and components required to build a complete car, apart from the bodywork, which is left to the creativity of the teams. The kit can be dismantled at the end of the season and used by other groups.

We considered very carefully the appropriateness of taking part in the enterprise and what the likely educational benefits for our pupils might be. We decided that it would provide, literally, a perfect vehicle for a meaningful STEM project. After discussions with the parent–teacher association (PTA), and a detailed exposition to them, they agreed to provide the near £1,000 of funding required to purchase a new Goblin kit car.

Starting out

The memory of our first involvement in the project remains with us vividly. There was great excitement when several boxes full of tubes, wires and tyres arrived with detailed instructions on how to build the car. Initially, we decided that the project would take place after school, outside of curriculum time, and would be run by teachers with the support of parent volunteers who had some interest in mechanical work.

The attendance for this was always free to pupils, but they had to commit to regular attendance. We thought that commitment would be an issue after the initial excitement had worn off, but we were pleasantly surprised by the numbers: all Year 6 pupils have wanted to be involved every year. From the outset, the target was to build the car in readiness for 'The Gathering of Goblins' at the historic Goodwood Motor Circuit.

Our first task is always to familiarise the children with the tools we will be using. This not only gives them the vocabulary needed to communicate with each other ('Please will you pass the 12 mm spanner from the socket set?'), but it also ensures that they know how to use the tools safely.

Building the car

To get the full value out of constructing the cars, the sessions are led by members of the senior leadership team. We feel that this ensures the quality and equality of the learning process and keeps the sessions focused on the objectives that this venture offers. It is only when the car-building starts that the real learning begins. We encourage the children to build from the plans unaided. This is when teamwork and cooperation is really developed. It is rewarding to hear children asking a friend for a 13 mm ring spanner or something from the socket set, when only a few weeks previously the only tool in the toolbox they could identify was a hammer.

Although we suggest the stages of progression in building the car, we are very hands-off; we allow the children to make mistakes and learn from them. An example of this is the construction of the car frame: this involves screwing together over 20 tubes using Allen keys, and it is almost inevitable that some will be upside down or the wrong way round and will need to be refitted. This does mean that building the car takes longer than it might, but we feel the benefits far outweigh the extra time required.

Once the frame has been built, the next set of tasks are to fit the front and rear axles, the steering column, brakes, motor, drive belt, seating, wiring and finally the bodywork. The bodywork is designed and made by the children every year. Typically, we use recycled, lightweight boarding (we are unsure of the material but it was previously used as advertising boards!), but at times the children have chosen to use unwanted CDs for the side panels, and on another occasion they chose two-litre plastic drinks bottles, for which we were awarded a prize for the 'most eco-friendly car' at Goodwood.

In the making of the car, we see pupils:

- Benefitting from the school ethos of risk-taking.
- Developing commitment (modelled by teachers).
- Developing shared responsibility.
- Learning basic life skills (handling tools and knowing their names).
- Acquiring an understanding of engineering.

- Developing an awareness of the methods needed to assemble an element of the kit car (e.g. steering assembly).

- Appreciating the qualities of the materials used for the components.

- Developing an awareness of the health and safety precautions to be taken during the assembly process.

- Working as part of a team.

The evidence of the pupils' learning has led us, in recent years, to include the construction and practice sessions within the school day as part of the curriculum for all Year 6s. We feel that everyone should benefit from the learning opportunities this project provides. Therefore, if it is good enough to do as an after-school club, then it is something that all children should take part in. This is in line with our philosophy at the school: doors should be opened for all children. We have always considered the project to be suitable for Year 6s only, however – this is because there is an element of physical strength required and the cars have been developed to suit a child of this size.

Driving the car

Once the car has been built, which takes about six weeks, we are ready to develop driving skills on the school playground. This can be very exciting, as most children have no experience of what is required. For safety reasons we begin with just a single battery. With this amount of power the cars will travel at 6–8 mph, allowing for the children's confidence to grow; many of them are very nervous and some extremely overconfident.

After a few sessions we introduce the second battery, which increases the top speed to around 15 mph. If you are driving and manoeuvring at this speed, as an 11-year-old, with your bottom only 6 inches off the ground, this is a thrilling experience. After the initial cautious runs, we lay out sprint and slalom courses so the drivers can hone their skills. At this stage the children become increasingly competitive, but some quickly learn that finding the 'racing line' is more important than seeing how fast you can go.

The very first race meeting we attended was near Bristol on a disused airfield. We were all very keen and green; we didn't realise how competitive many of the other teams would be. It was an amazing success and the children had a fantastic time! The other teams there were very helpful, as were the organisers. It has to be noted that this is always the case at any meetings we have attended. There is a strong camaraderie among all the competitors.

The Gathering of Goblins

During the first year we went to our first 'Gathering of Goblins' at the Goodwood track. Race day at Goodwood is quite an event, and up to 90 cars normally attend. This is the day that the children get to showcase their product and skills. There are generally six to eight children with each car, plus parents, friends, mechanics and teachers. The place is always buzzing with excitement. The event provides an arena where the children are challenged physically and mentally, but they know they have the support of the team around them. The exhilaration is transferred to other pupils back at school as news of the Sunday at Goodwood spreads, and this helps uptake for the following year.

One year we had a larger than usual Year 6 class, and were presented with the problem of too many children wanting to attend the Goodwood meeting. The solution was to run our own event in addition to the big meeting. This proved to be an enormous success and it is something we will repeat annually. Every Year 6 pupil took part and most had a member of their family watching.

The format of the 'Gathering of Goblins' has remained fairly similar during the years that we have been attending. With competitors having to arrive for registration at 8.30 a.m., and an hour-and-a-half's journey for us, it is an early start. After the drivers' safety briefing and the handing out of wristbands (only drivers and two adults are allowed in the pits), the morning's events begin at 9 a.m. Each car has six turns at each discipline: the slalom, the drag and the sprint. The children take it in turns to drive the car, perform the push start and manoeuvre the car back to the starting point each time.

For these 10- and 11-year-old novice drivers who have had limited experience in driving the car at school, the first drive at Goodwood – performing in front of a large crowd and racing against other cars (normally in groups of three) – is a nerve-wracking experience and a steep learning curve! Some cope better than others. Many of the children have produced near-perfect drives under this pressure. However, several others have ploughed through cones, collected many time penalties and thoroughly tested the durability of the car. It is at these testing times that team support is essential.

At the end of the hectic morning's racing we stop for a peaceful picnic lunch with the children and parents. It is at this point that the drivers' names go into a hat and the luck of the draw decides which children will have the privilege of driving 'The Lap of Champions'. This involves all the cars at the event being on the track at the same time, fitted with a sensor to time the lap and racing a full 2.4-mile circuit. This part of the day has provided us with lots of highs and lows!

Highs and lows

On our first visit to Goodwood, we watched from the spectators' bank, expectantly peering into the distance as our car came into sight. It appeared to be running very well in comparison to those around it when a catastrophe unfolded before our eyes. As our car raced into the final bend, we could see that it was slowing and continued to do so until it finally came to a stop. To the driver's embarrassment, the car was rescued by the breakdown support vehicle and towed back to the pit lane. The drive belt had snapped.

Perhaps the most exciting final lap involving one of our children was when our car was being driven by a particularly competitive Year 6 girl. She didn't take kindly to some questionable overtaking tactics on the final straight. She responded, after some bold manoeuvring, by gently easing her adversary into the pit wall and then sailing on to the finish line – it was like watching those international racing stars, Vettel and Hamilton, going head to head!

Our visits to the Sussex track are seldom trouble free. There are always mechanical issues, successes and disappointments. Some of these are caused by the drivers, some by wear and tear and some by overly helpful parents. Our most dramatic incident falls into the latter category. On our arrival at Goodwood, we have to unload the cars and equipment and then remove all vans and trailers to a distant car park. We then have to check everything is in order before the officials inspect the car, ensuring that it is safe and compliant with all the rules.

It was just before the official reached our car that disaster struck. An enthusiastic parent volunteer had completed the final stages of the wiring. Unfortunately, he attempted to connect the final wire to the wrong battery terminal. Suddenly, whoosh! The flames shot along the wires, sending helpers leaping all over the place. The offending connection was removed and the flames died down relatively quickly – thankfully, a fire extinguisher was not required. However, we were left looking at a car with smouldering plastic wires in need of replacement with just 15 minutes left before all cars needed to be on the start line. The event organisers came to the rescue and provided a new set of wires to attach, and with just minutes to spare we arrived on the starting grid!

Ongoing developments

Our annual car construction is now an established part of the curriculum for Year 6 children. But a rich, cross-curricular undertaking such as this should be a rich experience for all, not a select few. Not all children can race the cars at Goodwood in the annual

'Gathering of Goblins', so any child who cannot make the race day (it is always a Sunday) is able to compete in an after-school event at school which is run by staff.

All teachers enter the profession wanting to make a difference to the children they meet, but unfortunately time restrictions and unforeseen workloads can dampen these ideals. We try very hard to encourage members of staff not to see these opportunities as add-ons, but as part of the rightful expectations of our children's education. As always with long-term school projects, a dedicated team of adults is required. These adults must see the value of the task and be committed to the whole-school ethos. As this project is part of the school curriculum, it is members of staff who coordinate it, apart from one reliable ex-parent, Martin Simmons, who is our resident expert on race day at Goodwood.

We are now in our seventh year of car construction and the popularity of the project has meant that we had to invest in a second car three years ago. The number of children studying at the school has steadily increased over recent years, and the growing numbers dictated that we return to the PTA to ask for funding for a second car. We managed to find a second-hand one and the PTA provided the cash. This has meant we have been running two cars at Goodwood for the last three years – and have had to upgrade our mode of transport to the track.

Conclusion

If we think of words to sum up what we are trying to do at The Hendreds, it is making the curriculum aspirational, optimistic, ambitious and intellectually demanding. Our expectations of the children and staff are high – another saying gleaned from a consultant was 'a low-level conversation is a low-level conversation'; you can substitute education for conversation. We have a 'can do' attitude; we want relationships and experiences to be authentic.

The extra meeting, the weekend trip to Goodwood, building the cars, sourcing parts and transporting the vehicles all takes time and commitment from members of staff over a period of years. However, we feel that the gains for the children are so plentiful that it is well worth these extra hours. The children are involved in a project that is real, not a scenario invented by teachers. They work as a team when they build it, drive it and compete in it.

The Goblin car project has enabled us to deliver the STEM subjects in a meaningful and practical way. The children are involved in a purposeful project in which they achieve an end product and learn life skills, possibly career-inspiring ones.

Further reading and useful links

Department for Education (2013). Design and Technology Programmes of Study: Key Stages 1 and 2: National Curriculum in England (September). Available at: https://www.gov.uk/government/uploads/system/uploads/attachment_data/file/239041/PRIMARY_national_curriculum_-_Design_and_technology.pdf.

Department of Education (2011). *Success Through STEM: STEM Strategy. In Response to the 'Report of the STEM Review'*. Available at: https://www.economy-ni.gov.uk/sites/default/files/publications/del/STEM%20Strategy-Success%20through%20STEM.pdf.

Department of Education (2012). *Success Through STEM*: *One Year On*. Available at: http://www.economy-ni.gov.uk/sites/default/files/publications/del/Success%20through%20STEM-One%20Year%20On.pdf.

Flinn, E. and Patel, S. (2016). *The Really Useful Primary Design and Technology Book*. Abingdon and New York: Routledge.

Ignotofsky, R. (2017). *Women in Science: 50 Fearless Pioneers Who Changed the World*. London: Wren and Rook.

Morgan, R. and Kirby, C. (2016). *The UK STEM Education Landscape*. London: Royal Academy of Engineering. Available at: https://www.raeng.org.uk/publications/reports/uk-stem-education-landscape.

Ofsted (2016). The Hendreds Church of England School Report (25 November). Available at: https://reports.ofsted.gov.uk/inspection-reports/find-inspection-report/provider/ELS/140473.

Greenpower Education Trust: https://www.greenpower.co.uk

About the contributors

Liz Tansley

Liz Tansley's early childhood experiences of schooling in Scotland shaped her deep interest in how education makes or breaks life chances. A master's degree with the Open University, working with a local authority for many years on moderation audits, reviewing children's literature for the journal *Signal* and an abiding commitment to an inclusive education have all informed her work. She moved on from her role as deputy head of a large (400+) primary school in 1990, taking up the challenge of a small school. She has since taken The Hendreds Primary School from 60 pupils to 140, and she is still as passionate as ever about the enriched curriculum.

James Veness

James Veness' first role at The Hendreds was as a sports coach, a post he held at the school while completing his sports and coaching degree. Having had his talent spotted by the head teacher, he then embarked on a teaching degree alongside his training at The Hendreds and has subsequently gone on to become a senior teacher and a member of the senior leadership team. With the team ethic being essential to the success of initiatives at The Hendreds, James has also become an integral part of the Goblin car project.

Christopher Savage

Following a successful early business career, Christopher Savage arrived at The Hendreds as a student teacher in 2005 and has since then taught every age group in the school and risen to the position of deputy head teacher. A wealth of coaching skills from his sporting background, which includes a black belt in judo, has informed his pedagogy in raising standards through engaging the whole child.

Chapter 16
A Creative Approach to History in the Curriculum

Stephanie Daley, head of curriculum development, London Fields Primary School, Hackney

London Fields Primary School holds the prestigious Gold Quality Mark award of the Historical Association, which is secured only after comprehensive and rigorous scrutiny and assessment. In making the award, the assessor felt it appropriate to note: 'The school has a challenging context with FSM [free school meals], MEG [minority ethnic groups] and EAL [English as an additional language] all far in excess of the National Average' (2015: 1). This emphasises the extent of the achievement of teachers and pupils in relation to the quality of history education and learning that were observed, and the notable progress made by children, many of whom lack the material resources and cultural experiences of their more advantaged peers.

The Historical Association's review – which covers the curriculum, teaching and learning, pupil achievement, the style and form of leadership, monitoring, evaluation and assessment – refers to particular aspects of practice and performance that are dealt with only fleetingly in Stephanie Daley's account. One feature it highlights, in particular, is the wide-ranging discussions which were witnessed, during which pupils drew upon examples from local and national history to illustrate their knowledge and understanding.

It may be worth highlighting one further observation from the report on the range, depth, quality and impact of the school's enrichment activities: 'As a result of one project a pupil's work is being displayed in the Museum of London. This exemplifies the high quality work that emerges from enrichment and reflects the enthusiasm students have for history education at their school' (2015: 6). Pupils also engage their parents in their history study and pursuits and win their interest and participation.

Background

London Fields is a large primary school where most pupils belong to minority ethnic groups and approximately half of the pupils speak English as an additional language (EAL). Just over half of all pupils are eligible for support through pupil premium funding, well above the national average. The head teacher is a national leader of education (NLE) and the deputy head teacher is a specialist leader of education (SLE). London Fields works closely with several schools in a supportive capacity, including one in a neighbouring authority. The school has achieved the Gold Artsmark and Primary Science Quality Mark awards, as well as the Historical Association's Gold Quality Mark.

Studying history

History has always been a subject which we are passionate about at London Fields. Studying history gives pupils the opportunity to develop an understanding of why the world and its people are the way they are today. They begin to ask questions as they explore the diversity of human experience, past lives and societies. As a school in an urban environment, we continuously audit our curriculum for cultural bias and tailor the topics and discussions within them to meet the questions and issues our pupils may have about their heritage and identity. We ensure that we discuss important societal shifts, who made them possible and why they are important to us today.

We devote time to helping the children appreciate the uncertain and fallible nature of history: the likelihood that the passage of time, or deliberate misrepresentation by the powerful or victorious, may well obscure the truth or accuracy of what happened in the past.

We encourage the children to consider and suggest:

- Why historical figures may have wanted to misrepresent things as they really were.

- The danger, injury and wrong arising from such manipulation.

- Possible occasions or events in history that might have been falsified or distorted.

- Contemporary events that might be open to misrepresentation.

- The power of the written word to shape opinion.

- Factors that make it more difficult in the modern age to misrepresent the facts.

- The importance of historians and history in our lives.

Developing metacognitive thinking and deep learning

From September 2014, we have followed the new history curriculum which focuses on British history. The intention is that by the end of their primary education, the children will have a chronological understanding of British history from the Stone Age to the present day, and be able to draw comparisons and make connections between different time periods and their own lives. Interlinked with this is the need to look at world history. At London Fields, the children explore the ancient civilisations of Egypt, Greece and Benin, developing their understanding of trends over time and across concurrent civilisations.

At London Fields we teach history through investigation and enquiry. The children develop an understanding of how history has had an impact on our lives today, locally, nationally and internationally. While it is important for the children to have awareness and knowledge, we wish to encourage independent and critical thinking which will foster an understanding of 'why' as well as 'who', 'what', 'when' and 'where'. Lessons are planned so there is time for discussion and debate, fostering an environment of enquiry which enables the children to revise and justify their opinions, as well as encouraging them to ask, as well as answer, questions about history.

Our aims and objectives in history are designed to encourage pupils to relate concepts and issues from their exploration of the past with their present-day lives – here are two examples:

■ To enhance children's appreciation of spiritual, moral, social and cultural (SMSC) issues through the study of history – giving pupils a historical education that draws on their knowledge and experience and makes regular and purposeful links with SMSC issues, both in the past and in present-day society.

■ To develop a sense of chronology – ensuring that dedicated curriculum time is given to exploring the chronology of the civilisation being studied (including the duration) to develop the children's sense of period, continuity and change and the bigger picture of history of the world.

Curriculum provision

Because history is so highly valued by us, it is granted significant curriculum time. Most year groups spend two terms a year studying a history topic. Although there is a notable focus on British history, the study of ancient civilisations allows the children to make links and connect cultures in terms of both time and tradition. An effort is made to increase the relevance of the topics studied by making links, where possible, with life in modern Britain – for example, connections between current issues and emotions surrounding immigration and the settlement of Huguenots in east London in the 17th century.

As part of our cultural bias overview, we have examined our curriculum and designed lessons which will excite and fascinate young learners, but also help them to debate and reflect upon historical events and build up a greater sense of their own values and identities. In 2017, we introduced a 'Heritage Week' to enable all the children to connect with, and be proud of, their personal and national histories. This allowed us to dedicate curriculum time to boosting cultural self-esteem and developing an understanding of the diverse history of Britain. This was such a successful unit that we have now developed a new unit for Year 6 around some of the areas of study.

Through working with the Black Cultural Archives in Brixton, I have developed a better understanding of how important it is to teach topics from a wide range of perspectives and to teach the children to investigate the reasons behind these perspectives, particularly when the event is perceived as 'wrong' or 'negative' in modern times. We hope that this will give them the toolkit to empathise and challenge viewpoints they disagree with, both now and in the future.

An overview of the history curriculum

We believe that history should be an interactive subject which strives to ignite children's natural curiosity. All pupils are provided for in lessons, regardless of gender, race, disability or the financial cost of external visits or visitors to the school. History forms part of the school curriculum policy to provide a broad and balanced education to all children. We recognise the fact that in all classes there are children of widely different abilities in history, so we seek to provide suitable learning opportunities for all pupils by matching the challenge of the task to the capability of the child.

Each unit includes opportunities for the children to investigate and handle artefacts, analyse pictorial evidence, view historical footage, take part in role play activities, visit relevant sites and museums and, where appropriate, experience oral history, engaging with historical characters and ways of life. The table below shows the history topics that are currently being delivered across Key Stages 1 and 2.

	Year 1	Year 2	Year 3	Year 4	Year 5	Year 6
Autumn term	Geography	Great Fire of London and Plague	Ancient Egypt	The Romans in Britain	Ancient Greece	Second World War
Spring term	Significant People in History	Changes Within Living Memory	Life in Britain from the Stone Age to the Iron Age	Britain's Settlement by the Anglo-Saxons, Scots and Vikings	Ancient Benin	Immigration in Britain
Summer term	Geography	Geography	Geography	Geography	Geography	Geography

At present, our curriculum provides a rich variety of topics that cover everything from the Stone Age to entering the European Union. Each topic has an overarching question which the children refer to at the end of each lesson to see how different events and actions can accumulate to build a deeper understanding of a historical period. They explore this question using a variety of investigative skills, engaging and becoming more familiar with historical methodology, such as analysing and debating the reliability of sources, making comparisons between historical periods, devising historically valid questions, drawing conclusions from sources and making links between events. Underpinning this is an emphasis on the children understanding the world around them, their country and their values. Some examples of overarching questions are set out in the tables below.

Key Stage 1			
	Autumn	**Spring**	**Summer**
Year 1	Geography Unit	Why do we remember famous people through the ages?	Geography Unit
Year 2	What can we learn from the plague and the Great Fire of London?	Geography Unit	How has daily life changed within living memory, and what does this tell us about Britain's history?

Key Stage 2			
	Autumn	**Spring**	**Summer**
Year 3	Were the Ancient Egyptians a great civilisation?	Geography Unit	Did humans make much progress between the Stone Age and the Iron Age?
Year 4	Did the Romans impact life in Britain?	Geography Unit	Was life better under the Anglo-Saxons, the Scots or the Vikings?
Year 5	Were the Ancient Greeks ahead of their time?	Geography Unit	How can we portray Benin's history accurately?
Year 6	How did the Second World War affect daily life in London?	Geography Unit	When did Britain become diverse?

All topics are mapped out in a SOLO (structure of observed learning outcomes) framework, showing questions which we will be able to answer by accumulating information and which will require deeper learning. We also ask the children to self-assess their learning from each lesson on a SOLO map, so they can see which type of learning allowed them to progress and understand what individual steps they need to take to progress in the next lesson.

The SOLO taxonomy and framework

The SOLO framework is designed to develop pupil thinking and learning and promote metacognition – that is, their capacity to identify where they have arrived in assimilating, accommodating and mastering a particular element or phase in the learning process; understand how they have got there (i.e. recognise the processes and strategies that have brought them successfully to that particular stage); and determine and clarify the skills and knowledge they must utilise to progress to the stage beyond that.

The framework (devised by the Australian psychologist John Biggs and his colleagues) has some resemblance to Piaget's theory of cognitive development and is scaffolded on sequential phases of the 'learning journey'. It is comprised of five levels of development, from a *prestructural phase*, where the pupil's knowledge or understanding of what is being studied is minimal, through to escalating levels of understanding. These culminate in a fifth and final phase, sometimes referred to as the *extended abstract* phase. Mastery of this stage represents the capacity to organise related ideas in a logical sequence, indicative of abstract thinking.

The SOLO framework is designed to achieve the following important objectives in relation to the learning process:

- To enable pupils to identify learning or knowledge, perhaps slight in content but significant in terms of understanding and progression, and to recognise what they have learned or mastered to arrive there.

- To help pupils consider, in a constructive way, what the next steps in their learning will be.

- To involve pupils in a process of linking their previous and future learning.

- To provide pupils with readily comprehended criteria for success in their deliberations.

The framework, correspondingly, supports teachers in mapping pupils' learning and identifying learning intentions for them.

Learning intentions

We use four key historical learning intentions or objectives (based on work by Chris Quigley) that the children will explore over the course of their education at London Fields:

1. To investigate and interpret the past.

2. To build an overview of world history.

3. To understand chronology.

4. To communicate historically.

These help the children to make connections with skills used in previous lessons or previous years.

We believe that getting the children to communicate historically and engage with the curriculum means that they need to have opinions, while also being able to see other points of view. Lessons involve them having to make their own decisions about which events were the most important by either debating their point of view or having to order events in a graph or 'diamond nine' shape, starting with the events which they believe were the most significant, decisive or influential.

Key debating skills can also be taught when a group of students are asked to debate the side of the argument with which they don't agree. This allows them to think more deeply about why certain things happened in history or which values participants in events must have held to make certain decisions. Some example debates have been: should the British Museum give back the Benin Bronzes? Should the UK have taken more evacuees from the *Kindertransport* in the Second World War?

Learning walls and visible learning

We use learning walls to show how history lessons contribute to finding answers for our overarching questions. We put up a range of evidence, from sticky notes of questions or issues which surprised or puzzled the children to photographs of the pupils investigating or role playing. There might also be copies of the children's writing or mind-mapping sheets. Pupils are encouraged to conduct further research at home and this is presented to the class and added to the display. This provides the children with a visual reference of their learning and their increasing knowledge, and an understanding that learning is a journey.

As part of our visible learning journey (Hattie, 2012), we want to build up the children's understanding of key learning behaviours: curiosity, independence, creativity, resilience and embracing challenge. Visible learning can be briefly summarised in the following terms:

■ Visible teaching and learning occurs when there is a clear goal and deliberate practice aimed at attaining mastery of that goal.

■ Feedback is visibly given and sought.

■ Teachers are encouraged to see learning through the eyes of students. Students see teaching as the key to their learning, but they are aware that they can help to teach themselves. Hattie's evidence shows that the greatest effects on student learning occur when teachers become learners of their own teaching and when students become their own teachers.

■ Visible learning students self-monitor, self-evaluate, self-assess and self-teach.

We believe that a key way to do this is through a history curriculum in which we could set the children carefully planned independent tasks and encourage them to embrace the challenges and think creatively to find links or solutions. We also talk a great deal about being wrong and how historians have made mistakes in the past, and how part of being a historian is guesswork.

A lot of our units contain a lesson based around artefacts and clues. The children have to apply their learning to debate whether or not an object is from the period of time they are looking at, what it is and who might have used it. During one lesson, the children were looking at artefacts from the Anglo-Saxon period. They worked together to form a hypothesis and then tested this as more clues were revealed to them by the teacher. Groups of pupils referred to prior learning in their exercise books to piece together their enquiry. In one example, the pupils were given specific dates as a clue; some of them recognised the dates as something they had already learned about. They then researched their exercise books and were able to link King Alfred to their artefact (the Alfred Jewel).

Cross-curricular links with history

Each unit incorporates many cross-curricular links with maths, literacy, geography, art, ICT, personal, social, health and citizenship education (PSHCE) and religious education.

There are strong links between history and the arts at London Fields. Our termly art and design and technology weeks relate to a considerable extent to history topics, with the children developing their artistic skills through historical themes – for example, using kerbstones to build a prehistoric burial site or creating clay versions of the Benin Bronzes. Similarly, music is used as an opportunity to explore the cultural heritage of the civilisations being studied. Each unit will look at an aspect of art from the era, such as Roman pots or Second World War propaganda posters. This allows the children to reflect on how art can help us to build a picture about the past.

We also ensure that there are dedicated writing lessons in each history unit which give the pupils a chance to write a more in-depth account of something they have studied. This helps to develop vocabulary and understand the perspectives of other people involved in the historical events being studied.

Geography is an integral part of history because land use and location are central to why certain historical events happened. Many of the tasks our children tackle in history lessons draw upon this understanding. The tasks help the pupils to appreciate how borders and kingdoms expand and contract and that the idea of boundaries is a fluid concept.

Literacy

History contributes significantly to the teaching of literacy in our school, not least by actively promoting the skills of reading, writing, speaking and listening. Children develop their oracy through discussing historical questions with partners or in groups or presenting their findings to the rest of the class.

In each unit, the children complete a piece of history writing based on literacy targets. This enables them to use the vocabulary they have learned creatively, as well as familiarising them further with the range of writing types and genres they have encountered and are required to employ in other areas of their learning.

For instance, during a week when Year 2 have been learning about the Great Fire of London, they might write a first-person diary entry detailing what they saw. Or Year 4, having studied a range of sources on the Vikings, Scots and Anglo-Saxons, might write a persuasive letter to our head teacher asking for the Vikings to rule us as life was so good under their leadership. During a week when Year 5 have been finding out about Victorian migration from the countryside to the towns, they might write a persuasive letter to a relative to convince them to move to a Victorian town. Or Year 4, having examined a collection of sources on life in Henry VIII's court, might write a setting description based on what they have learned.

As well as being an opportunity to consolidate their writing skills and reapply them in an alternative and more independent context, this type of activity also allows the children to put themselves in the shoes of the historical characters they are learning about and approach their learning from an unfamiliar perspective. We have found this to be an effective way of revising learning from the lesson, while also progressing with writing.

The examples below were written by pupils in response to historical issues.

The Blitz:

Which jobs were necessary during the Blitz to help protect people?

When the bombs fell, the firefighters rushed towards the area and tried their hardest to put out the fire. Like the firefighters, nurses did a vital job too, when people got hurt they would nurse the people and try to save people's lives.

What strategies did the government use to boost morale?

During this horrible situation, the government did whatever they could do to not give up. Such as in this photo there are firefighters in the background trying to put out the fire when the milkman is still carrying on with his job whistling along the streets. They used different methods of propaganda, like they took clips of people whose house was bombed and saying that they will never give up.

Year 4 and 5 pupils

A speech to be delivered at the Acropolis:

My amazing Athenians,

I have called you here today to talk about a building that we will call the Parthenon if we build it. Today I will like to tell you how and why it's important and why we should build this wonder.

Are you aware that we just won a war that will go down in history? Don't we deserve a building that will take you back to our victorious win? We should give the Athenians something to treasure, to have a great time. Athens is a great city, look at the ruins of the Acropolis. We all deserve this building. Isn't that the least we deserve?

Year 4 and 5 pupils

Numeracy and ICT

History teaching contributes to the teaching of numeracy in a variety of ways. Children learn to use numbers when developing a sense of chronology through engagement in activities such as the construction of timelines. The children learn to interpret information presented in graphical or diagrammatic form – for example, when they study in graph form the Vikings' gradual assumption of control over the Anglo-Saxons.

We use ICT in history teaching where appropriate and we meet the statutory requirement for children to use ICT as part of their work in history at Key Stage 2. The children use ICT in history to enhance their skills in data handling and in presenting written work, and they research information using the Internet. Children can use tablets to blog their history learning and later to comment on each other's work.

PSHCE

History contributes significantly to the teaching of PSHCE. The children develop self-confidence by having opportunities to explain their view on a variety of social questions, such as how society has responded to immigration over time. They discover how to be active citizens in a democratic society by learning how laws are made and changed (e.g. by exploring and considering the significance of the Magna Carta), and they learn how to recognise and challenge stereotypes and to appreciate that opinions change over time. They learn how society is made up of people from diverse cultures and enlarge their tolerance and respect for others.

In our delivery of a balanced history curriculum, we help the children to deepen their understanding of global issues by making links between current international issues such as human rights (linking to Mayans) and the Ebola epidemic (linking to the plague). This enables the children to see the relevance of historical issues in a contemporary context as well as widening their vision and understanding of the world as an entire entity. In this way they can see their own place, not merely as an individual but also as a member of a continuous yet changing society.

British values

In line with national curriculum requirements, we actively promote the fundamental British values of democracy, the rule of law, individual liberty, and mutual respect and tolerance of those with different faiths and beliefs as critical components of our pupils' personal, social, moral and cultural education. Over the course of their schooling, pupils visit the Houses of Parliament and a court of law, as well as places of worship for each of the world faiths. Our weekly 'Manners Focus' ensures that children develop the essential skills of listening, respecting other's views and courtesies and positive modes of behaviour, such as table manners. They experience democracy through voting for their own school council representatives, and more recently learning about the general election and the introduction of the Magna Carta. We mark Remembrance Day annually as a school, and in 2014 each year group went to visit the 'Blood Swept Lands and Seas of Red' exhibition at the Tower of London.

Evaluating progression and impact

History planning is undertaken by the subject leader who plans for progression across the key stages. The subject leader conducts learning walks and book checks to ensure that planning is adhered to and to evaluate the impact that the teaching is having upon the children's learning. The results are then fed back to the staff, either formally or via the staff update. Members of staff also complete a competency-based survey, from which staff meetings and appropriate continuing professional development are designed to further the impact upon our pupils. The children are actively encouraged to blog their work, which can be found on our website, demonstrating the range of provision which they can proudly show to their parents.

Targets for history provision are created on an annual basis in the subject leader's action plan, based on termly assessed results and feedback. The history subject leader is also responsible for supporting colleagues in the teaching of history, for being informed about current developments in the subject and for providing a strategic lead and direction for the subject in the school. The history policy is evaluated and reviewed by the individual coordinator and senior management, and is agreed by governors.

Assessment

At the end of each lesson, the pupils complete a journal task which asks them to reflect on their learning from that lesson. The question is left very open to encourage the children to draw upon any information or ideas that they think are relevant. This has enabled us to have a much clearer understanding of their learning, and whether they are able to make connections and suggest reasons for things. We have been able to identify much more easily those children who are working at greater depth and those still working at a surface level. These are marked by the teacher and feed into our formal teacher assessments.

Teachers are also able to scaffold the children's understanding or challenge them to extend their thinking by asking personalised questions about what they have written. The children then respond to these with a green pen. This personal dialogue has been effective in ensuring the children's progress.

Resources

Pupils at London Fields benefit from extensive resourcing to support teaching and learning. A sizable proportion of funds is spent each year on developing this. We ensure that our children have access to:

- ■ A wide range of high quality non-fiction and fiction texts to further learning in the topic.
- ■ A variety of tactile historical sources and objects to engage and inspire the children to make historical connections.
- ■ Class sets of tablets to ensure the development of ICT skills in history.
- ■ Visits to external sites in and around London, linked to the topic, which expand their realm of experience.

Historic sites and museums offer cultural resources and opportunities, and our teachers are constantly looking for new experiences that will enrich the learning of their pupils. We believe that fieldwork trips are valuable for cementing historical understanding and bringing history to life. We are fortunate, of course, to be situated within easy access of some of the country's most prestigious cultural and historical venues, such as the British Museum and the Imperial War Museum, and even Pudding Lane itself, but history trips have also taken us further afield to Lullingstone Roman Villa and the Verulamium Museum in St Albans.

We also organise talks and workshops, some of which have a cross-curricular link (e.g. Egyptian dancing and instruments), where an expert comes into the school to share their knowledge with the children in a creative capacity. Recently we had a Mayan expert visit us with her archaeological tools to teach us about the Ancient Mayan civilisation.

History at home

Being an ancient city, living in London provides our children with a wonderful opportunity to discover more about the past. As well as the many museums, history is everywhere – in buildings, blue plaques and the many stretches of our original city wall!

However, evidence of the past can be found in every locality and community. The children can also learn a lot from personal stories of the past which allow them to understand that the world changes with each generation. At London Fields, we actively encourage the children to continue their research at home by interviewing family members, exploring local online archives and examining local architecture.

Conclusion

At London Fields, we believe that the study of history is essential for our children as they develop into well-rounded global citizens. The children develop their skills of enquiry, deduction, analysis, evaluation and inference while learning to question the world around them and starting to increase their understanding of the past – making links between civilisations and eras, as well as their relation and relevance to the present.

We have designed a history curriculum that draws upon a wide range of subjects from art to geography. The children can see that history influences much of the world around us. They are taught about inspirational figures to remind them that they do have the agency to change current affairs. They are taught to reflect on our present time and how it might be viewed in the future. We ask them what might have changed by then and why. In doing so, they not only understand history as it is so far, but they also develop a growing awareness that actions have consequences and history is being made at this very moment.

Further reading and useful links

Cooper, H. (ed.) (2016). *Teaching History Creatively* (Learning to Teach in the Primary School). Abingdon and New York: Routledge.

Dweck, C. (2006). *Mindset: The New Psychology of Success*. New York: Random House.

Hattie, J. (2012). *Visible Learning for Teachers: Maximizing Impact on Learning*. Abingdon and New York: Routledge.

Historical Association (2015). Quality Mark Final Report [London Fields Primary School] (7 July). Available at: http://www.londonfields.hackney.sch.uk/_site/data/files/users/2/policy/83839A047BA3698E47B2AABCBE263EBF.pdf.

BBC Schools Primary History: http://www.bbc.co.uk/schools/primaryhistory

Black Cultural Archives: https://blackculturalarchives.org

Chris Quigley Education: http://www.chrisquigley.co.uk

Historical Association: https://www.history.org.uk

History on the Net: http://www.historyonthenet.com

Show Me: http://www.show.me.uk

SOLO taxonomy: http://www.johnbiggs.com.au/academic/solo-taxonomy

About the contributor

Stephanie Daley

Stephanie Daley studied English and previously worked as an events coordinator. She qualified as a teacher in 2012 and has been working at London Fields ever since. She has taught across the school from Year 1 to Year 6 and has been the Key Stage 1 phase leader. She is head of curriculum development for the whole school, as well as head of history and geography, and is the joint literacy coordinator.

Chapter 17

Artists in School: Specialist Teaching in the Arts

Jo Acty, artist-in-residence, St Mary and St John CE Primary School, Oxford

Some schools believe so strongly in the importance of the arts in school that they employ a specialist art teacher to work with them on a regular basis. Jo Acty is the artist-in-residence at St Mary and St John CE Primary School. She supports the pupils on a regular basis and works with them on special projects. In this chapter, Jo gives her perspective on being an artist-in-residence, and then goes on to describe one specific art project which involved another professional artist and six groups of children from across the city.

Oxford's Churches Together initiated an ecumenical Unity Week schools art project involving Christ Church Cathedral, professional artist Nicholas Mynheer, pupils from five city schools (St Andrew's CE School, St Aloysius Catholic School, Rye St Antony School, St Barnabas CE School and St Mary and St John School) and a children's community art group (St Margaret's Art Group).

The theme, 'caring for the planet', centred on one of Nicholas Mynheer's paintings called *Creation*. The schools were invited to participate and consider an aspect of creation: air, water, land, shelter, light or sustainability. The themes, which could be expressed in any medium, aimed to capture the beauty and interconnectedness of life on Earth, as depicted in the creation story. The groups were asked to consider the challenges that creation presents to humanity in terms of its care and nurture of the world.

The final artwork, a series of six fabric panels, would draw connections between the story of creation from the Book of Genesis with the contemporary challenges we all face today as we try to care for the planet. The passage included references to plants and trees and the gifts they produce as sustenance for the creatures of the world.

With each school choosing their own medium, there was a great deal of freedom for interpretation. The pupils' choice of media was inventive and often surprising – from paint and textiles to earth, moss, feathers and even LED lights. While teachers and helpers assisted in the practicalities (mixing paints and cleaning clothes!), the creativity was entirely the children's.

Artist Nicholas Mynheer inspired the children by visiting each group to discuss the theme, scope and scale of the project. The five groups worked on their various panels in their schools. Each panel was a plain white cotton sheet measuring 2.2 x 1.2 metres.

Although the pupils knew that their panel would be part of a larger work (a six-panel polyptych), they did not see the final completed work of art until it was assembled in the cathedral, where it was the centrepiece during January 2017. The completed artwork remained on public exhibition for the following fortnight, and the installation was recorded for local television.

This project, and Jo's ongoing work at St Mary and St John School, provides compelling evidence of the value and impact of professional artists and specialist art teachers working in schools.

Background

St Mary and St John CE Primary (voluntary aided) is a vibrant urban school in east Oxford with 360 pupils and a distinctive Christian ethos – welcoming those of other faiths as well as those of none. With 28 languages spoken at the school, St Mary and St John is a multicultural, multi-faith school. The curriculum is broad and balanced and makes use of the city's cultural reserves.

We have the explicit goal of promoting friendship and understanding between the diverse communities of the area, with a special focus on our sizeable Muslim community. The school's mission statement emphasises that we offer an inclusive environment, fostering curiosity, spirituality, creativity and respect. At our school we want everyone to be valued, to explore the joy of learning and to achieve their full potential.

Art and creativity

Art and creativity is highly valued at St Mary and St John. The school participates annually in Oxfordshire's Artweeks event, when the school presents artwork from students, staff and friends of the school to the local community. We promote art through the Arts Council and Trinity College's Arts Award scheme. Parents and professional visiting artists regularly share their skills and expertise, including photography, wood carving, drama, dance and jazz. The parent–teacher association and I, as artist-in-residence, annually lead, design and deliver history of art themed lessons to help pupils produce exciting artwork for the school calendar, aimed at parents and the local community. This calendar is an important annual fundraising event, and always centres around a key theme or genre of art. In 2017, the focus was on contemporary female artists to celebrate the Turner Prize winner Lubaina Himid.

We try to make use of the many creative skills which can be found in our parent community. Thanks to parental input, the pupils have been able to experiment with new ways of using materials and have trialled techniques such as cyanotypes, dry point and variations on traditional lino printing. This is a practical and productive way to broaden the children's perceptions of what art can achieve and realise, and gradually empowers non-specialist teachers with a range of new art skills.

My colleague Helen Edwards, who works as a teacher in the school, also contributes to my weekend art classes. Helen has systematically introduced a wide range of visual literacy skills into her general art lessons. She has raised the children's awareness of key elements in art, which has given them the vocabulary they need to discuss and enjoy art from a more extensive knowledge base and with more informed perspectives. After four years of working in this way, the evidence can be seen throughout the school, and visitors often comment on the pupils' insightful questions and comments.

Helen and I are trained Arts Award advisers, and we offer this recognised qualification through Trinity College and the Arts Council. We have run Arts Award projects with the school and independently. Recently, we worked with the Oxford Science Museum, with Year 5 and 6 pupils, combining art and science in an exciting way. This culminated in an exhibition in the museum of the pupils' 3D artwork, which was inspired by the museum's collection.

Art-related continuing professional development is also supported at St Mary and St John. Three of the staff, including myself, are studying for a MA in education (Artist Teacher Scheme) which reflects on the nature and quality of art teaching practice combined with personal art development. The school regularly enters Take One Picture (the National Gallery's schools competition) and several members of staff have participated in National Gallery workshop days. As well as advising individuals, Helen and I are planning an INSET day on drawing and certain specific art skills which have been requested by class teachers.

It is important to note that the head of the school, Liz Burton, is very supportive of the arts, and the children's artwork is celebrated throughout the school. From my experience of working in schools, the message sent out from the head and senior leadership team determines the whole-school ethos. All our St Mary and St John colleagues attach a high importance to ensuring the children enjoy a broad, balanced and creative curriculum.

The role of the artist-in-residence

I am fortunate to have been employed as artist-in-residence at St Mary and St John for nearly four years. I have a shared space in the school's second hall where my main art materials are stored in three tall grey cupboards. My art sessions are visible to passing students and teachers. I also have an etching press installed in one corner, adding a new specialism to the art curriculum.

I have had my own teaching studio for many years, but to be part of a larger community has been a very rewarding experience. Despite being a part-time teacher, I feel very much part of the school, designing whole-school projects for inside and outside the school premises, for class projects and enrichment lunchtime groups, and after-school art clubs for each key stage. I also have an advisory role as joint art coordinator, so I can help teachers with their lesson planning and advise on materials and ideas, if needed.

I try to continue my own printmaking and painting practice on my non-teaching days. This adds up to a busy life, but I find that my own practice and enthusiasm for different media informs my teaching and vice versa. I hover between teacher and artist at school, spending most of my time working with smaller groups, which allows the space and time for discussion and the opportunity to develop ideas and demonstrate materials and techniques to a deeper level. Within this space, the children consider themselves artists – endowed with high personal expectations, a growing understanding of the value and reward of persistence and a strong sense of ownership of their work.

I also use the school to run private classes for young people aged from 7 to 18 out of school hours on Friday and Saturday and during school holidays. This brings in young people from all over the city as well as from the school community.

Every two years, to celebrate their artwork, these young out-of-school artists also participate in Oxford's annual Artweeks event. The head teacher allows the school hall to become an exhibition space, open to the local community, for two weeks. This really shows the commitment of the school to the arts, as the school timetable carries on around and among the artwork. Because many of the artists are secondary pupils, the exhibition introduces the younger children to artwork from older students, which inspires them greatly, as the remarks in the exhibition guestbook can testify.

Unity Week art project

Nicholas Mynheer, who specialises in ecclesiastical painting and stained glass, came to introduce his work to our two Year 5 classes, as inspiration for creating one of six panels for a polyptych display in Christ Church Cathedral for the Unity Week schools art project, which would involve six school groups altogether.

To start the project, Nicholas presented a PowerPoint of his work. The painter, sculptor and glass artist is one of the most distinguished artists in Britain. Largely biblically inspired, his paintings, stained glass and sculpture can be found in cathedrals, churches and public institutions all over the country and worldwide. The art critic Sister Wendy Beckett says of Mynheer: 'He loves life and makes its Holiness visible.'

The children were intrigued and asked questions about the size of his artworks and the religious symbolism. They gasped when, in the classroom, he unrolled a huge pencil sketch of his First World War window for Southwell Minster. At 4.5 metres long, this was very impressive. He shared and explained the stages of the creative process required to create such a window, and we learned how the composition was arranged to accommodate the lead structures that would be needed to hold the stained-glass pieces together. Nicholas's figures are quite stylised to enhance the symbolism he wants to convey, which in turn gave the children the freedom to move away from the rigours of a photographically representative response.

Nicholas outlined the children's role in the project and gave them an insight into their chosen theme of sustainability, taken from the story of creation in the Book of Genesis. We were all working to a tight schedule. Nicholas could only stay for an hour, and we had limited time available over the next two days. Each school was given a standard white sheet to cut to the size of the panel on which to create their design.

When I am working on a project, I like to involve the children in the process from the outset, as I find the plan that I might have in mind is always altered and enriched by their ideas. Their opinions are valid and worthwhile, and they deserve to have full involvement. I hope I have learned to let go and allow the act of informed creativity to lead the way. After Nicholas' visit, I made notes on the children's response to his painting and continued, with them, to mull over the possibilities within our theme.

Our theme: sustainability

I took a synthesis of the children's responses into the classroom the next day, working with the two classes separately. Together, each group produced mind-maps about the Bible passage and what it meant. The discussion soon turned to sustainability, and how the planet was struggling through global warming and human excess. We talked about well-known creatures that are close to extinction, but to make it feel more relevant to us personally we looked at the balance between food production in the UK and British wildlife. After some research, I found a list of endangered species in the UK – taken from the national Biodiversity Action Plan.

The next day I brought in more than 60 images of endangered species in the UK. We discussed techniques of drawing and observation, including squinting and turning both the image and the drawing upside down! The children produced some sensitive drawings and were clearly inspired by the subject matter and emboldened by breaking down the drawing process into manageable steps. Together, the children created 60 drawings of great quality.

Choosing the techniques and media

In response to the delicate quality of the drawings, I decided that a silk painting method using gutta would help to preserve that quality. Gutta is a thick latex-like substance which is produced by trees from the genus *Palaquium*. It is used for painting on silk or other fabrics. The method of containing the separate colours with a thin black raised out-line of gutta would also reference the lead work seen in Nicholas' Southwell Minster stained-glass window.

As we only had two days to design, transfer and paint the panel, I decided to work with three groups of six for the design and preparation. The first group worked as a team, organising the 60 enlarged photocopied drawings into a cohesive design which included every child's drawing. We talked about flattening the perspective, as Nicholas had done in his compositions, to ensure the design was balanced. The children then placed each of the drawings carefully under the stretched fabric and traced them lightly in pencil. The next group went over the pencil tracing with clear lines of gutta. I then worked with small groups from both classes to fill in their own creature with Brusho paint, so eventually every child had their 'touch' on the piece.

The design was already looking very strong, so we deliberated whether we should leave it with a white background. One of the children thought it might be an innovative idea to show the different habitats – water, land and sky – and this led on to the introduction of food crops such as cereals and a fruit tree. In a slightly back-to-front way, the last group of six designed the background around the already placed animals, birds, insects, fish and reptiles.

We managed to finish on time and a group of the children were invited to see their panel placed in situ in the cathedral. They were very proud of their achievements.

The learning outcomes

The children acquired many skills during the process. They learned how to generate ideas through mind-maps and discussion, both in class groups and in pairs. They learned about designing a collaborative artwork, making aesthetic choices along the way in response to the brief, and how to work together cohesively to a deadline. They learned drawing skills that have raised their confidence in their own ability. They enjoyed the opportunity to work on a large scale and to use the technique of silk painting, where the paint spreads beautifully across the fabric up to the gutta outlines.

The children always respond well to visitors to the school and the experience stays with them. The fact that Nicholas brought in his working drawing and painting had a profound effect on them and made a real difference to their attitudes. They were fascinated by how an artist works through ideas en route to a finished piece. The drawing showed how Nicholas had edited the design and that beginnings don't have to be perfect; a lesson well learned, and a reminder to be kind to yourself in the early stages of producing any kind of creative piece.

I think producing art is still seen as slightly magical by many young people, and even some adults, so being close to an artist and learning from them about their processes provides a privileged view into their creative world.

The final artwork

The most extraordinary moment was seeing the six panels, all in different media, working perfectly as one unified work of art. The finished piece was an artistic testament, and proof that a team working together (or in this case a team of teams) can produce a result that is greater than the sum of its parts. The unity of purpose that these children exhibited produced an artwork that truly encapsulated what Unity Week stands for.

The six panels drew connections between the story of creation in Genesis with the contemporary challenge to care for the planet and to overcome enmity and division. The groups captured, each in their own way, the beauty and interconnectedness of life on Earth, in the face of so many threats to life, and how we might work together to nurture, restore and reconcile the world.

At the end of the Unity Week project, Nicholas commented: 'It was extraordinary to see how enthusiastically the schoolchildren took this project to heart. Not only did they instantly connect with the various themes, but they had genuine concerns for the challenges that mankind faces and extraordinary vision in seeing paths forward.' He said he often finds that working with children is 'a little like prayer; in the sense that you start off thinking you want to say something but end up being told something. In that sense, it is humbling.'

Our head teacher was greatly impressed by the St Mary and St John panel and referred to 'the unmistakable joy and sense of creative achievement gained by the pupils from the visible evidence of their effort'. She asked to have it returned after the exhibition and it now hangs in the parents' waiting area, on permanent display for all to see and enjoy.

Further reading and useful links

Buzan, T. and Buzan, B. (2008). *The Mind Map Book*. Harlow: BBC Active.

Eisner, E. W. (2002). *The Arts and the Creation of Mind*. New Haven, CT: Yale University Press.

Gopaul, A. (2017). *Bloomsbury Curriculum Basics: Teaching Primary Art and Design*. London: Bloomsbury.

Harding, A. (2005). *Magic Moments: Collaboration Between Artists and Young People*. London: Black Dog Publishing.

Hewitt, J. (2014). *Learning Through a Lens: It's All About Photography*. Carmarthen: Independent Thinking Press.

Hickman, R. (2005). *Why We Make Art and Why It Is Taught*. Portland, OR: Intellect Books.

Hobbs, J. A. and Rush, J. C. (1997). *Teaching Children Art*. Upper Saddle River, NJ: Prentice Hall.

Robinson, K. (2001). *Out of Our Minds: Learning to Be Creative*. Oxford: Capstone.

Wenzel, A. (2013). *13 Art Techniques Children Should Know*. Munich: Prestel.

Access Art: https://www.accessart.org.uk

National Society for Education in Art and Design (NSEAD): http://nsead.org/home/index.aspx

Unity Week at Christ Church Cathedral: https://www.youtube.com/watch?v=2Mj8bf8Q9vM&feature=youtube

About the contributor

Jo Acty

Jo Acty is currently based in Oxford, where she has been an artist-teacher since 1989. She has worked in Oxford and Devon in schools, hospitals and with community groups, as well as running private art classes as ArtWorks School of Art. Jo trained in fine art at Winchester School of Art and Brookes University and specialises in painting, drawing and printmaking, but she also enjoys exploring a full range of materials including sculpture, mosaic and installation. Jo is a self-taught teacher but is in the process of taking an MA in education (Artist Teacher Scheme).

Chapter 18
The Reclaimed Curriculum

Sue Tomkys, head teacher, with Sam Conway, Francesca Jenkins, Alison Seddighi, Jess Tweedie, Vivien Weekes, Edina Wemeser, Edwina Vernon, Maria Prodromou, St Joseph's Catholic Primary School, Marston, Oxford

In a school notable for high achievement in more than one subject – from the performing and creative arts through to chess and design and technology – St Joseph's Catholic Primary School is most remarkable for the breadth of curriculum it offers.

As well as all the national curriculum subjects, the school provides additional opportunities and areas of learning which the staff regard as indispensable to the education they provide. The main contributory factors in the structuring of what they describe as 'an enriched curriculum' include:

- Constant and rigorous evaluation of the quality and effectiveness of provision.

- The very evident enthusiasm and specialist expertise that individual members of staff bring to particular subjects and areas of learning.

- Access to and recruitment of additional specialists.

- High quality learning environments, such as those offered by the school's forest garden, and the opportunity to experiment and take risks in the expansively furnished and equipped children's kitchen.

- The provision of clear and challenging goals, such as when preparing for a competition, production, performance or presentation, or aiming high to achieve personal goals across the curriculum.

The cliché commonly called on to convey children's enthusiasm for their learning is 'a buzz of excitement', but this idea really comes to life at St Joseph's, where pupils from across the school describe the work they are engaged in with incredible eagerness – a telling indicator of their motivation and delight in learning.

Background

St Joseph's is a two-form entry Catholic primary school located on the outskirts of Oxford, where it serves three parishes. Its proximity to several local hospitals means that many of the pupils' parents work in healthcare and this has led to a significant increase in the percentage of pupils from ethnic minorities (70%) and with English as an additional language (EAL) (51%). Approximately 6% of pupils are eligible for free school meals, 11% are eligible for pupil premium funding and just over 12% have special educational needs (SEN).

The school offers extended wrap-around care from 8 a.m. to 6 p.m., catering for up to 60 pupils each day. This is staffed by school personnel, thus the income generated goes into the school budget rather than to an external provider. This significantly assists us in financing our diverse curriculum.

The school is a strategic partner in the Oxfordshire Teaching Schools Alliance.

A nurturing environment

Our school mission statement is the foundation stone of all we do at St Joseph's. One part of it emphasises that we aim to provide 'a nurturing environment, with the best possible educational facilities and opportunities for our pupils'. Our curriculum is deliberately broad and rich: it is designed to foster a love of learning and to prepare pupils for their life in the wider world.

Some time ago, Sir Ken Robinson's 2007 TED Talk, 'Do Schools Kill Creativity?', struck a chord and galvanised us, as a staff team, to make sure that all talents are valued, appreciated and nurtured in our school.

A topic-based approach

In each department, the curriculum is centred on a topic each term, which allows us to be flexible around the interests of pupils and staff. Some topics which have been very successful are revisited – for example, our upper Key Stage 2 film topic, where the children study the history of film from early moving pictures and Charlie Chaplin through to modern-day cinema, including Bollywood.

High quality texts are chosen, and these have proved crucial in immersing pupils in the topic (e.g. Brian Selznick's *The Invention of Hugo Cabret* (2007) for our film topic and Eva Ibbotson's *Journey to the River Sea* (2014) for our Africa topic). Using key texts means that all enjoy a shared experience and are engaged and enthusiastic. It is important that the curriculum remains fresh and relevant.

We have just begun setting topic homework tasks where there is choice, so that parents and carers can also choose which tasks best fit their family's talents. This has been received with great enthusiasm, and has resulted in the sharing of high quality outcomes and products – such as model volcanoes, working gas masks and collective recipe books – in open sessions for pupils and families. These mainly take place immediately after school to enable more parents/carers to participate. Children are the most powerful motivators for parents to become involved, so we can increase parent–school liaison by involving parents in class project homework and inviting them to share their ideas with the children.

An enriched curriculum

Great care is taken to ensure that, while pupils are learning about a diverse range of topics, all areas of the national curriculum are taught and statutory requirements are met. Curriculum coordinators monitor their subject areas and standards, but, like most schools, we are determined to offer additional opportunities beyond the national curriculum.

Specialist teachers and smaller groups are used to promote a greater depth of high quality learning – for example, in the Forest School and design and technology suite. The curriculum is further enriched by activities such as Philosophy for Children (P4C), music (e.g. recorder and brass instrument tuition for all), choir, orchestra and chess.

Standards in SATs are maintained at very good levels despite the high priority given to the diversity and richness of the curriculum. We believe it is difficult for children to write high quality texts unless they have had memorable, high quality experiences. For example, Year 3s learn to build models and program them using LEGO WeDo, and in Year 6 they use LEGO MINDSTORMS and take part in Robotscool (a competition similar to BBC Two's *Robot Wars*). The range of activities provided is varied and extensive to appeal to all interests and to challenge children to broaden their experiences.

A diverse curriculum

The curriculum is designed to celebrate our multicultural diversity. Parents often contribute to enrich topics, such as a visiting history expert talking about the Second World War or scientists and other experts sharing their knowledge of subjects as wide-ranging as Indian dance, cooking and religious traditions.

The diversity of ethnic groups and languages at St Joseph's has led us to introduce several of the opportunities we now offer. In our Key Stage 1 planning, preparation and assessment (PPA) time, we encourage teaching assistants and parents to initiate activities, such as classes celebrating cultures and specific languages which enable the children to teach each other about their culture or language. Families take pride in becoming involved – for example, by producing PowerPoints which they can present to the class.

Culture and language

At St Joseph's, we celebrate our many diverse cultures in several ways.

In Year 1, pupils participate in 'Celebrating Languages' as part of their activity afternoon on Fridays. Each week we learn some simple greetings, count to 10 and sing songs in a different language spoken by a member of the group. Each week the children ask, 'Which language are we learning this week?' The languages learned include German, Polish, Spanish, Malayalam and Tagalog.

In Year 2, the children take a more proactive role in teaching during our 'Celebrating Cultures' sessions. Each week a child from the group prepares a short presentation about one or more aspects of the culture from their home nation. We sometimes also enjoy culinary treats from different countries. We start by discussing what we already know about the country, and then consider other areas about which we wish to know more. Questions range from 'What do their houses look like?' to 'Did they have dinosaurs?' We then watch the children's home-prepared presentations, after which the child presenting can act as the expert and answer the other children's questions. In this way, we learn about festivals, food, animals and climates and read stories.

In Years 3–6 we learn French, but we do not limit our cultural outlook to France – we also learn about French-speaking Africa. Language learning takes the form of games, songs, colouring, art, watching DVDs and short performances. The children learn some basic grammar and can say a few short sentences about themselves within a few weeks. In Year 4, the children enjoy describing their pets, while Year 5 and 6 learn about Africa, theme parks, films and celebrations.

For the past three years, we have entered a competition entitled Love Languages, which takes place at St Helen's and St Katherine's School, Abingdon. The competition involves a short performance in another language. The last play we put on showcased the languages in our school in a drama written by the children.

Residential and day trips

Residential trips have been carefully designed to complement our curriculum. Year 3 begin by camping out overnight in the school grounds, with an outside adventure company leading activities during the day – a gentle and not too worrying beginning for parents. Year 4 pupils go to a scout ground for two nights and engage in activities that develop teamwork and take the children out of their normal comfort zone.

In Years 5 and 6, the trips take place in alternate years so that one year, when upper Key Stage 2 is studying war, we go to France for a combination of historical and cultural experiences, including making croissants and visiting Vimy Ridge and the Wellington Quarry Museum at Arras. The alternate year involves an adventure trip to Pembrokeshire where the children experience a wide selection of 'real' outdoor experiences. We think it is important to climb on rocks, not a climbing wall, and experience sea-based activities such as surfing and coasteering. Some of our children may have never previously seen or been in the sea.

There is always financial support available from a range of sources – such as pupil premium funding for the relevant children and from uniform sales and class photograph income – so that no child is disadvantaged.

Creative thinking

Our approach to creative thinking in the curriculum has developed over the past 10 years. It began with a firm belief and conviction that, while teachers are in PPA, the children should enjoy enrichment opportunities.

We have four classes in each of Key Stage 1, lower Key Stage 2 and upper Key Stage 2, and we began by splitting these into six groups with 20 children in each. We also group across both our year group classes, since we believe that working with different groupings reduces the likelihood of bullying because the children get to know each other better. The timetable is complex to arrange, as some activities last two hours rather than one, and all children in any one year group must have the same range of opportunity.

The opportunities are chosen depending in part on the specific talents of the current non-teaching staff and the input of external specialists. We invite feedback from pupils to monitor the impact of each activity or programme.

In 2017/2018 the activities over the year are:

- Key Stage 1: Celebrating cultures, collage, design and technology structures, music, PE, dance around the world, Forest School, celebrating cultures, a longer design and technology project (Year 2).

- Lower Key Stage 2: French, Malawi (where our international link school is based), LEGO, art, library skills, PE, Forest School, food technology, a longer design and technology project.

■ Upper Key Stage 2: PE (at secondary school, to take part in sports which are not normally taught in primary school, such as trampolining), P4C, music, French, digital leaders, cooking, Forest School (off-site for the older pupils), Robotscool, puppet-making, scenery design and preparation for performance.

P4C

St Joseph's adopted P4C several years ago after the head teacher and other members of staff attended training with P4C specialist Will Ord. Further training with SAPERE has ensured that this approach is used as a tool for learning. We have been fortunate to employ a philosophy teacher (who also works with SAPERE) who teaches PPA sessions to upper Key Stage 2, as well as team-teaching with class teachers to model good practice and embed it in our school.

The goal of our P4C lessons is to develop communities of enquiry where children and teachers practise caring and collaborative discussion by listening and thinking about what others say and believe, building on each other's ideas, debating, challenging and agreeing (or disagreeing) respectfully with one another. We spend some time at the beginning of each lesson thinking about how to maintain thoughtful and worthwhile conversations.

The children are encouraged to consider which thinking skills we should be practising, and these become our lesson objectives. For example, in Year 4 we have been using P4C in our geography lessons. We have been thinking about, 'Which are the best countries to live in and why?' The children are encouraged to consider, 'What do we need to be doing to answer this question?' and they suggest agreements like 'listen to each other' and 'take turns to speak' but also 'we need to connect our ideas' and 'do some research'.

As well as caring and collaborative thinking, we develop critical and creative thinking, such as giving reasons, thinking of alternatives and evaluating our opinions and arguments in light of the dialogue we have had. The children are encouraged to come up with 'thinking questions' by reflecting on the big ideas or concepts behind what we are studying. In geography, this has triggered questions such as: 'What does it mean to be poor?' and 'If a country has a lot of money, does it mean that its people are happy and safe?' The children have been challenging the idea of gross domestic product (GDP) as a good indicator of quality of life because, as they said, 'Perhaps the money is not distributed equally.'

Sometimes, we explore a concept or book that the children are reading over a series of lessons, with each lesson informing the next. Last year we began by thinking about the big ideas in Beverley Naidoo's *Journey to Jo'burg* (1985), a picture book set in South

Africa. Some of the initial questions were: 'Why is there racism?' and 'When is it OK to protest?' These questions led us to think about power and its connection to racism, violence, wealth, power, inequality and freedom. Some of the questions the children created and discussed were: 'What is the impact of racism on people's lives?', 'Who deserves power?', 'Is wealth racist?', 'Is being rich having power?', 'What type of power do poor people have?', 'Do all creatures deserve to be free?' and 'How do people get power?' For our most recent lessons, we circled back to the question of racism and came up with definitions of racism informed by our discussions. The children were then given the opportunity to create posters that raised awareness about racism and its connection to some of the key concepts we had explored.

Global citizenship

Our global citizenship link with Chipili Primary School in Malawi started nine years ago and has been sustained with the support of the British Council's Connecting Classrooms programme. We have had three successful grants and have had teachers from Malawi visit us and our teachers visit Malawi, the most recent pair visiting in 2017. Sessions are taught during PPA sessions in lower Key Stage 2, and these encourage our children to examine joint topics with our link school on areas such as food, electricity and toys.

We strive for the relationship to be reciprocal and real and are constantly looking for ways to enhance the learning. Our recent grant from the British Council included training in critical thinking and this led to an exciting collaboration with P4C in our lessons. We found that by posing deep questions we were able to encourage our pupils to grapple with ideas beyond their lived experiences, challenging their own previously held assumptions. For many of our pupils it is also an opportunity to talk about their own extended families and experiences outside of the UK. On a teacher exchange visit, the icing on the cake was to be able to teach the same lesson to pupils in Malawi and then share the responses with our pupils here.

We generate a big idea for our lessons, combining class topics with core skills from Oxfam's and the British Council's global citizenship curriculums. An example of a big idea question came during a topic on toys. The question was 'What makes a toy?' We started by asking if children in Malawi had toys. The children automatically said no and reasoned that if the children did not have money then they could not have toys. We then did an activity where we placed a range of images on a continuum from 'toy' to 'not toy'. The children then discussed and debated whether items such as cardboard boxes, chairs and televisions were toys. By the end of the session we agreed that all the things could be toys – and yes, that children in Malawi would have toys. Then someone asked the question, 'Is a pair of scissors a toy?' This led to more discussion and debate. As a follow-up to this session, the children made plastic bag footballs and bottle cars as recycled toys (consulting videos of children from Africa making them).

This international link has been invaluable in helping the children relate to one another on an equal basis and share information with the link school. The pupils come to appreciate that they are all 'experts' in knowing about their own cultures and countries and benefit from a wider, more global understanding.

Design and technology

The design and technology curriculum includes textiles, mechanics, food technology, structures and electrics. At St Joseph's, we have chosen to employ a specialist teacher for four days a week to teach this subject, working with groups of 15–20 pupils at a time. In practice, this is organised by splitting Key Stage 2 classes into two for their design and technology lessons; the remainder of the class generally have art or computing in this 90–120-minute slot each week. Further design and technology in PPA time is also provided. This means the children are receiving specialist teaching in a purpose-designed area which includes a children's kitchen. This area was developed in 2017 by redefining the indoor space efficiently. The Year 6 leavers donated the cooker and the parent–teacher association also contributed.

The children progress, learning new skills during their time in the school, and can use their knowledge of other subjects to design, make and evaluate their projects. In textiles, the children make items from material, calling on mathematics for measuring and cutting and learning different joining methods. In mechanics, the progression is from simple sliders, levers and linkages through to axles, wheels and motorised cars (later to be controlled by a computer program).

Food technology is taught every year and includes food groups, nutrients, balanced meals, cutting skills using the 'bridge' and 'claw' techniques through to applying these to the preparation of fruit and vegetables and different dishes from around the world. The older children make seasonal soups and different breads. They adapt their recipes to change the appearance, taste and texture of their dishes.

In structures, the Year 1s make free-standing structures such as the Three Billy Goats Gruff's bridge, while the Year 5 pupils make an Anderson shelter linked to their topic on the Second World War. They use measuring, saws for cutting and glue guns for sticking and adding strengthening, all using methods they have learned. The children in Year 4 work on electrical circuits, reinforcing their scientific knowledge and making lighthouses or volcanoes. Year 5 children add alarm systems to their electrical skills.

The children work on projects which link to their class topics, and these are as exciting and challenging as we can make them. Some pupils are particularly able to excel in the subject due to it being very practical and requiring different skill sets from some other subjects.

Children of all ages find design and technology worthwhile, as they have the opportunity to use their hands and brains to make something innovative, which aids their learning and growth. Their work is valued through the use of high quality specialist exercise books which the children take with them throughout their time at St Joseph's. The children enjoy seeing how they have progressed in their knowledge, skills and techniques.

Forest School

We are passionate about outdoor learning at St Joseph's. We believe the children can learn more effectively if they are given opportunities to shape their own study by being allowed to follow their interests and explore and investigate at their own pace.

Our school is fortunate enough to have a woodland area surrounding the school grounds, which we decided to turn into an outdoor learning site. Our copse has a variety of native trees, wildflowers, birds and woodland animals and a pond that gives home to protected species, such as the great crested newt.

In 2009, we set up our own Forest School, piloting possibilities and effects on the children's learning by taking groups of 10 children into the forest on a regular (weekly) basis. After the first year's success we extended the Forest School programme, including Key Stage 1 and lower Key Stage 2.

The younger children take part in den-building, where their dens have to meet specific criteria, while children in Years 5 and 6 are challenged to build a bridge using three diverging beams and 10 wooden planks of the same length, which requires problem-solving and teamwork.

In Forest School, the children complete a structured programme of activities which engage them with nature. These allow the children to further develop their confidence and self-esteem and enhance their social and investigative skills, as well as explore their natural environment.

The children learn a lot about changes in the seasons, animals, plants and pond creatures through careful observation, investigation and identification. We engage in problem-solving and team-building activities, and learn, for example, different tying techniques to make sure the dens we build are safe. We learn about safe ways of using tools and making fire. We help our children to develop a sense of ownership about their Forest School site and stewardship of their environment. We also discuss safety in the woods, helping the children to develop the skill of assessing the risks around them.

Enrichment weeks

Enrichment weeks are used to immerse the children in specific topics. At the beginning of the school year, in Brain Week, we explore the wonders of the brain and encourage the children to develop a growth mindset (Dweck, 2012). We have also had an International Week, a Paint One Picture Week and, most recently, a Spirituality Week.

As a school we felt that it would be valuable for the children to be given the opportunity to express their spirituality in a variety of ways, not just through a written task. We wanted to assist the children in accessing the concept of faith through all aspects and dimensions of the curriculum, so we suspended much of the planning for that week (apart from phonics and maths). All classes provided the children with imaginative opportunities to access their faith in a range of ways (e.g. dance, art, music, design and technology, Forest School).

Feedback from the staff and the children indicated that this week has been an extremely liberating and valuable opportunity for all to make personal links between themselves and God. The quality of the work was rich, varied and thoughtful across all key stages. Representations of spirituality through the biology of the heart, expressions of their relationship with God through 'Pray Dough' and 'Pray Clay', a rap from Year 1 about how God makes them feel, dancing for joy in the Early Years Foundation Stage (EYFS) because God makes them feel happy, and children across the school learning how to use mindfulness techniques to come closer to God all contributed towards a worthwhile experience for staff and pupils alike.

Chess

At St Joseph's, we believe that competitions can provide children with a purpose and a goal to work towards and, as well as the joy of participating, the opportunity to have their achievements and talents recognised.

Chess at St Joseph's began about eight years ago with the Delancey UK Schools' Chess Challenge. This competition takes place internally within the school, but it results in age-group winners who go on to compete at a regional Megafinal. After five years, several players were becoming recognised at county level and around 70 children in the school were playing chess. We recruited an experienced coach to provide for diverse levels of engagement and ability, and entered the county U11 and U9 leagues.

We were delighted to win at the London Chess Classic schools event in both 2016 and 2017, and we were the first state school to win the U11 county league for 17 years. Families have become very involved in playing chess, and it has become as cool to be good at chess as it is to be good at football. We now have around a hundred children in the school who play chess, and it is difficult to keep up with demand.

Performance

Performance is very strong in the whole school with EYFS and Key Stage 1 producing nativity plays; Year 3 putting on a singing, recorder and poetry performance; Year 4 performing a play linked to their topic (and elaborated upon by our funny and able Key Stage 2 coordinator); and Years 5 and 6 putting on a full-scale production, bringing together the talent in singing and acting which have been nurtured over their time at St Joseph's. It is our policy that all children in Years 2, 4 and 6 will have a part to play, because we believe that everyone should have an experience of performance at primary school. The children also manage the lighting and sound for their productions in Key Stage 2.

We look for chances to build on pupils' strengths and give them new opportunities to develop confidence and enjoyment in their learning. We know that confidence built in one area of the curriculum feeds success in others. Pupils are carefully selected and invited to join the cast; the criteria for selection could be gifted acting but equally it could be the need for confidence building. The standard of the final performance is high: the talents of our cast always surprise us and the feedback from parents, pupils and staff is always positive.

The Shakespeare club

We have run the Shakespeare club for the last two years, providing our older children with the opportunity to perform a Shakespeare play to the public in a professional theatre (facilitated through the Shakespeare Schools Foundation). This has had a tremendous impact on their levels of confidence, resilience and empathy. It has been a privilege to witness the children break with their preconceptions about the language of Shakespeare being alien or even elitist. One group of children had become so comfortable with Shakespeare's iambic pentameter that they decided to open their production of *The Tempest* by rapping Sonnet 18 ('Shall I compare thee to a summer's day?')!

Performance offers the children a platform to confidently explore and use figurative language which can then be deployed in their own writing. In addition, Shakespeare club has also been a helpful transition tool for those children in Year 6 moving up to secondary school, by giving them exposure to texts which will be covered in Key Stage 3.

Through the inclusive nature of performance, Shakespeare club can successfully integrate different social groups (including children with SEN), creating friendships that might never have been realised otherwise. The club has provided children with the inspiration and ambition to seek out opportunities elsewhere and to further the drama skills learned from their performance. Several children have joined local drama groups and performed in amateur productions outside of school. Performance can instil aspirations and self-esteem, giving our children the confidence to see that the entire world is their stage.

Music

Music is at the heart of our worship, and underpins much of our competition and performance goals. Our music curriculum has been enhanced by our choir, orchestra, handbells group, rock band and brass group.

Every Wednesday and Friday morning at 8.25 a.m. the school hall is flooded with the sound of our 90-strong Key Stage 2 choir singing with great gusto. The children regularly sing together, clearly enjoying the thrill of being part of a creative group who are joyfully expressing themselves. They have performed at Christ Church Cathedral, Dorchester Abbey and at many other concerts in the local community.

The choir, orchestra and handbell players are performance-orientated groups, and venues range from international arenas such as the O2 Arena in London to the intimacy of carol singing in local community nursing homes.

A wide range of material is chosen to interest every taste, while also promoting a musical education. Music at St Joseph's owes much to the talent of the staff involved and the investment to support their vision and ambition, which includes the establishment of our own orchestra. Last year, the combined choir and orchestra were selected to play a medley from *Les Misérables* at Birmingham's Symphony Hall. The children's performance and arrangement of this medley resulted in the school being presented with a local Innovation in School Music award.

Every child is encouraged to develop musically, being supported and guided by a range of highly skilled professional mentors. When talent is recognised, either by the school or peripatetic staff, opportunities are given for further development, such as participating in gifted and talented music days locally and music scholarships with Jesus College, Oxford.

All performance groups wear a specifically designed 'Music at St Joseph's' T-shirt, which was designed by one of the children, proudly showcasing their individual musical contribution as well as being part of a fun, dynamic and creative school community.

Conclusion

At St Joseph's, our aim is to provide every child in our care with the opportunity to develop into a caring and positive individual who will make a valuable and lasting contribution in the future, in whatever way they choose.

Staff are given the chance to use their own personal interests and talents to enhance the curriculum for our learners. The central underlying and common values we all share is the opinion that our children deserve the very best. None of the broad curriculum the children enjoy would be possible without the passion, energy and commitment of all the St Joseph's staff, both substantive and peripatetic.

What we have created took several years, but it is now entrenched in our ethos. We change what we offer yearly as the staff change and different pathways present themselves.

Any school can begin to reclaim their curriculum by identifying openings which could be provided by staff who have a passion for something which will motivate and benefit the children. Schools can also look to local people or outside providers to broaden the opportunities available. The challenge then is to support staff, through training or non-contact time, to realise their vision. When talking to staff, it is often amazing how many unusual talents and interests have been hidden. Staff who are teaching to their own passions enthuse the children with their infectious excitement for the subject, and as a result are likely to feel more fulfilled professionally.

Further reading and useful links

Dweck, C. (2012). *Mindset: How You Can Fulfil Your Potential*. London: Constable and Robinson.

Gilbert, I. (2007). *The Little Book of Thunks: 260 Questions to Make Your Brain Go Ouch*. Carmarthen: Crown House Publishing

Ibbotson, E. (2014). *Journey to the River Sea*. London: Macmillan.

Naidoo, B. (1985). *Journey to Jo'burg*. London: HarperCollins.

Robinson, K. (2007). Do Schools Kill Creativity? [video] *TED*. Available at: https://www.youtube.com/watch?v=iG9CE55wbtY.

Robinson, K. and Aronica, A. (2016). *Creative Schools: Revolutionizing Education from the Ground Up*. London: Penguin.

Selznick, B. (2007). *The Invention of Hugo Cabret*. New York: Scholastic.

British Council – Connecting Classrooms: https://schoolsonline.britishcouncil.org/about-programmes/connecting-classrooms

British Council – Core Skills: https://schoolsonline.britishcouncil.org/international-learning/core-skills

Children's Food Trust: http://www.childrensfoodtrust.org.uk

LEGO Education: https://education.lego.com/en-gb/downloads

Love Languages: https://www.freemens.org/lovelanguages2018

Oxfam – Global Citizenship in the Classroom: https://www.oxfam.org.uk/education/resources/global-citizenship-in-the-classroom-a-guide-for-teachers

Philosophy for Children (P4C): http://www.P4C.com

Robotscool: http://www.robotscool.com

SAPERE: http://www.sapere.org.uk

Shakespeare Schools Foundation: https://www.shakespeareschools.org

About the contributors

Sue Tomkys

After an early career as a cost and management accountant, Sue Tomkys made the decision to qualify as a teacher and spent 13 years in the classroom at various schools in Oxfordshire. She has now been the head of St Joseph's Catholic Primary School in Oxford for over a decade. In 2011, she became a local leader of education (LLE) and system leader, and has supported schools and new head teachers in both Oxfordshire and the Diocese of Birmingham.

Sam Conway

Sam Conway has a background in drama and EAL and now leads a drama group as part of the Shakespeare Schools Festival. His highlights also include taking his students to be part of a Shakespeare flash mob at Westminster Abbey.

Francesca Jenkins

Francesca Jenkins has led the early years department at St Joseph's for several years and is now the assistant head teacher. She is passionate about fostering children's confidence in their creativity by providing an enriched, varied and exciting curriculum that is accessible to all learners.

Alison Seddighi

Alison Seddighi, a linguist with expertise in French and Italian, has been teaching languages for 10 years at St Joseph's and has recently started learning Persian.

Jess Tweedie

Jess Tweedie has a master's in education in curriculum development, and has worked in international and English schools. She is currently deputy head at St Joseph's and has been recognised as a specialist leader of education (SLE) for her work as an English and EAL coordinator. Her career has given her experience with different curriculum models and pedagogy, and has cemented a belief in a growth mindset and an enriched curriculum to develop the whole child.

Vivien Weekes

Vivien Weekes has taught in a wide variety of schools and is now design and technology coordinator at St Joseph's, where she can indulge in her creativity and pass on life skills in food technology and textiles to her pupils.

Edina Wermeser

Edina Wermeser, a Hungarian by birth, has always been passionate about the great outdoors as well as working with children. After gaining her qualification as a Forest School teacher, she set up an outdoor learning programme for St Joseph's – where she has been working as a Forest School teacher and outdoor learning coordinator for just over a decade, providing opportunities for children aged 4–11 to engage with nature.

Edwina Vernon

Edwina Vernon is a music practitioner and choir mistress based in Oxfordshire. She collaborates with conductor Caroline Hobbs-Smith on school musical events, such as *Les Misérables* and *West Side Story*, with St Joseph's school choir, orchestra and handbells group – with over 100 children performing.

Maria Prodromou

Dr Maria Prodromou, a philosophy practitioner and SAPERE teacher trainer, coaches and supports teachers and schools in embedding philosophical dialogue and enquiry across the curriculum.

Conclusion

The schools that feature in this book, though few in number, are wide ranging in terms of type, size, location, diversity of pupil intake, socio-economic features, history and heritage. They include state schools, faith schools, academies and a nursery setting. Of course, the schools also vary in terms of the leadership, management and organisation and, inevitably, ethos and philosophy. Some are more fortunate in terms of the resources available to them and the degree of parental support they can call upon.

However, the schools have significantly more in common than the differences and disparities that distinguish them from one another. The similarities can be summarised as follows:

- They are memorable and, indeed, enthralling places, characterised by imaginative and inventive educational provision and practice.

- They are rich in curriculum offer, set in carefully designed, attractive and inviting learning environments and adequately resourced to serve diverse learning needs.

- There is an emphasis on the personal development of the pupils – on their social, spiritual and cultural education. Their whole experience of life in school helps them towards an understanding of the nature of society and the part they will play in it.

- They have the capacity and willingness to call on specialist subject expertise, from both within the school community and beyond.

- Although the teachers would not regard themselves as exceptional, their teaching is consistently good (and often outstanding), informed by rigorous planning and underpinned by effective teamwork and a strong commitment to the development of the children's understanding and creativity.

- They share a vision about what the education of children at the primary stage should represent and provide in the 21st century, and a profound concern about the challenge of preparing them adequately for an unpredictable and uncertain world.

Most significantly, they share a commitment to the implementation of all that is best, and most worthwhile, in the national curriculum. Their determination to preserve every subject is evident in the education they strive to provide. In all cases, they continue to do so because they believe that what they desire for the children in their care can only be brought about by the provision of a broad, relevant and engaging curriculum.

They reject the notion of a diminished education focused on the attainment of limited aims across a narrow subject range, as barren in its ambition and aspiration as it is meagre in reach and substance. They are in no doubt that a liberal, progressive and democratic society should provide for all its children, without exception, the fullest and most rewarding education possible. It is surely significant that the schools – trusting as they do in the worth of a full and enriched curriculum, however demanding and challenging its implementation – are judged by Ofsted to be 'good' or 'outstanding', and their pupils consistently achieve above expected requirements in national tests.

For example, in the humanities and science, the schools encourage pupils to research and investigate, to question, speculate, debate, hypothesise and express themselves in both spoken and written form. They are convinced that a wide-ranging, creative, practical and fulfilling approach to language development – taking proper account of form, style and correctness – is more likely to be effective when pupils are engaging with interesting subject content, rather than an unrelenting concentration on repetitive, mechanistic and linguistically limited approaches to literacy.

A particular feature of much of the work described here is the carefully nurtured acquisition and mastery by pupils of subject-specific language. The children often needed precise, accurate, assured (even, occasionally, arcane) vocabulary for the purpose of communicating and explaining to groups of parents and other adults the nature of their study across a wide range of activities – in science, design and technology; making animations; constructing and manipulating robots; building and driving a kit car; and creating collaborative artworks.

An inspirational creative partnership

Before we sum up the exciting work that our colleagues have shared, we would first like to mention the project that helped to inspire the original concept for this book.

The pupils of Christ the King Catholic Primary School, in a culturally diverse area of Birmingham, had become interested in the art and history of stained glass, as a result of series of different learning experiences. Previous contact and links with Birmingham's Queen Elizabeth Hospital led them to explore the possibility of commissioning a stained-glass window that would adorn the hospital's inter-faith chapel. They wanted the window to tell their favourite bible story, in which a group of friends lower their paralysed companion through the roof of a house where Jesus is preaching in the hope that he will be cured.

The project was coordinated by the pupils' teacher, Grainne Tierney, and supported by the hospital chaplain. After some research, the children decided they would like to commission artist Nicholas Mynheer (see Chapter 17) to design the window. The children embarked on an intensive campaign to raise the funds needed to cover the financial outlay. Nicholas recalls when he went to visit the school to be briefed by the pupils: 'I was hugely impressed by the children's art history knowledge and appreciation.'

His window design shows the man having being lowered through the roof and Jesus in the act of healing him. On the left are two pupils of Christ the King School carrying someone on a stretcher, because as Nicholas explains, 'in commissioning the window and raising the money, they have become part of the caring process of the hospital'.

Once the first dazzling window had been installed, the children initiated the second phase of the project. Realising that their window sat alone in the middle of three windows, they approached a sister school, St Margaret Mary's, and invited them to join them in a further commission to complete two more windows. Nicholas returned and worked with both sets of pupils.

For their second window the pupils of Christ the King School commissioned the stories of Noah's Ark and the infant Moses in the bulrushes, because they felt these stories would inspire hope and offer encouragement and comfort to patients of all faiths, especially those from the Abrahamic tradition – Judaism, Christianity and Islam.

The pupils of St Margaret Mary's School, led by the deputy head teacher, Jane Logue, commissioned the third window, based round the image of the Sacred Heart, a symbol of Christ's love for all humanity.

Although this was primarily a project which involved Catholic primary schools and was rooted in Christian symbolism and values, it was very evident that the children were keenly aware that the medical care provided by the hospital embraced and catered to all faiths – and none – with equal dedication. Nicholas Mynheer said, 'The children wanted their gift of the windows to lift and sustain the spirits of all who gazed upon them, whether they be hospital patients, visiting relatives or staff.'

This project triggered our search for other colleagues who demonstrated a sincere commitment to ensuring a broad and balanced curriculum for all pupils, while sustaining high standards of academic attainment, teaching and pupil well-being. The pupils' engagement with the real world of medicine, design, art and fundraising seems to us emblematic of so many of the elements and much of the high quality and imaginative practice we have witnessed. These include:

■ The engagement of pupils in imaginative, creative and cognitively rewarding learning activities and experiences.

▨ Work that consistently arose from, and was inspired by, regular involvement on the part of pupils in relevant, diverse and challenging experiences.

▨ Learning that derived (notably in the project described here) from a fusion of teacher guidance and input and pupil-centred initiative of remarkable inventiveness and ingenuity.

▨ The acquisition of valuable new knowledge and the acquisition of fresh skills.

▨ The commissioning of, and engagement with, external expertise in the realisation of a project.

▨ The nurturing of pupils' capacity and sense of vision to understand and value the purpose of their learning, as well as the resolution to see it through to a successful conclusion.

▨ A gradually developing awareness on the part of many pupils of at least some of the elements that make for scholarship.

▨ A growing insight into, and sympathetic understanding of, human and social issues, enabling pupils to look beyond their own traditions and cultural values and empathise with those of other communities and beliefs.

▨ The shaping of pupils' ability and confidence to venture beyond their own school environment and collaborate with others in the learning process.

▨ Teaching and learning subtly and powerfully interacting to bring about a tangible legacy of educational value.

A broad and balanced curriculum

We have not attempted to describe the curriculum each school offers across the entire subject range, since to do so would be impractical and the outcome mere classification. We have, instead, invited colleagues to select areas of practice that seem representative and noteworthy. Some contributors have focused on individual subjects (although in every case, links have been forged with subjects such as English and maths), while other chapters have described teaching and learning that involves clusters of subjects and which makes important links between different areas of knowledge and skill.

In all, we are left with a remarkable range of study and learning that covers, in every school, all the designated national curriculum subjects, and does so imaginatively, creatively and, at times, with daring inventiveness. In many cases, the pupils engage in learning, research and scholarship *beyond* what is envisaged by the national curriculum, as the following cases, among others in the book, testify:

- Complex and intellectually challenging work in science, technology, engineering, art and mathematics (STEAM) involving ecology, biochemistry and robotics.

- A remarkable international business project that involves collaborative entrepreneurship with other institutions across the world.

- The employment of digital technology in ways that afford us an insight into models of teaching and learning that may have a major influence on forms of education well into the future.

- The engagement of pupils in the creative and expressive arts, stimulating them to come to terms with challenging concepts and ideas, experimentation, practice and performance.

- A growing emphasis on environmental studies, exemplified in pupils' practical engagement with the natural world and a developing sense of their stewardship of the land.

- An emphasis on languages, classical and modern, taught in a way that is rewarding and opens the door to pupils' awareness of other nationalities and cultures.

The genesis of the practice, study and work described in the preceding chapters lies largely, though not exclusively, within the national curriculum. Let us consider again, briefly, some of the features that make it critical to the provision of effective education.

In stressing that the national curriculum is just one element in the education of every child, the Department for Education's Framework Document contends that it provides 'an outline of core knowledge around which teachers can develop exciting and stimulating lessons to promote the development of pupils' knowledge, understanding and skills as part of the wider school curriculum' (Department for Education, 2013: 6).

Explicit in this statement is an emphasis on knowledge and skills, not simply as part of the wider school curriculum but as the very essence of learning. We are left in no doubt here, and elsewhere, that education is essentially about the acquisition and mastery of knowledge which explains and clarifies the nature of existence, and identifies the means and skills by which we can effectively respond to and engage with it. Knowledge, the determining and all-important element, is dependent, to a significant extent, on a range of skills for its acquisition, mastery and understanding; obvious examples being the skills of reading, computation and systematic investigation.

The national curriculum seeks to represent a comprehensive map of the essential knowledge at the heart of learning – critical concepts, ideas and related skills – in an ordered, sequential and progressive form. Learning, in turn, is about realising objectives and achieving goals in diverse domains, whatever the level of study we are engaged with. The programmes of study are designed to result in sound understanding and competence in relation to the guiding objectives and to prepare pupils to progress and move to the next stage. Important concepts and skills are not to be ignored or only partly understood.

A notable feature of the work described in this book has been the schools' determination to bring to a defined and recognisable conclusion what had been intended and planned for at the outset, however ostensibly minor and short-lived or ambitious and demanding. We know, of course – as you will recall from the account in the introduction of the flight project at Mandeville Primary School in Hackney – that carefully planned initiatives will often yield riches and advances in learning far beyond what was originally envisaged.

The following two examples, drawn from differing contexts, illustrate the concerns of teachers, and the eagerness of pupils, to discover, 'What will happen if ...?' and 'What will happen at the end?' – the aims of seekers of knowledge down the ages.

- The children at Boldon Nursery School – Outdoor Nursery who, in a single continuous process, identified willow twigs in their wild garden; cut, stripped, prepared and heated them (following scrupulous safety precautions) in an iron grill over an outdoor fire pit; and then finished the session by writing with their newly created writing implements.

- The construction, over a period of weeks, by upper junior pupils at The Hendreds School of the engine and chassis of a kit car that they learned to drive (carefully supervised) and subsequently raced in competitions.

Both of these very different educational projects were seen through to a visible and successful conclusion. Although disparate in scale and undertaking, they share an element of risk and gave the children a sense of ownership and responsibility. Both examples were motivated by specific learning intentions, underpinned by: clear educational vision; careful planning and organisation to ensure their successful implementation; recourse to essential guidance and expertise; the utilisation of appropriate and essential resources and materials; the ability of the children to work collaboratively; and the need, maintained throughout, for discussion, enquiry, review and evaluation.

These two examples exemplify a critical difference between the best of contemporary teaching and learning and some of the flawed practice referred to in the introduction. However worthwhile and engaging in certain important respects, the potential value of that work was not always realised, due to a failure to identify the guiding educational aims and objectives to be achieved, together with the absence of a clear sense of what knowledge and concepts might be learned and what skills might be mastered. These shortcomings were largely due to the relative scarcity of whole-school curriculum mapping and the resulting uncertainty on the part of teachers with regard to subject specialisms, especially at the upper primary or junior stage.

Specialist teaching in the primary curriculum

The new national curriculum maps areas of knowledge and understanding and provides both for progression in learning and for differentiation matched to stages of cognitive development. It represents a secure educational inventory with the potential to support and promote a broad and balanced curriculum. The reclaimed curriculum, however, is significantly dependent on the input of specialist subject knowledge. This is provided by teachers whose specialist knowledge, enthusiasm and skill equip them to operate at advanced levels of competence, supporting the widest range of ability but also ensuring appropriate challenge for the most able pupils.

In every school, we observed teachers leading practice in their specialism, self-assured in their work across the broad curriculum. Management structures provided for them to do so, and even went beyond in order to ensure a constant momentum of pedagogical creativity and invention, contributing to enrichment in every aspect of teaching and learning. Forward-looking, enlightened and enabling leadership fostered individual enterprise on the part of staff. We have seen teachers, inspired by individual vision and insight, who were confident that their ideas and suggestions for the curriculum and learning would be sympathetically considered, adopted or adapted, integrated and implemented – to the advantage of all.

In every school, innovative curriculum work was founded on supportive and aspirational staff interaction. Everything of consequence in the life of the school was a matter of collaborative vision and general ownership. The leadership and management made sure that everyone was on board and in the know; individual contributions would be heard and valued.

In such schools, teachers revel in and celebrate one another's skills and successes, and grow professionally to the benefit of all in their learning community. We have also seen teaching assistants, non-teaching staff, parents and external specialists make crucial and empowering interventions in whole-school projects or specific areas of learning, calling on their personal skills, expertise and enthusiasm.

Engaging with specialist expertise beyond the school

In a number of cases, schools have formed links with institutions, experts or speakers of other languages, whose particular expertise and knowledge have become transforming influences. In other instances, they have secured the involvement of parents with specific capacities and skills to contribute to educational programmes in ways which might be beyond the school's pedagogical or financial resources. Many schools find subject expertise through links to local organisations or centres of excellence, such as their local university, art gallery, orchestra or museum, which can provide high quality and inspirational inputs and resources.

The creative projects and work described in this book strongly suggest that subject specialisms and insights are vital and indispensable to a curriculum, reclaimed from a narrow and prescriptive perspective of education, in order to ensure the best and most relevant teaching and learning.

What we have documented here are notable initiatives and developments that captivate and enthral, but we also witnessed – and this is characteristic of many good schools – much of enduring value that might well go unnoticed by the hurried observer.

One final example was a chance encounter with a ballet group, which we came across as we moved around a school from one exciting initiative to another. This group, composed of Year 3 girls and boys, all in ballet shoes, were practising in a side room, where they proceeded to demonstrate a sequence of accomplished movements which they eloquently explained to us. It was memorable, not only for the graceful and assured competence of the children, but for the almost incidental nature of the encounter; just another of the enthralling happenings we witnessed that day.

It was simply a ballet lesson, a curriculum opportunity that is unlikely to be experienced by most primary schoolchildren, but it was provided by a professional ballerina who visits weekly to teach children across the whole age range. It was so routine and unconnected with the agenda for our visit that it might not have featured on our itinerary. But it seemed to us emblematic of the marvels inherent in the whole curriculum and the immeasurable richness it offers the children fortunate enough to experience it.

We would like to thank most warmly the colleagues who have contributed to this book. They have generously provided us with valuable insights into their everyday but inspirational practice. They have explained how they try to harness the potential of their specialist subjects to motivate and enthuse their pupils. They have demonstrated how they use their projects and initiatives to contribute to the development of literacy and numeracy, to encourage pupils to ask questions, to research and to express themselves orally and in writing. These colleagues are firmly convinced that wide-ranging, creative and enquiry-driven approaches to teaching and learning are more effective and memorable than strategies confined to a narrow range of subjects.

We hope that the chapters in this book offer inspiring examples of schools determined to reclaim the curriculum and provide environments, contexts and opportunities for teaching and learning which make for the very best of primary education.

Further reading

Department for Education (2013). The National Curriculum in England: Key Stages 1 and 2 Framework Document. Available at: https://www.gov.uk/government/uploads/system/uploads/attachment_data/file/425601/PRIMARY_national_curriculum.pdf.

About the Authors

Bill Laar

A former primary school head teacher, Bill Laar has worked as an inspector and adviser for several local authorities including London, Birmingham, Walsall and Oxfordshire. He was a registered Ofsted inspector and served as chief inspector and deputy director of education (primary and secondary) in the City of Westminster in London. He has also worked with schools and teachers across the UK and overseas as an adviser and consultant. Bill is a visiting fellow at Oxford Brookes University and for many years was patron of National Primary Heads (NPH).

Bill continues to lecture and write on a wide range of educational issues – including leadership, curriculum, literacy, narrative and creativity – and has written a number of books and materials for teachers, including *Primary Heads: Exceptional Leadership in the Primary School*.

Jackie Holderness

Jackie Holderness has taught at primary, secondary and master's level. After several years working as a teacher in the Netherlands, and as a deputy head teacher and Ofsted inspector in Oxfordshire, Jackie was appointed senior lecturer in education (language and literature) at Oxford Brookes University, where her specialisms also included EAL/TESOL, international education, teaching, learning and curriculum design.

In 2012, while working as materials director with Achievement for All, Jackie helped to found Europa School UK, a 3–18 state school which offers a multilingual European curriculum. In her current post, as the education officer at Christ Church Cathedral, her focus is on spiritual and heritage education – but her role also complements her involvement in several local initiatives, which include storytelling, the creative arts and bringing children and books together. She has also written a wide range of education books and materials, for pupils and teachers, on language, literacy and EAL.

Primary Heads

Exceptional Leadership in the Primary School

Bill Laar

ISBN: 978-184590890-4

Primary Heads contains lessons on leadership from a group of highly successful primary head teachers. The book starts with an overview of current thinking on good leadership practice and then takes the reader through the personal stories of 11 head teachers who have, sometimes in the face of extraordinary adversity, transformed their schools. Each has a very personal view on what it has taken for them to succeed and what successful leadership in primary schools should look like. Bill then draws out the key elements from their accounts and details how primary schools and primary heads can create the best possible environment for learning by concentrating on the identified aspects of exceptional leadership. This detailed translation of theories into notably successful practice, presented through the personal accounts of a group of outstanding head teachers, will have a particular resonance for practitioners engaged in the challenging business of education today.

For all primary school leaders. The book will be relevant, too, for administrators, school governors and those involved in teacher training and continuing professional development.